MADAME DE POMPADOUR

I dreamt of love and fame; I strove.—Ernest Rhys

It is neither by marble nor bronze ... that her image must be transmitted to posterity; for this woman so fragile, a figurine of Sèvres will suffice; it will be at once a portrait and an emblem.

—Émile Campardon

Madame de Pompadour, from a painting by
François Boucher. Reproduced by permission
of the Trustees of the Wallace Collection,
London.

✵

MADAME DE POMPADOUR :

Mistress of France

DAVID MYNDERS SMYTHE

WILFRED FUNK · New York

DESIGNED BY JOHN KING

To Steve,
and to the memory of Maggie

CONTENTS

ILLUSTRATIONS

viii

FOREWORD

THE NAME Pompadour is as familiar to most readers as the real character of the woman who bore that name is unfamiliar. Because Madame de Pompadour was the most famous of the Mistresses of Louis XV, her name has come down to us as a synonym for flagrant immorality, shameless parasitism, and inept petticoat rule.

But to render so harsh a judgment upon this fragile courtesan is inaccurate; worse, it is unfair. No historical figure can rightly be judged by today's standards; the portrait will inevitably emerge distorted and unbalanced if it is not framed in the standards of judgment of its own time. By the standards of eighteenth-century France, Madame de Pompadour was not a vile woman, baser than any other—she was, in alertness of mind, kindness of heart, and even in moral conduct, superior to most of her contemporaries at the Court of Versailles.

Why, then, has her real nature been so often pictured out of focus? Surely not merely because she was a King's brilliant Mistress? Henry IV had his Gabrielle d'Estrées, Louis XIV his gentle Louise de la Vallière and imperious Madame de Montespan—and yet those monarchs and their mistresses never incurred the popular odium and fierce hatred which were the lot of Louis XV and Madame de Pompadour.

The answer lies with those Frenchmen who wrote during and after the French Revolution. In their frenzied efforts to blacken the *Ancien Régime* they impatiently dismissed the ineffectual Louis XVI, and ferociously attacked the reputation of his grandfather, Louis XV. What more natural than that the dead King's most conspicuous Mistress, she who had reigned the longest, should also have her reputation shredded for posterity?

Every biased and malicious memoir penned by Madame de Pompadour's enemies was scanned for salacious evidence against her. That is how such preposterous libels as the "orgies" in the Little Apartments and the "harem" in the *Parc aux Cerfs* were born. When enough lies could not be uncovered, those who wrote from the Jacobin viewpoint did not hesitate to invent them.

In the realm of politics, cried these denouncers, Madame de Pompadour's unforgivable crime was leading France into the Seven Years' War on the side of Austria. It is true that the war was an uninterrupted disaster for France, and military defeat is one thing that the usually tolerant French have shown themselves unable to forgive. But Madame de Pompadour, while wholeheartedly supporting the Austrian alliance, did not create it. Even if she had, was she mistaken in her passionate determination to destroy Frederick the Great? Do not 1870, 1914, and 1940 vindicate her hatred of Prussia? Historians now generally agree that in the middle of the eighteenth century Prussia had succeeded Austria as the chief German threat to France. "Her" war, despite its dreary pattern of inexcusable favoritism and abysmal defeats, was not so disastrous for France as the reckless adventures of the two Napoleons.

Since 1900 the trend among French biographers, brilliantly pioneered by Pierre de Nolhac, has been to refute these astigmatic attacks upon Madame de Pompadour and to unveil Louis XV's Mistress in a more truthful light. No American biographer has followed in their footsteps, and so this book has been written in the hope that it reveals Madame de Pompadour as the charming and cultivated woman she was, the typical product of the graceful, skeptical eighteenth century.

She was Paris, not Versailles, and in a striking sense she was the vanguard of the Revolution. She was the first of the middle class successfully to storm the ramparts of the ancient Monarchy, and her presence became the rallying point at Court for the New Ideas.

It was true that she appeared to the people as a soulless parasite, and they hated her as personifying the viciousness of Absolute Monarchy. Consciously, without any doubt, she believed herself Monarchy's defender; unconsciously, protecting and patronizing Voltaire, Montesquieu, Diderot, and other critics of absolutism, she carried within herself the seeds of the Monarchy's ruin.

Telling accurately the story of Madame de Pompadour does not require the application of whitewash to her fragile figure. Her faults cannot—and need not—be denied. They were obvious enough without her enemies having to invent more. Cold, calculating, sometimes vindictive, practicing to perfection the exhausting wiles of the social climber, she was at the same time tender, generous, sometimes warm, and always considerate.

Successful beyond belief, she came in the end to be melancholy beyond endurance.

David Mynders Smythe

Principal Characters

Jeanne Antoinette Poisson, Marquise de Pompadour   1721-1764
Louis XV, King of France and Navarre   1710-1774
Marie Leczinska of Poland, Queen of France   1703-1768
Louis, Dauphin of France   1729-1765
Maria-Rafaéla of Spain, Dauphine of France   1726-1746
Marie-Josèphe of Saxony, Dauphine of France   1731-1766
The Sons of the Dauphin:
   Duc de Berri, later Louis XVI   1754-1793
   Comte de Provence, later Louis XVIII   1755-1824
   Comte d'Artois, later Charles X   1757-1836
The Daughters of the King:
   Madame Elizabeth (The Infanta)   1727-1759
   Madame Henriette   1727-1752
   Madame Adélaïde   1732-1798
   Madame Victoire   1733-1802
   Madame Sophie   1734-1800
   Madame Louise   1737-1787
Philippe, Duc d'Orléans and Regent of France   1674-1723
Maria Theresa, Empress of Austria and Queen of
   Hungary   1717-1780
Frederick II (The Great), King of Prussia   1712-1786
George II, King of Great Britain and Hanover   1683-1760
Augustus III, Elector of Saxony and King of Poland   1696-1763
Stanislaus Leczinski, ex-King of Poland   1677-1766
Charles Edward Stuart, The Young Pretender   1720-1788
Maurice de Saxe, Marshal of France   1696-1750
Duchesse de Châteauroux, predecessor of Mme. de
   Pompadour   1717-1744
Comtesse Du Barry, successor of Mme. de Pompadour   1743-1793

Marquis d'Argenson, Foreign Minister   1694-1757
Comte d'Argenson, his younger brother, Minister
    of War   1696-1764
Comte de Maurepas, Minister of Marine   1701-1781
Machault d'Arnouville, Keeper of the Seals   1701-1794
Comte de Stainville, later Duc de Choiseul   1719-1785
Duc de Richelieu, Marshal of France   1696-1788
Charles de Rohan, Prince de Soubise   1715-1787
Abbé de Bernis, Foreign Minister and later Cardinal 1715-1794
François Quesnay, Physician and Economist   1694-1774
Jean François Marmontel, Writer   1723-1799
François Boucher, Painter   1703-1770
Crébillon, Dramatist   1674-1762
Voltaire   1694-1778

The Family of Madame de Pompadour

François Poisson, her father   1684-1754
Madeleine de la Motte, her mother   1699-1745
Abel Poisson, Marquis de Vandières and Marigny,
    her brother   1726-1781
Charles-Guillaume Le Normant d'Étioles, her hus-
    band   1717-1799
Alexandrine d'Étioles, her daughter   1744-1754

PROLOGUE

N AUGUST 10, 1744, Madame Le Normant d'Étioles presented her husband with an infant daughter. Five days later the twenty-two-year-old mother suffered a grievous relapse. The doctors said it was childbed fever. Possibly they were right—at least in part. But there was another reason for Madame d'Étioles' grave state, one which the doctors could not discern for they could peer neither into her brain nor her heart.

Only the frail patient herself knew that her illness was linked to that of one more august than she—august and infinitely remote. None other, in fact, than His Most Christian Majesty, Louis XV, King of France. For Madame d'Étioles, seemingly a devoted wife, had dreamed a dream for many years, indeed from childhood, of becoming the official mistress of the King. Serenely confident, unswervingly faithful to what she believed to be her charted destiny, she knew herself capable of overcoming a thousand barriers of birth and rank. She was convinced that only one thing could block her path—death. Her own death or that of Louis XV.

News had just reached Paris of the dangerous illness of

the King in the frontier city of Metz, and its crushing effect on the beautiful Madame d'Étioles was shared by the average citizen of the capital, with a feeling almost as personal as hers.

"The news of the King's danger," wrote Voltaire, "reached Paris in the middle of the night. The inhabitants rose from their beds and ran about in their excitement, without knowing whither they went. The churches were opened, although it was midnight; nor did people any longer pay any regard to the hours of sleeping, waking, or taking their meals. All Paris seemed to have gone mad, and the houses of persons of condition were surrounded by crowds. The public squares were also thronged with people, who all kept crying out: 'if he dies it will be for having marched to our relief. . . .' " In many churches the priests who read prayers for the King's recovery were forced to pause through emotion, the people responding with sobs and cries.

The people of France feared the apparently inevitable death of their King not only because they dreaded the inexperience of his untried son but because, in spite of his scandalous behavior, they still loved Louis. If God spared him, they reasoned, he would change his ways and return to the respectable life of his early married days.

Indeed there were many ways in which Louis could change, the better to please his subjects and his God. As he lay burning with fever in Metz, prey to the religious terrors which always pursued his morbid soul, he must have reviewed over and over his many lapses from morality. Stricken in distant Paris with physical illness and a debilitating fear that the King's death would cheat her of her goal, Madame d'Étioles, too, must have reflected on the life of open promiscuity the King had led for more than a decade. It was a chronicle she knew by heart.

Married at fifteen to a wife seven years his senior, Louis had been a devoted, even an ardent husband for seven years. Marie Leczinska, daughter of the exiled King of Poland, had never wildly dreamed of becoming Queen of France. No one else had dreamed of her becoming anything at all. She and her father, former King Stanislaus, existed in Alsace in genteel poverty on a pension provided by the French Crown. Marie busied herself with music and reading, of which she was very fond, and with her religious duties, which she adored.

And then, in 1725, the quiet Polish Princess was chosen to be the bride of Louis XV. At once Stanislaus' pathetic little court became the center of frenzied activity, messengers from Versailles followed one another constantly with costly presents, and the happy Marie readied her trousseau for the greatest day of her life—her marriage to the King of France.

The life together of the young sovereigns was at first happy. Marie was not pretty, but neither was she ugly. Her eyes were penetrating and shone with intelligence. Her nose was slightly irregular but she had a kind and humorous mouth. During the few years of her happiness her appearance was gentle and charming. Louis thought his wife the most beautiful woman at Versailles, and no one confided to him that his opinion was unique.

Royal children arrived in such rapid succession that the Queen once described her life as *toujours coucher, toujours grosse, toujours accoucher!* A baby girl who died, then twin Princesses, Elizabeth and Henriette, and at last, in 1729, the most precious of all—a son, an heir to the Throne, a Dauphin of France. The King was humbly grateful to the Queen for this greatest of gifts she could bestow upon his House.

Ten children were born of the Royal marriage of whom six daughters and one son lived. Such fruitfulness began to tell upon the Queen's health and appearance. She rarely felt well enough to dress, much less to amuse the King. And above everything else Louis had to be amused, to be distracted from his innate boredom.

Although Marie Leczinska was intelligent and the King's senior, she was in awe of him, never quite at ease before him. Their tastes were dissimilar. She enjoyed a small quiet group of friends with whom she could chat in the evenings; the King preferred gay late suppers at which there was much gambling and drinking. After one of these parties Louis, who had drunk too much champagne, noisily demanded admittance to the Queen's apartments. The pious Marie, to whom physical relations were more a duty than a pleasure, was disgusted and refused to let him in. Louis was chagrined and thought again of his wedding night, which his prudish wife had spent on her knees in prayer.

These widening differences between husband and wife were eagerly watched by malicious eyes at Court. Many of the courtiers had long since tried (and up to now, in vain) to introduce the King to their own vicious habits. These self-seeking parasites had nothing to gain through a virtuous Queen but could hope for much if they sponsored a successful mistress. They did not have long to wait.

"It is impossible to say," wrote the triumphant Duc de Richelieu, "when or where or how the King ceased to be the best of husbands; but after he had been married seven years he realized one fine morning that he was only twenty-two, and seven years younger than his wife."

The woman who stole the King's heart was the Comtesse de Mailly, eldest daughter of the Marquis de Nesle. Her two sisters and the other mistresses who followed them could never wound the neglected Queen as she had done, for she was the first. And yet Madame de Mailly was not an evil woman. The same age as Louis, she loved him for himself alone. She was kind and gay, with an ordinary, sincere mind which was outspoken in its frankness. Tall, with a wide mouth made more noticeable by many large teeth, she conducted herself in an unconsciously graceless manner. Proud, she nursed a long memory for snubs. But she was not a schemer, and she totally lacked the mercenary instinct.

Even as the King's Mistress she was poor. "Her chemises are all wearing out and in holes," an observer noted incredulously, "and her maid is ill clothed, which reveals real poverty." Of all the mistresses who were to follow Madame de Mailly, she, the first, was the only one who loved Louis unselfishly. The King remembered this as he writhed upon his sickbed in Metz.

Unfortunately for the happiness of Madame de Mailly,

she had a younger sister Pauline who was anything but ingenuous. Pauline was determined to displace her sister in the King's favor and persuaded the kind Madame de Mailly to summon her to Versailles. As scheming as her older sister was not, Pauline was soon involved in an affair with the susceptible King. She became pregnant, and Louis hastily married her to a complaisant nobleman, the Marquis de Vintimille, who accommodatingly took himself off to the provinces immediately after the ceremony.

The new Madame de Vintimille, long of neck and exuding an *odeur de singe,* was now undisputed ruler of the King's heart. Madame de Mailly, doubly wounded by her lover's fickleness and her sister's treachery, bore the humiliation bravely and continued to live on at Versailles as *maîtresse-en-titre.*

The parsimonious Monarch showered gifts upon the new Mistress as he had never done upon the old. He bought for her the château of Choisy-le-Roi, near the Forest of Sénart, and furnished it richly in blue and gold. But Madame de Vintimille enjoyed her new luxury only a short while. A few days after she gave birth to a son, she was seized with terrible convulsions and died in agony. The King was almost overcome with grief, and turned for consolation to the faithful Madame de Mailly; together they wept for the lost Mistress and sister. (The son of the dead woman was given the title Comte du Luc. As he grew older his resemblance to his father became so marked that he was popularly known as *le demi-louis.*)

Madame de Vintimille's body was laid out in a house in the town of Versailles, watched by servants to protect it from the populace. During the night, however, the guards slipped away to drink, and an infuriated mob broke in, screaming insults and hideously desecrating the corpse of "the King's whore."

Two years passed, and Madame de Mailly continued to live with the King. Her sister's harrowing death frightened her into repentance; she washed the dirty feet of the poor and bestowed upon them what little money she had. But she still had not learned the danger of being kind to her sisters.

Marie Anne de Nesle, widowed Marquise de la Tournelle, was the youngest of the Marquis de Nesle's daughters. Unlike her older sisters, she was beautiful, with a full oval face and only the hint of a double chin. Her proud blue eyes were unusually large, her nose was straight and haughty, and her mouth was Botticelli. The sensuousness of her face was accentuated by a large full bosom. She too persuaded simple Madame de Mailly to invite her to Versailles, and she too succeeded in attracting the King's interest. Like her Mazarin grandmother, she was ambitious and ruthless. Before yielding to the infatuated Louis, she forced him to agree to her terms: disgrace and dismissal of her sister and the title of Duchesse for herself.

And so Madame de Mailly crept from Versailles where she had known so much misery, and Marie-Anne succeeded her as *maîtresse-en-titre* with the title of Duchesse de Châteauroux. The new favorite was savagely haughty and at once made a host of enemies. The most bitter was the Comte de Maurepas, Minister of Marine, whose acid pen etched scathing verses at her expense. Try though she would, she could never persuade the King to dismiss his favorite Minister—it would take a stronger woman than Madame de Châteauroux, one far more clever, to accomplish that.

Nevertheless, she had her way in most things. She was mercenary, loving not the King but the power and luxury he gave her. Though passionate and domineering like Madame de Montespan, the Duchesse had at least a glorious conception of what kind of King Louis XV should be. Lazy as he was, she incessantly prodded him into action, trying vainly to inspire him to emulate Louis XIV. She liked political affairs, took an active interest in the War of the Austrian Succession, and in 1744 insisted that Louis lead his army to Flanders in person. "You kill me," the King remonstrated.

But Louis went, and the Duchesse and her fat jolly sister, Madame de Lauraguais, soon followed. Madame de Lauraguais amused the King with her good nature—sometimes so much that he took her to bed instead of the arrogant Favorite. These sisters were never serious rivals; there was no question as to which one was in undisputed control.

The scandal of the King's life became so open that even the Army was outraged, and Louis and his companions abandoned the surly troops for the greater comforts of the city of Metz. They had hardly arrived before the King fell ill on August 8th and by the 12th the doctors had given up hope.

All this Madame d'Étioles knew, but she could only

guess, apprehensively, what was actually happening at the Royal sickbed.

The throng of nobles and priests surrounding the King's bedside clamored for the dismissal of the hated Mistress. Frowned upon by the clergy, feared and envied by the Ministers of State, detested by the populace, the Duchesse still held the King's affections. Always vacillating, Louis sought to postpone his answer, hoping desperately that he would recover. Instead he continued to sink. The fanatical Fitz-James, Bishop of Soissons, mercilessly played upon the King's fears and threatened to withhold the Sacraments unless he rid himself of Madame de Châteauroux. Louis, finally overcome by his intense terror of Hell, gave in; the Duchesse received her orders to depart. The banishment included the amiable Madame de Lauraguais as well.

And so the two sisters, surprisingly dignified in their disgrace, were driven from Metz by the relentless priest. Though guarded by an escort of soldiers throughout the long journey back to Paris, they were in real danger of their lives from the indignant attacks of the peasants along the way. The ordinary people of the country, far from impeccable themselves, bitterly resented vice in those whom they had been taught to respect and obey. The people of France still respected Louis XV, and miraculously he escaped the fury which struck only at the fallen Favorite. The King was dying; they could forgive and pray for him. At least the harlot was gone.

The day after Louis was forced to part from his Mistress the Bishop of Soissons administered the Sacrament to him.

Still unappeased by his triumph of the previous day the
prelate stepped forward and announced to the courtiers
crowding around the bed:

"Princes of the Blood and Nobles of the Realm, the King
charges his Lordship, the Bishop of Metz and myself to
assure you, on his behalf, of his sincere penitence for the
scandal which he has caused by living as he has done with
Madame de Châteauroux, for which he now asks pardon
of God and man. He is informed that the lady is now some
leagues from here, and he commands that in future she
shall remain at a distance of fifty leagues from the Court."

"And," murmured the dying King, raising himself on
his pillow, "her sister the Duchesse de Lauraguais as well."
At that moment of imminent death Louis meant it.

But the austere Bishop was soon to regret that he had
overplayed his hand, and the others who had taken a less
prominent part in the King's public humiliation hastily
and emphatically attempted to dissociate themselves from
it. As for Louis himself, he burned with shame at this
forced abnegation and twice in later life, when dangerously
ill, firmly declared, "This will not be another Metz affair."

For the unthinkable occurred: the dying did not die.
The King recovered. An obscure retired army surgeon,
living on his pension in Metz, asked to see the patient. As
the Royal doctors had already abandoned hope, the humble
man of medicine was ushered into the sickroom. He examined the frightened King and then asked permission to
administer an emetic. To universal astonishment Louis
improved at once; his fever declined, and in four days he
was convalescent.

Meanwhile the distracted Queen was traveling without rest along the great road from Paris. When she arrived in Metz she found, instead of a corpse, a rapidly recovering husband. The King at first seemed abashed and sincerely begged her forgiveness for the unhappiness he had caused her.

Some of the Queen's friends exaggerated the intensity of the King's penitence and with more naïveté than good sense arranged two pillows in the hopeful Queen's bed— and waited. They continued to wait, vainly. As Louis' health returned, so did his coldness toward his wife. When he was well enough to return to the military campaign, Marie timidly begged to accompany him. "That will not be necessary, Madame," he replied, and coldly bade her good-by.

When the news of Louis' recovery reached Paris the citizens were almost delirious with joy, and "the city for many hours was nothing but a vast enclosure full of madmen." The number of prayers for the King's recovery was now equaled by the *Te Deums* which were ordered, and a poet of the people named Vadé, a kind of eighteenth-century Villon, bestowed upon Louis the tender sobriquet *"le Bien-Aimé."* Well-Beloved in truth he was; only in unhappier years was the pretty phrase to be uttered with derision.

The King made a triumphal entry into Paris on November 13, 1744, welcomed by crowds massed along the route of the Royal procession. First a troop of cavalry, sabers gleaming, galloped past, followed by a regiment of the Swiss Guard, shining in their white dress uniforms. Directly behind them the Royal Coronation Coach rolled majestically along, drawn by four blooded horses whose proud heads were topped with graceful plumes that nodded in the breeze.

Inside the coach the King sat in full view, and his subjects saw that he was happy and touched by their frenzied devotion. His handsome face, which ordinarily wore an impassive bored expression, was lighted by a charming smile. Never had he been received with such enthusiasm in Paris where he always felt ill at ease. And never again, alas, were King and Capital to love each other as they did that day.

The lines of waving, smiling people shouted *vive le Roi, vive le Bien-Aimé,* and more than once the astonished Louis said, "What have I done to deserve it?"

What, indeed? He had recovered his health, consigned his unpopular Mistress to deserved obscurity, and publicly reconciled himself to his loving and neglected consort. That was enough to satisfy the Parisians, who believed the King was truly theirs again and almost burst with prideful affection at the sight of his manly beauty.

Louis XV had all the appearance of a King more usually found in stories and legends than among the monarchs of the earth. He was the handsomest man in France, possibly the handsomest in Europe, and at the age of thirty-four he was in the prime of his life. Casanova, a skilled reporter, described him:

"Louis XV had the finest head in the world and he carried it with equal dignity and grace. No painter, however skillful, has succeeded in capturing the expression of that splendid head when the monarch turned to look kindly at anyone. His beauty and grace made one love him at first sight."

The common people and those not so common loved him on that November day—ordinary people who were gazing at him for the first time, and others who had seen him many times. No one loved him more than Madame Le Normant d'Étioles, radiant at the double joy of the King's recovery and his dismissal of Madame de Châteauroux.

She stood in a window of her house in the rue St. Honoré watching the procession, and her eyes, strikingly large and brilliant, were fixed tenderly upon Louis. Dressed in a gown of pale blue silk, she leaned forward, but not too boldly, and her lips molded themselves into a subtle little smile. She hoped the King would see her, would recognize her.

Did he? Did he see, in that vision of blue silk, the image of the nymph in rose taffeta who so often—so suspiciously often—had crossed his path a year ago in the Forest of Sénart? Did he recall the fair charioteer in the blue phaeton who followed the Royal Hunt with the same unerring sense that the Royal Hounds followed the boar?

Possibly not. For Louis was growing tired now, and there still remained the fireworks and banquet at the Hôtel de Ville, and his public appearance on the balcony of the Tuileries. The Royal Coach moved on, and with it moved that day of joy, irreversible.

That night the King slipped out of the Palace of the Tuileries and secretly made his way to the house of the

Duchesse de Châteauroux in the rue du Bac. There must have been a full reconciliation between the lovers, for less than two weeks later Louis dispatched a letter recalling her officially to Versailles. Her apartments in the Palace and all her honors and privileges were restored to her; the enemies who had rejoiced at her disgrace were to be punished. The Bishop of Soissons was forbidden to appear at Court, and it was Maurepas, whom the Duchesse hated most of all, who had to carry the King's letter and face her accumulated fury.

Paris was outraged that the King so disdainfully flouted public opinion. "One cannot," recorded the Duc de Luynes, "describe the effect upon the people of the recall of Madame de Châteauroux." The honest fishwives acidly expressed their change of heart by swearing that "now he has taken back his Harlot he will not find a Paternoster on the pavements of all Paris."

But Louis, anticipating the resumption of unmarital bliss, cared little for the opinion of his people, and the vindictive Duchesse cared less. Madame de Châteauroux, however, was never to enjoy the heady flavor of vengeful triumph. She did not know it, but she faced an enemy more powerful than the people of Paris; that enemy was Death.

Before she could return to Court, she became suddenly ill with violent headaches and a malignant fever similar to that recently suffered by the King. Some whispered that Maurepas had poisoned her, but the rumor was ill founded, and her malady was very likely typhus. She suffered horribly, shrieking in the agony of her convulsions. There was time left to make peace with the Church before she expired in delirium on December 8th. It was her Saint's Day, the Day of Mary, and since she was a little girl she had expressed the wish that she might die on that day.

The King did not conceal his grief and spoke of the Duchesse as "the only Mistress he ever loved." He withdrew from Versailles with her few friends, spurning the Christian offer of the Queen to console him. "Our poor Master," wrote d'Argenson to the Duc de Richelieu, "has a look which makes one tremble for his life." The King's heart had been wounded but time, and very little of it, would heal his hurt.

I

THE TRAP IS SET

*T*HE KING of France was giving a ball in his Palace of Versailles to celebrate the marriage of his only son the Dauphin. The Dauphine was a younger sister of the Infanta who once had been intended for Louis XV himself but who had been tactlessly rejected. No one alluded to the fiasco which had so angered Spain. Everyone hoped that the new marriage would heal the estrangement between the two branches of the House of Bourbon. "Les Pyrénées n'existent plus," said the courtiers, as had been said when Louis XIV's grandson became King of Spain.

This was the climax of a brilliant series of balls given by the King to honor the young couple. Never in his reign had Versailles shown so resplendently. To the guests coming from Paris it seemed as though the Palace, brightly lighted at every window, was a great casket glittering with fire and jewels.

The Queen rose from her game of *cavagnole* at nine in order to dine in public with the King. At midnight the masked ball was to begin, and to it had been invited the *bourgeoisie* who ordinarily did not have access to Royalty's sacred precincts. It looked as though half of Paris had come to be the King's guests. An endless line of carriages rolled into the outer courtyard, their gaily dressed occupants alighting and presenting themselves at the entrance to the Marble Staircase.

No cards of admittance were required. One member of each group raised his mask, gave his name and the number in his party to the usher, and all were allowed to enter. Anyone harboring ill intentions toward the Well-Beloved would have found no obstacles in his way; police precautions were nonexistent; but on this 25th of February 1745 everyone was lighthearted. The heavy barriers of oak were pushed aside, and the throng jostled its way through the State Apartments. Some paused to listen to the musicians stationed in each room or to sample the rich foods and wine which weighted the buffets, but most were intent on struggling through to the Hall of Mirrors. The great *Galerie* was the crowning glory of Europe's most magnificent royal residence, and tonight it presented an almost indescribable spectacle. Fortunately Cochin has left us a matchless engraving of the scene.

Throughout its length of two hundred feet the Hall of Mirrors swarmed with a swirling pushing crowd of maskers —Turks, jugglers, jesters, mandarins, magicians, shepherds, and savages—all reflected and reproduced in the lofty Venetian mirrors which were set opposite each window. The whole pageant was brilliantly lighted by more than three thousand wax candles, which burned in crystal chandeliers and heavy silver candelabra and flickered in the girandoles placed near the windows.

The Savonnerie rug which usually covered the floor had

been removed, and some of the guests sat on the polished surface eating and drinking without embarrassment. The soft rustle of the women's skirts and the sharp tap of the men's high red heels filled the room with a strange contrapuntal rhythm.

In the center of the hall the maskers perspired, but those standing near the tall windows shivered as the cold wind rattled the glass panes and swept through the cracks. The white silk curtains, embroidered with golden *fleur-de-lis*, billowed and swirled as they were caught by fitful gusts of the night air. It almost seemed as though the elements were warning of future storms for the gilded celebrants. But tonight Versailles sailed heedlessly on, like a great lighted ship ignorant of the icebergs beneath the surface.

From the *Salon de la Paix* an unmasked group of the Royal Family emerged, led by the Queen. Marie Leczinska was only forty-two, but already she had the fussy look of an old lady. Like many neglected women she overdressed, loading herself with innumerable ribbons, bows, and ornaments. Though her kind face smiled at the guests, no one was interested in the Queen. Where was the King?

Behind the Queen walked the young married couple. The fifteen-year-old Dauphin bore an elusive resemblance to the King. The same regular eyebrows, the same dark eyes—but these eyes were not soft and tender like the father's. Their expression was timid, almost furtive, as though their owner was constantly afraid of doing some displeasing act and being caught. The Heir to the Throne was costumed as a gardener and his bride as a flower girl. Maria-Rafaela of Spain, three years older than her husband, wore a grave expression. She was plump but not offensively so. Her skin was delicate and fair and went naturally with her beautiful red hair. But this she carefully concealed, even from her husband. "That color," said d'Argenson, "is dishonoring in France."

Suddenly there was a stir in the crowd. The doors of the King's Apartments opened and eight tall figures entered, dressed exactly alike as Yew Trees. A loud murmur of excitement ran through the room. One of these fantastic creatures was surely the King, but which one?

A group of women swarmed around the Yew Trees, teasing, coaxing, seeking to learn behind which mask the Royal face was hiding. The Yews all acted alike and continued to play their evasive game. Madame de Portail, the wife of a Président, was sure she had identified one of the mysterious eight as the Monarch. She flirted with him, and was enraptured when the figure beckoned her to follow him into the King's antechamber. When they reached the small dark room the tall masker made passionate love to her. Madame de Portail, convinced that she had obtained what nearly every woman in France wanted, offered little resistance and in a matter of moments had surrendered herself to her ardent suitor. When she reappeared in the Hall of Mirrors, still smoothing her disheveled dress, the Yew Tree lifted his mask, smiled mockingly, said "Thank you, madame," and disappeared. Poor Madame de Portail was overcome with mortification; it was not the King at all but merely one of his gentlemen.

Most of the beautiful women clustered around the Yew Trees would willingly have done the same. Over two

months had elapsed since Madame de Châteauroux had
gone unmourned (except by the King) to her tomb and
still no successor was in sight. Whom would Louis choose
this time? Surely he had forgotten his grief by now!

There were many who placed their bets on the Duchesse
de Lauraguais. She was certainly no stranger to the King.
And to Louis, always a slave to familiar things, that was
recommendation enough. Moreover it was obvious that
her aimless prattle and unvarying evenness of temper
pleased him. Louis shrank from scenes, especially scenes
with women. However one point counted against Madame
de Lauraguais—she was of the nobility. Louis' experience
with her three sisters, especially Madame de Châteauroux,
made him wary of choosing his next Mistress from among
the Court. Almost any noblewoman in the Hall of Mirrors
that night would have renounced Heaven itself if by doing
so she could become *maîtresse-en-titre*.

But Louis was no fool. He had observed that the ladies
of the nobility were scheming, mercenary, and domineering. Probably he would never have summoned the will to
dismiss Madame de Châteauroux had death not done it
for him, but now that she was gone the cautious King had
no intention of enslaving himself again. Once enslaved,
never free—especially Louis, who never was known to break
a habit in his life.

No, it seemed wiser to stoop to the *bourgeoisie,* to pick
a new Mistress from that cultivated wealthy middle class
with which he had had little personal experience but about
whose lives he knew a great deal. Had not the Duc de
Richelieu, always his preceptor in immorality, excited his

curiosity with tales of amorous conquests among the fair Parisiennes? Had not Louis himself read fascinating secrets of their private lives in letters selected from the mails for his amusement?

There was a stronger advantage than novelty to recommend a bourgeoise. Raised from a class as yet unadmitted to Court, she would owe everything to the King. She would have no powerful family urging her on to more and yet more demands for money, position, and power. Such a woman would love Louis for himself alone (as had poor Madame de Mailly) and would not dare meddle in politics or attempt to dominate him.

So ran his thoughts in the empty weeks after Madame de Châteauroux died, and sometimes he voiced them aloud to his valets Bachelier and Lebel. These men were with the King constantly and knew almost all the secrets of his private life. Frequently they assisted him in his assignations, and could wield great influence in the choice of the next Mistress. It was not they, however, but another, the Sieur Binet, first *valet-de-chambre* to the Dauphin, who was fated to play a crucial role in replacing Madame de Châteauroux.

Binet had free access to the King and remarked one day, when Louis was particularly restless, that he knew a lady of the *bourgeoisie,* young and beautiful, who worshiped the King, who lived only for him. In fact she was the wife of Binet's own relative, Le Normant d'Étioles.

The name struck a chord in the King's memory. Madame d'Étioles—was she not the enchanting woman who had attracted his attention last year in the Forest of Sénart?

Did she not live with her husband near the Royal château of Choisy? Yes, answered Binet, His Majesty was correct. It was the same lady.

The King could not know that destiny was about to play a trick in the Hall of Mirrors and that the outcome would alter irrevocably his reign and the history of France. He could not foresee that a beautiful little bourgeoise not so unambitious as the one of whom he dreamed, would enter his life that night. Could he have known that she would bind him to her as no one ever had done he might have fled; but could he have glimpsed the love and companionship she was to lavish on him, he would have certainly remained.

A slender, graceful form costumed as Diana the Huntress had been watching Louis through the rose silk mask which half covered her features. Now she advanced toward him, sure that she had penetrated his disguise. Although the upper part of her face was concealed, Louis saw a high pale brow crowned with glorious chestnut hair in which sparkled many diamonds. Her bare arms and hands were the most beautiful he had ever seen. Her walk was stately, yet graceful, quite unlike the peacock strut of most ladies of the Court.

Now she was beside the King, who begged her to unmask if only for a moment. The Unknown laughed melodiously and taking an arrow from her quiver placed it to her bow, playfully aiming at the King's heart. "It is your charms, not your darts, that I fear," said Louis and moved toward her. Diana lowered her mask for an instant, and the King

saw what some instinct must have told him he would see—
the smiling, the incomparable face of Madame d'Étioles!

She replaced the mask and, as she turned to flee, dropped
her handkerchief. To the consternation of all the ladies,
noble and middle class alike, the King stooped, picked up
the wisp of silk and lace, and threw it after her retreating
figure. Madame d'Étioles had won!

Three nights later, on the Sunday before Lent, the City
of Paris returned the King's hospitality by giving a ball in
honor of the Dauphin. The arms of France and Spain were
emblazoned wherever one looked, on buildings and on the
handsome pavilions which had been erected in the Place
Louis-le-Grand (Vendôme), Place de la Bastille, and Place
du Carrousel. In these pavilions free food and wine were
dispensed and a noisy cheerful crowd filled the streets, their
natural enthusiasm for the Royal celebration heightened
by the spirit of Carnival.

The ball itself was held at the Hôtel de Ville. In the
courtyard a luxurious room, gilded and mirrored, had been
constructed to provide extra space—but it was not enough.
"There was a great crowd and terrible confusion," Barbier
disgustedly recounted. "It was impossible to go up or down
the staircases. Everyone crowded into the rooms, where it
was disagreeable and suffocating. There were six buffets
scantily laden or badly provided for; the refreshments gave
out three hours before midnight. There is only one opinion
in Paris of the mismanagement of this ball; after having
displayed so much particularity in choosing those who
would take part, they must have not only given out in-

numerable invitations, but to all kinds of people, and no doubt to all the workmen and tradesmen of the town, for there were a lot of boors."

The Prince de Croÿ diplomatically refrained from commenting on the discomforts and confined himself to the innocuous verdict that "as far as the decorations of the hall and the illumination, it was the prettiest thing that I have seen today."

The Dauphin came alone to thank Paris for the tributes paid to his marriage. His speech over, he went downstairs to the main ballroom and was almost crushed in the crowd. With difficulty his twenty-four bodyguards retrieved him and cleared a way through the throng to his carriage.

The King, wishing to leave the full honors to his son, had delayed his own departure from Versailles until one in the morning. At Sèvres his carriage met that of the Dauphin returning from Paris. The Dauphin warned the King how crowded the ball was at the Hôtel de Ville, and the two separated, the son hurrying home to savor the joys of what the father had long since forsaken—the marriage bed.

Hoping the multitude at the Hôtel de Ville would thin out, the King with the Duc d'Ayen went first to the ball at the Opéra. They dismissed the Royal carriage in order to better conceal their identities, paid their admission like everyone else, and mingled unrecognized with the masked dancers. Louis was enjoying the freedom of a private gentleman for the first time, and he danced with several ladies who never suspected that their masked partner was the King of France. Thirty years later the young and impru-

dent Marie Antoinette was to slip away in disguise to many
of these same Opéra balls—but she was not to be so successful in concealing her identity.

When the King and the Duc arrived at the Hôtel de
Ville there was still a crowd of guests. Louis had an assignation with a young woman of good family, and he searched
impatiently for her among the dancers. She was not there.
The Abbé de Bernis, who knew her parents, had warned
them of their daughter's danger and they had forbidden
her to keep the appointment.

Several gentlemen of the King's suite noted their master's irritation and went to the parents' house to rouse them
from sleep. They begged them to send their daughter to
the King; but cajoleries, bribes, and even threats fell un-
heeded on the ears of the respectable parents. By some
unaccountable reasoning, they failed to appreciate the
honor of permitting their daughter to share a bed with
His Most Christian Majesty!

But if Louis was disappointed by one young woman he
was gratified by another. For Madame d'Étioles was at the
Hôtel de Ville. Somewhat disheveled by the pressure of the
crowd and the long hours of uncomfortable waiting, she
managed to assume a seductive air, and Louis was delighted
with her. They retired to a private room where the King,
now enraptured, was allowed a few kisses, a few caresses.

But Madame d'Étioles, contrary to the accounts of some,
did not on that night become the Mistress of the King.
Those who believe she did understand little of her essential
nature. To have yielded completely to Louis at that first
rendezvous would have been to break every rule fixed in

her cool brain. She did not intend to be the King's amusement for one night and then forgotten. She wanted to be
the Declared Mistress, and her calculating instinct told her
that surrendering herself like a milliner's apprentice was
not the way to achieve her goal.

And so the King of France, like an untried schoolboy,
took his new love home—not to her husband, who was still
ignorant of his wife's dazzling prospects, but to her mother
who knew and approved of everything.

The rue de Richelieu, where Madame Poisson lived, was
some distance from the Hôtel de Ville, and the crowds in
the streets slowed their hired carriage almost to a walk.
Coming to an intersection which was blocked by a police
barrier placed there to control the crowds, the frightened
driver refused to go on. The King leaned toward the Duc
d'Ayen and said impatiently, "Give him a *louis*." The Duc,
knowing more about the relative value of money than a
King who never had need of it, objected to the excessive
tip: "Your Majesty must protect yourself. The police will
be informed, they will make inquiries, and tomorrow will
know who we were and where we went." He tipped the
driver a mere six livres, and the cab proceeded unhindered
to the rue de Richelieu where Madame d'Étioles was seen
safely into her mother's house.

It was eight-thirty in the morning when Louis returned
to Versailles. Sleepy as he was, the King changed his coat
and went at once to the Chapel to hear Mass. In this he
saw nothing inconsistent. His private life was one thing—
and he realized how far it strayed from the precepts of
religion—but in his public capacity as the Eldest Son of the

Church, Louis XV was always devout. There was no hypocrisy here. Louis believed firmly in the teachings of the Church, even if he knew himself incapable of living up to them. When once urged at Easter to accept an unconsecrated wafer (since he was not in a state of Grace) he was sincere enough to reject the subterfuge. If he was in his carriage and met a procession carrying the Host, he would descend and kneel in the mud. He was always attentive at Mass, even on this Monday morning when his prayers must have been repeatedly interrupted by the beguiling vision of Madame d'Étioles.

II

REINETTE

*I*N *1721 PHILIPPE,* Duc d'Orléans, was Regent of France, and Paris adopted his morals—or lack of them. The Sun King, Louis XIV, had disappeared below the horizon, and his place on the throne was occupied, if not filled, by a handsome boy who bore the title of Louis XV. But it was the Regent who ruled.

Philippe d'Orléans, although entirely untouched by morality, was not really a bad man; he was only vicious. Still in his forties, he was witty, brilliant, and affable— charming to those with whom he came in daily contact and kindness itself to the boy King, who adored him. But the stench of his private life floated from the windows of the Palais-Royal and infected the entire capital. Never before had Paris given itself up to such unrestrained debauchery.

A shocked contemporary passed judgment: "Immorality is general and frightful. All the young people of both sexes . . . are living the most reprehensible of lives. . . . They comport themselves like the beasts of the field. . . ."

This was not entirely the fault of the Regent. During the last years of Louis XIV France had fought a costly war of attrition. Economy was fashionable among all classes, indeed was a necessity. The old King and his pious Madame de Maintenon frowned upon levity, let alone license. And so when peace came, and then the Regency, a reaction was only to be expected.

But this reaction seemed to have no bounds. Extravagance and speculation were everywhere. The brilliant and unsubstantial Scotsman John Law was promising to restore the kingdom to solvency and to make millionaires of all who bought stock in his *Compagnie de la Louisiane et de l'Occident*. People stormed the brokers' offices fighting and trampling one another in their frenzied craze to exchange money for Law's certificates. Lackeys became millionaires and tried to assume the airs of noblemen. And then inevitably the bubble burst and millionaires became lackeys trying to retain the airs of noblemen. Thousands of investors were ruined, and morals became worse than when thousands had been showered with sudden wealth. Barriers of class were crossed and recrossed on this appalling economic seesaw.

In the midst of this quick vulgar wealth and quicker brutal poverty, the great noblemen of France quarreled like children over questions of petty precedence. Each looked to the State to replenish his own pocket—Philippe d'Orléans more than any other. The common citizens were filled with contempt for the blue-blooded scavengers of the Royal Treasury and filled with fury at the imminent prospect of national bankruptcy.

The young King slept lonely in the gloomy Palace of the Tuileries, while across the street the chandeliers of the Palais-Royal blazed until dawn. There the Regent gathered nightly with his intimates and abandoned himself to drunken revelry. Husky guards barred the doors to intruders, and the noble company was free to wallow in privacy. The champagne was inexhaustible, and by morning everyone was near insensibility. They staggered off to whatever beds they intended to occupy knowing the next evening the performance would begin all over again.

Philippe was a Freethinker, and religion did not, any more than decency, set bounds to the range of conversation at his table. Every member of the clever company vied to outdo the others in relating some outrageous anecdote, obscene jest or blasphemy. The Black Mass was celebrated in the Regent's presence, Paris whispered. Whether this was true or not, he continued to drink the nights away, surrounded by his mistresses and the Duchesse de Berry, the daughter he loved too well. Dipsomaniac, drinking until she reeled and vomited on the floor; nymphomaniac, picking up lusty men from the streets and alleys of Paris, this beautiful horror broke her father's heart by dying at the age of twenty-four.

Such were the times in which the mother of the future Marquise de Pompadour progressed from adolescence to womanhood. Not that Madeleine de la Motte knew the interiors of the Palais-Royal; she was only a bourgeoise, and not even *haute bourgeoise* at that. Daughter of a contractor who supplied meat and other provisions to the *Hôtel des Invalides,* she could hardly expect to move in the exalted circle of His Highness the Regent. But from adolescence she inhaled the prevalent air of amorality, and she was to transmit to her daughter her own agnosticism of right and wrong.

No authentic portrait exists of Mademoiselle de la Motte, but she was considered one of the most attractive women in Paris. Barbier, the ubiquitous lawyer who knew everything that went on in the middle-class circles of the capital, wrote that she was "a beautiful brunette, with very white skin, one of the most beautiful women in Paris, with all the spirit imaginable."

This enchanting girl, the target of many hopeful suitors, chose at nineteen to marry an unprepossessing admirer named François Poisson, who came originally from the diocese of Langres in Champagne. Beyond the fact that he was one of nine children and the son of a well-to-do weaver, little is known about Poisson.

When Madeleine de la Motte married him Poisson was already a widower in his thirties and showed unmistakable signs of a dissipated life. His new wife must have been attracted by his kindness and sense of humor, although when drinking his coarseness and lack of breeding became all too obvious.

And yet Poisson was not the drunken buffoon he has been painted by his daughter's enemies. He drank, yes, admittedly he liked to drink. What man did not? But it is impossible to accept him as a chronic alcoholic when he held so many positions requiring a clear shrewd head.

He was a trusted employee of the four Pâris brothers who specialized in contracting to supply provisions for the account of the Government. He acted capably as their agent in supplying the army of Flanders and earned an

honorable record in supplying troops during a plague in
Provence. These transactions involved a high degree of
financial risk, and it is hardly likely that bankers as astute
as the Pârises would have assigned such duties to an
habitual drunkard. He was neither a sot nor a fool.

On December 29, 1721, while the Regent was giving a
supper party and Louis XV was suffering through his lessons, Madame Poisson gave birth to a daughter. The Poissons lived in the rue de Cléry, and next day, in their Parish
Church of St. Eustache, the infant was christened with the
name Jeanne Antoinette.

Some four years after Jeanne Antoinette's birth, her
brother Abel was born. (An infant sister had intervened,
but did not survive.) The parents adored their bright children, and the little girl and boy from childhood felt a
tender affection for each other. When the little girl was
a few years old it became evident that she had inherited
her mother's great beauty. Her hair, however, was not the
sable hue of Madame Poisson's but rather a soft light shade
of chestnut.

Of course Madame Poisson had lovers, among them a
foreign Ambassador, the Minister of War Le Blanc, and
Jeanne Antoinette's own godfather, Pâris de Montmartel.
But the affectionate happiness of this stable middle-class
household remained unaffected by such minor deviations.

Shortly after Abel's birth, M. Poisson found himself in
serious trouble. In the previous year, 1725, he was assigned
to supervise the supply of grain to the capital, where a
famine threatened. The transaction incurred the displeas-

ure of the Treasury, and as the Pâris brothers enjoyed high protection at Court, M. Poisson became the scapegoat. A commission of inquiry examined his accounts; Poisson could not on sudden notice recover the advance payments he had made for the purchase of supplies or repay the loans he had necessarily incurred. He was found guilty of defalcation and condemned to be hanged. Foreseeing the sentence, Poisson managed to flee from France, remaining for eight years an exile in Germany.

His name, however, was later cleared completely. Thanks to Madame Poisson's insistence, Pâris de Montmartel and the Marquise de Saissac (who was well connected at Court) persuaded the Prime Minister, Cardinal Fleury, to cancel his conviction. In 1734 he was allowed to return to France, and years later Jeanne Antoinette paid 400,000 livres (about $800,000) into the Treasury to balance her father's accounts.

After his return home he was sent, in 1741, to Cologne on a confidential mission by the Minister of War, and on the same trip handled with his usual ability another army contract for the Pârises. This vindication and subsequent employment in positions of trust *preceded* his daughter's liaison with the King.

During her husband's exile, Madame Poisson, who had always lived comfortably, found herself with resources too slender to educate her two children. Fortunately, her principal lover at that time was Charles Le Normant de Tournehem. His portrait by Tocqué hangs at Versailles. It shows a stout gentleman, handsomely attired in a coat of crimson velvet heavily encrusted down the front and around the pockets and cuffs with gold braid. His face is full but not heavy; it is the likeness of a man kind and affluent, and Le Normant de Tournehem was both. He came of a good Orléans family, and succeeded his father as a Farmer-General, one of that wealthy group of financiers who advanced cash to the needy government and received in return the right to collect the taxes.

A Farmer-General was wealthier than many nobles, and Le Normant de Tournehem was fully able to assist Madame Poisson in maintaining her household and in providing for the education of her children. And he was devoted to them, especially to Jeanne Antoinette. The little girl already showed signs of that ineluctable charm which was to remain her greatest gift throughout her life. By then she had acquired the piquant sobriquet of Reinette—Little Queen —and until she ascended into the golden world of Versailles her family and friends called her by this pretty name.

The Farmer-General, on his frequent visits to Madame Poisson, placed Reinette in his lap, talked to her in his grave kind voice, and treated her as though she were his own daughter. In the years to come, when Reinette had become the Marquise de Pompadour and M. de Tournehem had become Superintendent of His Majesty's Buildings, her enemies spread the rumor that she was. But there is no doubt that François Poisson was her real father. Le Normant de Tournehem might pay for Reinette's education, but the absent Poisson supervised it and kept himself informed of her progress.

When the child was seven she was sent to the Ursuline

convent at Poissy, where two of her aunts (Madame Poisson's sisters!) were nuns. Even at that early age Reinette
radiated an irresistible fascination. Like the other girls at
the convent she dressed in printed calico, but she wore it
as though it were taffeta. At once poised and lively, she
strove always to please, and those around her came under
the dominion of her winning manners and her cool intelligence. One of the good nuns wrote to the anxious Poisson:
"Your dear pleasing daughter is very graceful and behaves
herself very well . . . she is not at all bored with us; . . . the
writing-teacher is working hard with her so that she can
write you herself and express her love for you. All she
wants is to have the honor to see and embrace you."

This letter must have been bitter-sweet to the lonely
father in Hamburg, who seemed more concerned about
Reinette than was Madame Poisson in near-by Paris. Worried about money, still young and beautiful, she lived the
loose life she preferred and probably gave little thought to
her daughter. Sometimes, however, she intercepted and
opened letters from Poisson to the convent, as the following indignant message from her religious sister to the
absent father indicates:

"Our Reverend Mother is very surprised not to receive
news of you; she wonders if anyone holds back your letters.
All I know is that my sister Poisson sent us one already
opened. It is only natural to think that she reads them all
before she sends them on; therefore, my dear brother, I
suggest that you write more by the post; it is the safest way
if you do not want my sister to know what you do for your
dear child. Under the pretense that she imagines that you

give a lot, she does not give anything except for bare necessities." Where was M. de Tournehem's money being spent
—on Reinette's needs or Madame Poisson's back?

In the same letter the Ursuline tries to explain Madame
Poisson's lack of generosity as being forced by straitened
circumstances, but soon explodes once more in solicitous
wrath: "... but the child is very delicate; right now she
has a terrible cold; therefore she needs delicacies. The
louis that you sent has been spent, and I have advanced her
an *écu;* our mother superior has made a note of it; if you
can send her anything else, do not do so by my sister. ...
Reinette is always sweet, she speaks to me often of you,
she told me the other day that she knew that you love her
very much, and that she has not a heart big enough to love
you as you deserve, but that she loves you to the full extent
of her little heart, and that as she grows up she thinks that
her affection for you will grow with her."

These letters say a great deal, and by implication they
say much more. It is clear that at eight the ties of affection
which bound Reinette to her father were the strongest in
her life, and she expresses her love for him in phrases unusually mature for a child. Child she must have been, and
child we know she was, at least physically. But nowhere is
there an indication that she ever had childlike reactions
to the people who surrounded her. It was as though she
passed from babyhood straight into adolescence without
ever touching childhood.

It is easy to see that Madame Poisson, while undoubtedly
loving her daughter, was too busy with her own life in
Paris to pay much attention to her. Furthermore, much

of her time was taken up in working for her husband's vindication. Not that she was so fond of Poisson; her chief motive in clearing his reputation was the advancement of Reinette. Madame Poisson did not love her daughter as her husband did—gently, protectively; she loved her fiercely and possessively. And she saw in Reinette's increasing beauty her chance to live vicariously the life she herself could never attain.

As Bernis wrote, "She [Mme. Poisson] did not have the fashionable manner, but she had spirit, ambition, and courage." Her middle-class origin prevented her pushing upward into the fashionable salons of the capital, but Reinette's beauty and charm offered her mother a way to satisfy her intense longing—the aching, frustrating longing which every unsuccessful social climber knows. If Madame Poisson had her way she would push her daughter upward, ever upward, from one social gradation to another, into marriage, into the fashionable world of the rue St. Honoré, and—who knew?—perhaps even higher.

Once when Reinette was sick with one of her frequent colds her busy mother came and took the child away from the convent. She never returned; her religious instruction was finished at the age of eight. It was not to count heavily in her future career, but she never forgot those who had been kind to her. Many years later, as the King's Mistress, she granted a pension to her Aunt, now the Abbess Madame Sainte-Perpétue, and donated money to repair the old convent. Perhaps she did so in memory of a charming little girl, delicate and courteous, intelligent and pleasing, who answered to the name of Reinette.

In the Age of Enlightenment, the world of fashion turned from the superstition of religion to the superstition of sorcerers. Fortunetellers of all kinds were the rage in Paris. One afternoon in 1730, shortly after Reinette left the convent, her mother took her to the noted Madame Lebon. The fortuneteller sat quietly for a long time, staring intently at the alert child before her. At last she spoke, a strange smile hovering at the corners of her mouth:

"Ma chère, vous serez presqu'une reine!" My dear, you will be almost a Queen!

There are those who do not believe in such things and never will; and there are those who do, and nothing can shake their belief. The scoffers dismiss the prophecy, suggesting that the scheming Madame Poisson briefed the fortuneteller in advance. That will never be known. But it is clear—and this is the important thing—that Reinette was deeply impressed and believed from then on that her destiny was bound by those compelling words. So much so that in the meticulous account book of the Marquise de Pompadour there is an entry which reads: "To Madame Lebon, for predicting that I would be the King's Mistress, a pension of 600 livres."

It was hardly credible, even in the Age of Enlightenment, that a nine-year-old girl could understand all the implications of becoming mistress to the King. The sexual drive is weakest in the years immediately preceding puberty, and Reinette certainly did not grasp the full import of the prophecy; to think that she did is to impute to her a depravity which she never possessed even in the full tide of her success.

Nevertheless, Madame Poisson's ample imagination soared. She noticed that Madame Lebon's words caught the child's fancy, and she played upon it. Beyond the fashionable world of Paris, beyond the sparkling salons rippling with witty and well-bred conversation, upward, through the gilded gates of Versailles itself, she visualized her daughter's progress into the very bedroom of the King.

And so Reinette began a new education, quite different from the one she had received at Poissy. This time it was her mother who established the curriculum. Madame Poisson, beautiful though she was, knew from her own full experience that beauty alone is not enough to hold a man's interest for long. What a man demands in a woman is variety, and perfection in that variety. Reinette must excel in all the arts and graces of her day.

Le Normant de Tournehem was in full agreement with Madame Poisson's ambitious plans and referred to Reinette as *un morceau de roi*. Only the best teachers would satisfy him, and he agreed to assume the expenses of this second and more wordly education.

Crébillon the Elder, one of the great dramatists of the last reign, instructed her in elocution and recitation. Crébillon was poor and sometimes inclined to be unsociable, but he loved Reinette and imparted to her something of his own gentle wit and irony. She learned dancing from Guibaudet; most important of all, Jélyotte, the great singer of the Opera and immensely popular with the public, trained her voice. In her youth singing was her greatest talent.

She studied the art of engraving, and although she was never more than a skillful amateur, the practice was in no small part responsible for her perfect sense of line and color. Surprisingly for one so delicate, she was an expert horsewoman; she loved horses and managed the most spirited with easy skill. In short, she possessed all the graces and accomplishments of a young goddess, save one —the knowledge of the difference between good and evil.

But does the fault lie with her? Despite the traditional strength of family ties in France, the eighteenth century was not an age which exalted conjugal love. That was a rarity and, in Paris at least, unfashionable. It was common for husbands and wives to ride in separate carriages and to frequent different salons. Many lived apart and announced their visits to each other in safe advance. Everyone who was anyone agreed that the moral side of love should be ignored. Love was a game, a series of adventures rather than a grand passion.

Imbert de St. Amand caught this spirit perfectly: "Look at the Cupid of the reign of Louis XV; the noisy insolent victorious Cupid, who scoffs at the love of former times as a malicious and ill-bred child mocks at an old man." The Parisians and courtiers who played with this mischievous Cupid were not beasts, not savages. They were the most cultured people in Europe, courteous and kind in their dealings with one another. But in their sexual habits morals played no part; they simply did not exist.

Throughout the Christian era society has not lived up to the standards it sets for itself. The inevitable result is that we take the Janus-face of hypocrisy for granted. The eighteenth century did not. Its greatest thinkers pretended neither to Christianity nor morality. They paid much attention to form and little to feeling. They had many vices but prudery and hypocrisy were not among them. They knew *themselves* and agreed with the Marquis d'Argenson that "the heart is a faculty of which we deprive ourselves daily for want of exercise, whereas the mind becomes keener day by day."

In Reinette's own family circle there was no one who exemplified virtue, no one who pointed out the desirability of her retaining it after becoming a woman. When she was thirteen her father returned and resumed his place in the house, if not the bed, of his wife. M. de Tournehem without the slightest tinge of constraint continued to be a steady visitor. M. Poisson did not resent these open attentions to his wife; on the contrary, he and the amiable Farmer-General formed a friendship which lasted as long as they lived.

There is no evidence that Poisson offered any objection to the road which his wife and her lover had marked out for Reinette. Not because he did not love her; we know that he did. It was simple enough in his mind: if Reinette could win the King's heart and become his Mistress, it would be the greatest fortune that could come to her—and to her family. Fortune, yes. No one gave happiness much thought. It never entered her father's head that there was anything shameful in such a relationship. Since none of the affectionate family told her it was wrong, since none of them thought it was wrong, how could Reinette be blamed for pursuing a dream that was embedded in her during childhood?

The girl, now adolescent, knew all the gossip of the

Court, and in the constant indulgence of her fantasy she laid the cornerstone of her future life. With her this fantasy was not play-acting but deadly serious. Already she was thinking of herself as the King's Mistress. She owned a portrait of the handsome young Louis who was only eleven years older than she. In her mother's salon she listened eagerly to gossip of the King's growing estrangement from his plain Queen and of his taking for the first time (1732) a mistress, Madame de Mailly.

Madame Poisson and Le Normant de Tournehem and Reinette herself were all aware that the odds against them were heavy. Naturally there was nothing unusual in a King of France having a mistress; what was unusual, indeed unheard of, was that she should come from outside the nobility. From time to time a King might pause in the magnificent routine of his life to honor some little bourgeoise with his tender attentions but such an affair was merely transitory. It could not last. Tradition opposed it. The barrier betwen the middle class and the Privileged Orders was too great for an ordinary woman to surmount.

But Mademoiselle Poisson was no ordinary young woman. As she passed her middle teens, the beauty of childhood changed into a fragile, an almost divine beauty of young womanhood. Her gentle harmonious disposition and her exquisite taste concealed the obsessive ambition to scale the social heights which her mother had imparted to her.

Meanwhile, during these years of preparation and training for her future, what kind of life did she live? There is little record of it. Did she have girlhood friends? Young girls need friends in whom to confide, with whom they can share their hopes and dreams. If Reinette had such a friend, her name has not survived. Young men? Suitors? No, it was not customary for a genteel young Frenchwoman to receive male callers before she married.

As it is for most children who have been almost entirely with older people, life within her family was sufficient for Reinette during these years. She loved her father deeply, and since Madame Poisson was merely friendly with him Reinette did not suffer the jealousy which so many daughters feel toward their mothers. She was congenial with her mother, in fact very fond of her, and she began to absorb some of Madame Poisson's driving characteristics. Her brother Abel, who adored her, had grown into an intelligent boy, modest and quiet. And there was always the affectionate sustaining presence of the family's good angel, M. de Tournehem, who never for an instant forgot his interest in her future.

It is quite possible that one reason for her absorption in her family was her frail health. In spite of her many activities Reinette was never robust. She was slender, and her beauty had a fragile, almost ethereal quality. Although she could be animated when she wished, her vitality was made possible only by regular periods of rest. She suffered chronically from colds, and her chest was delicate. There was a still more disturbing factor in her health. It is almost certain that during the trying years of adolescence menstruation was abnormally delayed. This might have been caused by glandular disorders and a tendency to anemia. In any event, to her perpetual mortification she suffered throughout life from marked irregularity in her periods.

This infirmity probably goes far to explain why she was never, in the usual sense of the word, a passionate woman. Tender, charming, sympathetic, light, and amusing—she was all of these. And beneath the soft exterior was a steely determination to pursue her ambition at any cost. That was passion of a kind, but not sexual passion.

At eighteen her beauty had flowered, and Madame Poisson lost no time in launching her campaign to push Reinette into a higher social sphere. Some of the great houses in the rue St. Honoré willingly opened their doors to her fresh youthful talents, conveniently overlooking her comparatively low birth. But Reinette could not always secure entrance for Madame Poisson. There is something infinitely pathetic in the spectacle of the great world of society accepting the beautiful daughter while smiling patronizingly, even contemptuously, upon the mother whose driving force had propelled her upward. Poor Madame Poisson!

The eighteenth-century salon was a particularly feminine institution. The salon revolved around a woman, and women exercised within its confines enormous influence, guiding conversation and making or ruining many a career. It might be the aristocratic Duchesse de Choiseul, clever and virtuous, abounding with common sense, never taken in by the contrived simplicity of Rousseau; it might be the obscurely born Madame Geoffrin, wife of a rich glass manufacturer, ugly and ignorant but possessing a genius for collecting authors (she did not bother to read their books) and managing their clashing temperaments with tact and finesse; or it might be the Marquise du Deffand, ironical and easily irritated, whose gatherings were diplomatic and political as well as literary, and where no one was admitted unless he had a great reputation.

Reinette was welcome at the house of Madame de Tencin, who presided over one of the most successful salons. It was there she met Montesquieu, Duclos, and Fontenelle. Among the group was the young and then unknown Marmontel, who saw "a woman of excellent talents and profound judgment, but who, enveloped in her exterior of plainness and simplicity, had rather the air of the housekeeper than the mistress. This was Madame de Tencin." She was the sister of a Cardinal whom she loved almost incestuously, and had been mistress to the Regent (now dead) and to Cardinal Du Bois. She took an immediate fancy to Reinette. This was fortunate; with her great influence at Court and her practiced ability to pull strings, she was to prove a valuable future ally.

Although Madame de Tencin's salon was considered one of the most exclusive, it soon disillusioned the observant Marmontel, who lamented, "It was a question of who should most quickly seize the moment as it flew, to place his epigram, his story, his anecdote, his maxim, or his light and pointed satire, and to make or find this opportunity the circuit they took was often unnatural." With each guest striving to be the center of attention, it was impossible for the conversation to hover long on any subject, and the hostess used a firm hand to keep her literary menagerie in order.

It was in these surroundings that Reinette first came into contact with the sharpest wits and deepest intellects of Paris. The *philosophes,* that collective term which included most of France's famous writers during the eighteenth century, were delighted with her quick mind and clever tongue no less than with her beauty. They did much, these Voltaires and d'Alemberts, to influence her attitudes and shape her thoughts. They formed her (with little difficulty) into a typical woman of the Age of Enlightenment and filled her unreligious mind with their own cynical skepticism of God and Church.

Reinette's voice was in demand as much as her beauty and wit and one day at Madame d'Angervilliers' her hostess begged her to sing. Although Reinette was clever enough to appear modest of her talents, nothing pleased her more than to demonstrate them. She sang the enchanting "Enfin il est en ma Puissance" from Lulli's *Armide,* her light clear voice moving everyone with its tenderness. Madame de Mailly, who was present and who had already been superseded in the King's affections by Madame de Vintimille, was overcome with sadness, and embraced Reinette with tears in her eyes.

Reinette had made visible progress up the social ladder, but the ascent was too slow to satisfy her mother or herself. Too many great doors still remained closed, too many families of fashion and wealth still disdained the little bourgeoise. Jeanne Antoinette Poisson had gone as far as she could go. What was needed now was more money, a secure position, and—another name. In a word, marriage.

III

MADAME LE NORMANT D'ÉTIOLES

NCE AGAIN Le Normant de Tournehem came to the rescue. Never losing sight of Reinette's ultimate goal, he looked around for a suitable husband who would smooth her path and found in his own nephew the perfect choice. Charles-Guillaume Le Normant d'Étioles was the son of Le Normant de Tournehem's brother, the Treasurer of the Mint. In the Le Normant family it was customary to distinguish one member from another by adding the name of each member's estate to the surname.

Le Normant d'Étioles was four years older than Reinette. Red-haired and undersized, he was neither handsome nor graceful, but his manners were unmistakably those of a gentleman. As son of the Treasurer and nephew of a Farmer-General, his future was assured; moreover it was likely that the closeness of family ties would make him amenable to M. de Tournehem's—and Reinette's—wishes.

But the marriage plans struck a snag at the beginning. M. d'Étioles was cool and more than cool, unwilling. He did not deny Reinette's charm and beauty; he could not. But in his opinion her charms, varied as they were, did not offset the disadvantage of uniting his blood with that

47

of Poisson or of acquiring for mother-in-law a woman whose morals caused even Paris to murmur. The combined blandishments of M. de Tournehem and the threats of his own father were necessary to persuade him to change his mind.

Once persuaded, the young man had to admit that the marriage offered advantages as well as drawbacks. The Poissons did not stint themselves in their efforts to reassure M. d'Étioles that the marriage would be financially as well as personally enjoyable, and the marriage contract shows that Reinette's dowry amounted to the considerable value of 120,000 livres. Thirty thousand was paid in precious stones, jewels, linen, and wearing apparel, while the remaining 90,000 was represented by a good house in the rue St. Marc. The dowry also included an annuity of 141 livres.

But as usual it was Le Normant de Tournehem who showered wealth upon the couple. He gave them 83,500 livres in cash and agreed to house and feed them (with five servants) and to provide carriages and horses—for his lifetime! He further promised that at his death he would bequeath them 150,000 livres in addition to what they would ordinarily receive as heirs. In the unlikely event that this love match dissolved in separation, the generous uncle bound himself to pay to each 4,000 livres a year in lieu of supporting their establishment. It is small wonder that the realistic Parisians again speculated on the parentage of Reinette! Aside from affection, M. de Tournehem was merely interested in furthering her career, and she was to repay him a hundredfold. On March 9, 1741, the wedding was celebrated in the Church of St. Eustache, where Reinette had been christened fewer than twenty years before.

After the marriage M. d'Étioles ruefully remembered his reluctance to consent to the match and wondered how he could have been such a fool. He fell deeply in love with Reinette, and there was no way he could know that only then was he being the fool. Her delicate beauty was enough to arouse any man's passion, a quality in which M. d'Étioles was not lacking. Reinette was a born coquette, expert at stimulating the interest of men, and her innate sexual coldness, which she tried to conceal, was just evident enough to tantalize and inflame still further her ardent husband.

Thanks to the marriage terms the young couple lived on a princely scale. In Paris, although they had a house in the rue Croix des Petits Champs, they lived at M. de Tournehem's luxurious hôtel in the rue St. Honoré. Here they entertained lavishly and often. No decent young woman is truly sought after in France until after she is married, and Reinette (as she was still called) became one of the most popular women in Paris. Many men begged to become her lover, but she gently refused them all, disarming them with her tact and grace and invariably retaining them as friends. The amiable M. d'Étioles was not jealous and he had no reason to be—of any ordinary rival.

As Madame Le Normant d'Étioles, Reinette's beauty was at its height. No portrait painted at this time can so well describe her as the words of Georges Le Roy, who, as Master of the King's Hunt, saw her many times: "She was," he says, "rather above middle height, slender, supple, and graceful. Her hair was luxuriant, of a light chestnut shade rather than blond, and the eyebrows which crowned her magnificent eyes were of the same color. She had a perfectly formed nose, a charming mouth, lovely teeth, and a ravishing smile, while the most exquisite skin one could wish to behold put the finishing touch to all her beauty. Her eyes had a singular fascination, which they owed perhaps to the uncertainty of their color. They possessed neither the dazzling splendor of black eyes, the tender languor of blue, nor yet the peculiar keenness of gray; their undecided color seemed to lend to them every kind of charm, and to express in turn all the feelings of an intensely mobile nature."

To these physical charms were added others more lasting: a keen intuition, and an extraordinary ability to adapt herself to the person of the moment and to become at will lively or serious, gay or grave, witty or profound. Hers was that most precious of all social gifts—the art of pleasing.

Before her marriage Reinette had met the influential Madame Geoffrin but had never been invited to her salon. It was different now; to the wife of Le Normant d'Étioles many doors swung open in the rue St. Honoré. Madame Poisson, however, was still an embarrassing problem. "One day," says Madame Geoffrin's daughter, "to my great annoyance I saw Madame Poisson and her daughter arriving at my mother's house...." Reinette, Madame de Ferté-Imbault admitted, was pleasing and "merited a few courtesies," but Madame Poisson was "so disreputable that it seemed impossible to follow up this acquaintance."

These cruel snubs must have wounded deeply both

mother and daughter, but they did not stand in the way
of Reinette's progress. She quickly won Madame Geoffrin
to her side, flattering the ugly old woman and taking the
utmost care not to attract too much attention to herself.
Madame Geoffrin was not witty, but she had an abundance
of common sense and "knew when to keep quiet, and to
speak only of subjects she knew." If the conversation
threatened to become unruly or to take a dangerous turn,
Madame Geoffrin's piercing black eyes flashed, and with a
peremptory "Come, that's all," she steered the talk into
another field.

Her salon was the best organized and most complete in
the rue St. Honoré. Every Monday there was a supper for
the painters and every Wednesday one for the *philosophes*.
Voltaire came, and Montesquieu, and the popular and
entertaining d'Alembert. In spite of the cynicism which
infected her guests, Madame Geoffrin herself was secretly
devout and Royalist. She might tolerate within her walls
chatter about a Constitution and freedom of religion and
listen to frantic advocacy of the "New Ideas," but she
never accepted them. As for M. Geoffrin, he merely paid
the bills. No one paid any attention to him or even noticed
when he left the table.

Reinette's social pace was soon slowed, but not halted,
by pregnancy. The always delicate balance of her health
was naturally disturbed, to the deep concern of her family.
"Do not," she wrote reassuringly to her father, "be uneasy
any more over my health. I assure you it is admirable at
present. I have had two attacks of fever but that was ten
days ago and I have not had it since. It has absolutely left

me. I have taken much quinine and so much other medicine that it has absolutely pulled me through. I tell you that to console myself for all of these vile drugs. I am going today to amuse myself at the Opéra."

Her son Guillaume-Charles was born in December 1741. Nothing is known of him except that his life was brief. Within six months he was dead, and Reinette, always a tenderhearted mother, grieved for her loss. But it was not good form in the world of fashion to grieve openly, and Reinette continued to live her pleasant careless life, keeping her sorrow to herself.

Winters were spent in Paris and summers in the country at Étioles. There M. de Tournehem had thoughtfully provided the same lavish accommodations for entertaining, and there during the long lazy months Reinette was truly queen of her surroundings. Country life in the eighteenth century was spacious and easy and above all informal. Etiquette was banished from the little château and Reinette begged her guests to leave formality behind.

The circle of her admirers was constantly growing. In addition to her old friend and tutor Crébillon, her admirers included the venerable Fontenelle, dean of French letters, Gresset the popular poet, Cahusac the dramatist, Montesquieu, author of *Lettres Persanes,* and, of course, Voltaire, as avaricious as he was talented. All these creative men paid willing court to their charming hostess and bowed to her gentle domination.

Reinette's mind was really cultivated. She was a true Parisienne, alert and interested in the intellectual currents which swirled about her. There was nothing affected in her love of literature, and she and her guests discussed and read the latest books, sometimes aloud.

But there were other diversions. Reinette loved the stage and was a consummate actress, both on and off the boards. M. de Tournehem built a small theater at Étioles, complete in every detail even to machinery for changing the sets. There she acted in plays for her friends' amusement and, as with everything she planned, was brilliantly successful. Président Hénault, irreproachably decorous and a friend of the Queen, met her at a dinner and was so carried away that he told Madame du Deffand he had "found one of the prettiest women I have ever seen; it is Madame d'Étioles; she knows music perfectly, sings with all possible charm and taste, knows a hundred songs, and acts comedy at Étioles in a theater as handsome as the Opéra. . . ."

She met other people too, some of whom bore great titles. The cynical Duc de Richelieu, one of the King's closest friends, returned to Versailles full of praise for the rich little bourgeoise at Étioles; the Chevalier de Brige, one of the handsomest men at Court and Master of the King's Horse, admired her passionately and was so constant a visitor that some suspected he was her lover. But Reinette was not susceptible to physical attraction and continued a placid friendship with Brige.

By all reason, Reinette should have been supremely happy. She had already risen far above the level to which she was born. She was very rich, and the radiant center of the group comprising the most intelligent men in France. She dressed in exquisite taste, and if it was "in the shade between the last degree of elegance and the first degree of nobility," she was nevertheless far better groomed than the ladies of the Court. Luxury surrounded her, and she was worshiped by her easygoing husband.

But she was not happy; at least she was not satisfied. High as she had climbed, it was not high enough. To a woman as ambitious as Reinette only the highest peak would bring satisfaction, and how could she, with her background, be expected to distinguish between satisfaction and true happiness? The words of Madame Lebon, *You will be almost a Queen* were stamped indelibly in her memory. They spurred her on even in those idyllic days at Étioles, and they were responsible for the conduct which robbed her mind and body of peace for the rest of her life.

How could she honestly have been in love with Louis XV when he had never spoken to her? How could a woman so level-headed, so free from hysteria, have surrendered herself to what must have seemed a hopeless pursuit? There are two factors which go far to explain her conduct: her mother's encouragement—the unceasing reiteration that she was *un morceau de roi*—and her own cool nature. Had she been a woman of strong physical passions, Reinette would have sought a lover from among the many men who besieged her and would have dismissed as a senseless dream any idea of capturing the King. Had she been lacking in ambition she would have lived contentedly with M. d'Étioles, a virtuous and honored wife, and gone to her grave unhated and unknown.

As she was both ambitious and sexually cool, her dream of becoming Louis' mistress spurred her on. And the

dream had the advantage of demanding no physical sacrifice. She was a narcissist with all the real charm and the
unvarying coldness of those who love themselves, and she
was true to type in weaving sensual fantasies around the
figure of the King before she had ensnared him. With the
King only an image in her mind, Reinette could honestly
imagine herself in love with him. She was an inwardly
glacial belle, out to capture a male for security and power
and, above all, for social position. Reluctant to surrender
her physical self, she was convinced that, when forced to
do so, no other woman could be more desirable.

Étioles lay not far from the Royal château of Choisy-le-
Roi and the Forest of Sénart where Louis XV liked to hunt.
The Monarch enjoyed and needed violent physical exercise, and he indulged in this sport several times a week.
The King and his gentlemen, dressed in Louis's favorite
blue with knives at their belts, were a handsome sight as
they galloped through the Forest after the hounds.

During the fall and winter of 1743-44 the King's path
was frequently crossed by a high-wheeled blue phaeton
drawn by a pair of magnificent chestnut horses. The driver
of this delicate vehicle was exquisitely dressed, sometimes
in light blue to match her chariot, sometimes in pink or
rose. She never paused long enough to allow Louis more
than a fleeting glimpse and then she was gone, dashing
down another path and into the woods. She handled her
horses with the casual grace which comes only from skill,
and she seemed to know the byways of Sénart as well as
the Royal hunters. When Louis, his curiosity aroused,

inquired who the fair charioteer might be, he was told that she lived near-by and was the wife of a rich bourgeois, Le Normant d'Étioles.

A few weeks later, in a gesture of gallantry, the King sent to Étioles the horns from a stag which he had killed. This gift caused a ripple of witty remarks among the guests at Étioles, but the master of the château was oblivious to any hidden significance that might lie in a pair of horns. Teased by her friends, Reinette replied airily that she was charmed by the King's kindness, that he was the handsomest man in the world, and that "only he could make me unfaithful to my husband." Everyone laughed at her insouciance, and none more heartily than M. d'Étioles.

Reinette's boldness increased and she drove more often to the forest to intercept the Royal hunt. Once she came so close to the glade where the King's party was enjoying a picnic that she could plainly see the *pyramides d'Égypte* (mounds of minced ham and spiced veal) which formed the main dish. Her sudden appearance startled the picnickers; she paused for a moment, looked straight at the King and then, striking her horses lightly with her blue-ribboned whip, she and the phaeton vanished into the Forest.

This was going too far. The Duchesse de Châteauroux could not fail to notice the King's interest in a woman who might become a dangerous rival, and she sent word to the upstart Madame d'Étioles that it would be wiser to stay away from the course of the Royal hunts. Reinette could only obey; she was in no position to make an open enemy of the King's Mistress. The little blue phaeton did not appear again.

IV

THE TRAP IS SPRUNG

*L*ENT BEGAN on March 3rd, three days after Louis had escorted Mme. d'Étioles home to her mother. The series of brilliant balls came to an end, but the beginning of the season of penance had no perceptible effect, in fact no effect at all, on the King's new love affair. Neither he—nor Reinette—was inclined to let their feelings cool. Louis was not accustomed to unfulfilled passion, and Reinette had no intention of throwing away the advantages of so auspicious a beginning.

It is uncertain exactly when the King became her lover, but it was at Versailles, sometime between the night of the ball at the Hôtel de Ville and March 10th. On that date the Duc de Luynes wrote in his journal that "all the masked balls have given rise to talk about the King's new love affairs, and especially about a Madame d'Étioles who is young and pretty; her mother is called Madame Poisson. They say that *she has been here* [Versailles] for some time and that she is the King's choice. If that is true, it can only be a light affair, and not a question of a new Mistress."

The Duc de Luynes' wife was Lady in Waiting to the Queen, and although the Duc was also a member of Marie

57

Leczinska's dull, virtuous circle, he was an impartial observer of life at Versailles and wrote with fairness and discretion. What he lacked was imagination and a knowledge of human nature. It never occurred to him that Louis XV would pick a middle-class woman, no matter how seductive, to be *maîtresse-en-titre*. To the nobleman de Luynes, it was unthinkable that such an affair could last.

For a few days it looked as though his estimate was correct. Louis grew suddenly cold to Madame d'Étioles and she went back to Paris. She waited in an agony of doubt and mortification for another summons to the Palace, but none came. That week of slight and neglect must have been the worst of her life. To be so near the prize, to have it almost within her grasp, and to see it apparently withdrawn! To have given herself—perhaps for nothing! To be treated like a girl from the streets! It was maddening. She must have wept bitter tears of wounded pride and asked herself a thousand times, *Why?* What had she done to turn the King from her? Had he sensed her lack of passion—or something worse?

At Versailles the King confided to Binet that he had found Madame d'Étioles attractive, indeed charming. He did not deny her beauty or her intelligence, but he thought he perceived in her an undue ambition and desire for advancement. He wanted time to think, and he wanted to test her devotion. Louis was nearer the truth than he knew. By nature he moved cautiously, distrusted the motives of everyone, and was wary of hasty decisions. Binet pointed out that he must be mistaken, that Madame d'Étioles was already wealthy and could have no motive other than love for him. But the King remained unconvinced, and the instinct which warned him might have doomed Madame d'Étioles to obscurity had not assistance come to her from an unexpected source.

This was the interference of the Dauphin's tutor Boyer, Bishop of Mirepoix, the leader of the pious party at Court. Always respectful of the Church, the King took Boyer's advice on affairs of ecclesiastical administration, refusing to heed the fulminations of Richelieu and other nobles who hated and feared the zealous priest. Boyer was unquestionably able and honest, but his honesty was the unpleasant honesty of a bigot. Hot tempered, tactless, and indiscreet, he hated the useless nobility and the *philosophes* with equal fervor. His enemies blamed the revival of Jansenism on his rigid views and pointed to his intolerance as the cause of increasing religious bitterness.

Boyer wielded unbounded influence over the Queen and her children. He had even, said the King's friends, gone so far as to prejudice the Dauphine against her father-in-law because of the King's flagrant infidelities. Louis had twice invited her to the Private Apartments to see his collection of treasures, and each time the Dauphine failed to appear. The third time, when she did come, she entered with an air of pained embarrassment, as though expecting to interrupt a debauch. Was not this the fault of Boyer? Had he not poured into the prudish ears of the Dauphin and his wife lurid accounts of the King's love affairs in those lovely *Petits Cabinets*? Up to now Louis had ignored these poisonous hints. He was far from blind to the motives of those around him. He realized that the Duc de Richelieu and his cabal were self-seeking and vicious. Besides, he respected the Bishop. Perhaps he feared him too.

The furore over a new Mistress was far more than mere jealousy and gossip. It was a matter of state, of high policy, for the past showed that whoever controlled the new Mistress would most likely control the King. The last thing that the Duc de Richelieu desired was that the King should have *no* Mistress. That would imply a relapse into the hands of the Devout and an end to the Duc's own iniquitous influence. True his candidate was Madame de Lauraguais, his own niece. But if the King preferred Madame d'Étioles, then let it be Madame d'Étioles! Let it be anyone, just so it was someone!

The Bishop saw the danger clearly. The scandal at Metz, the outrageous affront of Madame de Châteauroux's recall —those were bad enough. But this new one, this Madame d'Étioles, was worse. She came from the salons of Paris and was known to be the friend of the *philosophes*—Voltaire who had referred to the Holy Church as the "infamous thing," Diderot who was an avowed atheist! What disasters might not lie ahead for the Monarchy, for the Church itself, if a woman sympathetic to such subversive ideas became the Mistress of His Most Christian Majesty? The Bishop was right. He was the first (but by no means the last) of the Sons of Loyola to tilt with this young woman who was a true child of the Age of Enlightenment.

Boyer was informed that Binet had first introduced Madame d'Étioles to the King's Apartments, and he confronted the valet-de-chambre with characteristic bluntness, threatening him with the loss of his post if Madame d'Étioles saw the King again. Binet was terrified and denied that Madame d'Étioles had desired anything except to ask the King to appoint her husband a Farmer-General. What was more natural than that Binet, her husband's own cousin, should be the intermediary? M. d'Étioles, said Binet, knew of this and had no objections. He assured the Bishop that Madame d'Étioles had received the promise she desired from the King and would not reappear at Versailles.

Boyer seemed satisfied though Binet could not rest. He feared for his own position, and in order to save himself told the King's friends of the Bishop's threats. Here, they thought, was their chance to confound the domineering priest and at the same time make up the King's mind to their own advantage.

Louis disliked making decisions, but he disliked even more any interference with his private life. At such times his weak will reversed itself and, typical of those who are by nature irresolute, he grew stubborn. He was indignant at the Bishop's ill-timed interference and determined to see Madame d'Étioles again. Binet undoubtedly warned her of the King's suspicions and advised her to appear less calculating and more enamored. It was also likely that Madame de Tencin, who had never lost interest in her young friend, assured the King of Reinette's love. But it was the blundering of Boyer that definitely charted the King's course—and France's.

Madame d'Étioles was seen again at Versailles, and the Prince de Croÿ noted on March 20th that the King was very much in love, although he "hunts all the same, three or four times a week, sups, these days upstairs with *her*, and spends the greater part of his time there. . . ."

On March 31st, Madame d'Étioles appeared in public at Versailles for the first time, at a comic ballet of Rameau's which was held on the stage of the Riding School. Invitations to this were eagerly sought, and her presence there openly confirmed her new status. The following night, at the *Comédie Italienne*, she was even more conspicuous. "The King was there in a small grilled box under that of the Queen. . . . One noticed that she [Madame d'Étioles] was there in a box in full view of the King and Queen; she was handsomely dressed and very pretty."

Ten days later, on Holy Saturday, the Duc de Luynes, faithfully recording all that he saw and heard, observed that the King "dines in private upstairs in his *Cabinets* or in some other place unknown, but no one is invited to dine with him. There are still rumors about Madame d'Étioles." Obviously the charitable Duc was not in the King's confidence or he would not have been so naïve. That same evening Louis invited a few of his friends, all men, to dinner to meet Madame d'Étioles. The party lasted late, and although the King dutifully attended Easter Mass the next morning, it is reasonable to assume that he did not receive the Sacrament.

M. de Luynes, whose chronology was more precise than his intuition, noted on April 22d: "One does not know precisely where she stays, but I think it is in the little apartment which belonged to Madame de Mailly and which adjoins the *Petits Cabinets*. She does not stay here all the time; she comes and goes from Paris, returning at

night." And on April 28th: "They say that she is hopelessly in love with the King and that this passion is
mutual." By then the Duc was convinced that a new
scandal was imminent, because he referred to the protests
of M. d'Étioles and remarked that although the King was
in love he still hesitated to name Madame d'Étioles as
maîtresse-en-titre.

And what of the amiable husband? Where was he during
March and April when his wife was journeying to and
from Versailles, sometimes remaining away from home
for several days? The problem of M. d'Étioles was handled
—not surprisingly—by that most astute of uncles, M. Le
Normant de Tournehem. The Farmer-General, advised
by Madame Poisson of Reinette's soaring prospects, prudently sent his nephew to the provinces on an inspection
trip and delayed his return as long as possible. The absence
of the unsuspecting M. d'Étioles gave his wife the freedom
she needed to spring the trap.

By Easter, however, M. d'Étioles was on his way home.
De Tournehem went to Magnanville to meet him and
there discharged the delicate task of informing him that
his wife had taken the King as her lover. De Tournehem
explained she felt an impulse so violent that she could not
resist it, and there was no other course for d'Étioles but to
consider a separation. Knowing from the beginning Madame Poisson's plans for her daughter, M. de Tournehem
would never have arranged her marriage if he had had
much affection for his nephew. Throughout the years his
first loyalty had been to Reinette. It still was.

As he was not an unfeeling man, however, he was

touched and frightened by the violence of d'Étioles' re-action. The young husband deeply loved his wife and had never for an instant suspected that she would ever leave him. He fainted from shock. When he recovered he became so violent that M. de Tournehem feared he might kill himself and ordered all his guns taken away. The betrayed husband talked wildly of going to Versailles to recover his wife, a piece of rashness which M. de Tournehem warned him was too dangerous a course and was completely out of the question.

The position of Madame d'Étioles was immeasurably strengthened by her husband's threats. She knew that de Tournehem could handle him and that in the end d'Étioles would acquiesce, but she pretended to the King that her husband was insanely jealous, that she was terrified for her life, and that only the King could protect her. She wept (tears were a most effective weapon against Louis) and begged him to recognize her position and to order a legal separation from M. d'Étioles.

What she really feared was not her husband's righteous wrath but the insecurity of her status at Versailles. She had had enough of the furtive secrecy of the past month, enough of being smuggled through secret doors and up hidden stairs. She wanted recognition, the sweet triumph of open acknowledgment as the King's Mistress. In the end the sight of her tears and the delicate flush of her fragile beauty overcame the King; he agreed to all her demands.

She was to be made *maîtresse-en-titre* when he returned from the army, to be presented at Court, and to have a title of nobility. Before the King's departure he bought for her the marquisate of Pompadour, an estate in Limousin which brought in an annual revenue of 12,000 livres. It had belonged to an ancient family which had become extinct only a short time before. The new bearer of its arms, three gold towers on a field of blue, would be known forever afterward by the pretty title of Marquise de Pompadour.

At twenty-three the former Mademoiselle Poisson had translated into reality the dream of her childhood and had justified the training of her girlhood—she was the official Mistress of the King. To others this might once have seemed an impossibility, but never to her. She was a born social climber, and, aided by her sometimes coarse but always shrewd mother, she confidently followed her undeviatingly upward path. If fierce triumph was hidden behind her quiet smile, who could blame her? She had reached her dizzy goal with what seemed a minimum of effort. To hold her place would eventually cost her beauty, her happiness, and finally her life. But had the new Marquise known the price of the future she would still have paid it. Nothing, absolutely nothing, was so important to her as recognition, the supreme accolade of the *arriviste*.

In spite of her calculating ambition, the Marquise de Pompadour had a tender heart and was generous and kind to those whom she loved. If she showed herself ruthless in the future to her enemies at Court, at least it can be said that they deserved it. She usually attempted to placate and win them to her side before their enmity made their destruction imperative. Only in the case of one friend, the

Abbé de Bernis, can she possibly be accused of ingratitude, and even in that instance there were arguments in her favor.

But there can be no excuse for her treatment of M. d'Étioles. She had repaid his years of adoration with a physical fidelity which cost her no effort, and which she cast away when at last she succeeded in drawing the King into her life. Mentally she was never faithful to her husband. For her, marriage was only an essential preliminary to a more important career, and without remorse she allowed Le Normant d'Étioles to fulfill the pathetic role of the necessary husband. Her cold-blooded desertion of the man who loved her was an irreparable flaw in an otherwise gentle nature, and her callous indifference to his sorrow was cruelty distilled.

Louis perceived this, and he was honest enough to respect the sorrow of a wronged husband even though he himself was the wrongdoer. During the latter part of April the Marquise received from M. d'Étioles a pitiful letter of forgiveness pleading for her return. In a rare moment of miscalculation she showed it to the King, thinking it would amuse him. Louis read it through silently. Its heartsick plea aroused in him the feeling of solidarity which one man has for another when woman is the adversary, and to the Marquise's surprise he returned the letter, coldly remarking, "Madame, you have an honest man for a husband."

The Law Court of Paris handed down a decree of separation on June 15, 1745, to Le Normant d'Étioles and the Marquise de Pompadour. By its terms the mother received custody of their infant daughter Alexandrine. Their community property was divided, the Marquise receiving back the house in the rue St. Marc which had formed the main part of her dowry and 3,000 livres in cash.

M. d'Étioles was sent on a trip to Provence in the hope that it would dispel his sorrow. Once at a dinner in his honor he was embarrassingly reminded of the wife he had lost; he was pointed out to a local official as "the husband of the Marquise de Pompadour." When the time came to propose a toast, the well-meaning provincial, ignorant of the intrigues of remote Versailles, raised his glass to "Monsieur le Marquis de Pompadour." As he sat down the silence was profound.

In time M. d'Étioles overcame his grief and put his faithless wife out of his thoughts. He did not suffer financially from the separation; in 1747, when Le Normant de Tournehem became Superintendent of the King's Buildings, he succeeded his uncle as Farmer-General and realized from his new post the enormous profit of 400,000 livres a year. A mature and wiser man, M. d'Étioles followed his wife's example and took a mistress for himself, Mademoiselle Rem, a singer from the Opéra. They were a devoted couple, had several children, and M. d'Étioles spurned the post of ambassador to Constantinople because its acceptance would have meant separation from his mistress.

Although Versailles hummed with gossip about the new Favorite, little was said openly. She had not yet been presented at Court and the King had not formally acknowledged her; it was safer to be discreet on so touchy a subject. The King so far maintained his reticence that he did not draw a draft on the Treasury to pay for the estate of Pompadour. Instead, the Duc de Luynes confided to his journal, "it is M. de Montmartel who furnished the money." Once again Pâris de Montmartel, court banker, onetime lover of Madame Poisson, and godfather of the new Mistress, re-entered her life at a crucial moment.

If the Court was afraid to discuss the King's new affair, Paris was not. The capital, always robust in its talk and uninhibited in its enjoyment of gossip, buzzed with details about the new Mistress. She was one of them, a true flower of the middle class, and Parisians felt a kind of pride that one of their own should rise so high and occupy a place hitherto reserved for the nobility. Soon their pride was to turn to pitiless hatred, but for the moment they were satisfied with the new Marquise—and so was she, as she relaxed and prepared to enjoy the happiest summer of her life.

V

SUMMER IN A SEA OF GLORY

*J*UDGING by the frivolities and celebrations of the past winter, one would hardly have thought that France was in her fifth year of the War of the Austrian Succession. In the eighteenth century wars were still fought according to more or less well-defined rules. To carry on a winter campaign, with its attendant discomforts, was unthinkable; by tacit agreement both sides halted operations in late fall and made no further moves until spring. The King and his general officers left the troops in camp and returned to the comforts and pleasures of Versailles.

The 6th of May 1745 was the date fixed for Louis XV to leave Versailles and rejoin his Army in Flanders. The Dauphin would accompany him this year, a privilege for which the young heir had long pleaded. The King dined *au grand couvert*, in public, on the eve of his departure. He later spent some tedious moments in the dull company of Marie Leczinska, listening to her banal remarks and drumming with his fingers on the window panes, a sure indication that he was irritated. Although he soon made his escape, he did not go to bed until three-thirty in the morning. What more logical presumption than that he was sharing a long farewell with his new beloved in the little attic apartments above his own? How the King must have hated to leave her! But this year he would not repeat the scandal of parading a mistress in front of his Army. Louis' road led to Flanders, but the Marquise de Pompadour's destination was much closer—her country house at Étioles, where she would spend the months of the King's absence.

At seven o'clock in the morning the King's carriage was ready, waiting for him in the little Marble Court of the Palace. The Dauphine was unable to appear; grief forced her to remain in bed. The Queen and her daughters were there to say a last good-by to Louis and his son. The women of the Royal Family had all opposed the Dauphin's departure, and some of the Ministers agreed with them, pointing out the excessive risks of exposure to battle. A mere two bullets, they said, could destroy the future of the dynasty, and the Crown would devolve to the branch of Orléans.

The Queen clung in tears to her son, kissing him again and again. The King was moody and silent and spoke only a few words to the Marquis d'Argenson. He said nothing to anyone else, neither his Ministers nor any of the courtiers. He was impatient to start and the farewells were cut short.

The King and his party traveled rapidly. They spent the first night at Compiègne and the second at Douai, where Louis got up at four in the morning and hurried onward, leaving the Dauphin still sleeping. News from Belgium spurred him on; the Army, besieging Tournai, was threatened by the relieving army of the Allies under the command of George II's son, the Duke of Cumberland.

The King reached Marshal Saxe's headquarters on May 10th. Although it was obvious that a great battle was imminent, Louis was in high spirits. In spite of the luxury to which he was accustomed, in spite of the bored indifference which was his usual mood, Louis rose to the stature of true kingship when with his soldiers. He and the Dauphin inspected the fortifications and mingled freely with the troops, who received them with wild enthusiasm. Louis never relinquished his dignity, but his manner to ordinary people was so natural and full of kindliness that his soldiers adored him; with their Sovereign present, they believed they could not be defeated.

The situation appealed to the King's acute historical sense, and he reminded d'Argenson that not since the battle of Poitiers had a King of France gone into battle with his son, and not since Saint Louis had any king gained an important battle from the English. He hoped, he added, to be the first to do so. The King was completely at ease with his officers, made jokes, and even sang a song consisting of many verses, which were, said d'Argenson, very droll. After that, Louis, like his soldiers, lay down to sleep on a pallet of straw.

Maurice de Saxe, Marshal of France, was not a Frenchman. Like many renowned soldiers he was a mercenary. He was a natural son of Augustus the Strong, Elector of Saxony, who had replaced Stanislaus Leczinski on the Polish throne. His mother was the famous beauty Aurora

Königsmark, whose brother Philip had been the lover of
the wife of King George I of England. Philip Königsmark
had been murdered by George's orders, and Maurice, in
memory of his uncle, bore a fierce hatred for the House
of Hanover.

When only twelve he had fought in the War of the
Spanish Succession, and in 1721, at the age of twenty-five,
he had entered the service of France, purchasing the
colonelcy of a regiment. Gold bought his commission, but
military genius qualified him to keep it. In the French
armies of the eighteenth century merely capable generals
were few enough; a real genius such as Maurice de Saxe
was phenomenal. After his death the Monarchy found no
one to replace him, and not until the Revolution did
soldiers as great as Maurice rally to the service of France.
Because he was a Protestant the King was long reluctant
to give him a Marshal's baton, but his rare brilliance
eventually overcame Louis' bigotry.

Maurice (or Comte de Saxe, as the King called him) was
harsh, tyrannical, and sometimes unjust. He permitted
his armies to plunder wantonly, but in that respect he was
no worse than many another general of his time. In his
private life he was as vigorous as in the field. In his youth
he had had a passionate affair with the actress Adrienne
Lecouvreur, and he never lost his preference for ladies
of the stage. It was said that every actress in Paris had at
some time been his mistress. Even on campaigns he kept
a troupe of ballet dancers to give performances and otherwise amuse him between battles.

Although he was not fifty when he won the Battle of

Fontenoy, his life of intense dissipation had affected even his iron frame. His face was pale and his body so swollen from dropsy that he could not sit a horse. He was pulled around the battlefield in a wheeled wicker chair which he called his "cradle," drawn by four gray horses. Some of his officers, alarmed at his physical deterioration and fearing that it might be mental as well, questioned the soundness of his strategy and complained to the King. Louis, who had the good sense not to interfere with his general, silenced their objections by turning to the Marshal and saying in front of them, "When I chose you to command my army, I intended that you should be obeyed by everyone, and I myself will be the first to set the example."

The Allied Army, composed of English, Hanoverian, Austrian, and Dutch forces, began the attack at six in the morning. Its objective was to break through the triple line of redoubts thrown up by the defenders and capture the village of Fontenoy, which would cut the French Army in two. The Allies advanced slowly in wedge formation, firing calmly and rapidly. The French desperately tried to halt their inexorable progress, but bullets seemed to have no effect on the enemy. The picked troops of France —the regiment of Normandy, the regiment of Hainaut, the regiment of Aubeterre, and the Swiss and French Guards—finally gave way in disorder under the steady pressure of Allied fire.

The King, who had been up since five, had taken his place on the crest of a small hill to watch the battle. Although he was within range of enemy shells, he refused

to heed his officers' requests to seek a safer spot. According
to the Dauphin, "he showed himself a true King all
through, but especially when it looked as if victory was not
going to light on his side." Marshal Saxe, in order to repair
his broken lines, ordered a temporary retreat, "which
afflicted him [Louis] exceedingly, but his countenance did
not change, and he gave his orders with a coolness which
everybody admired."

The young Dauphin was in a state of feverish excitement
at what appeared to be certain defeat and, drawing his
sword, tearfully begged the King for permission to lead a
charge of the Household Troops. Louis, the blood of a
hundred fighting ancestors stirring within him, was himself
inclined to plunge into the battle. Only reluctantly did he
bow to Marshal Saxe's peremptory refusal.

The English, apparently winning, were prevented by a
lack of cavalry from pursuing the fleeing French troops,
and now they had come within range of the Royal artillery.
French shells began to rip into the solid phalanx of the
enemy, who wavered in confusion. Pressing his advantage,
the French commander ordered a general attack, and in
ten minutes gaping holes were torn in every side of the
English column. The King's Household Troops made a
furious charge into the breach and the English fell back
in wild rout. After seven hours of bloody struggle, the
Battle of Fontenoy was won. It shone forth as a glorious
victory in a century marked by an almost unbroken succession of humiliating French defeats; it was the last of its
kind for nearly half a century. Not until the Revolution
did France win another victory so great as Fontenoy. It

paved the way for the fall of Tournai a month later, followed by Marshal Lowendal's capture of Ghent and Ostend, and the fall of Bruges and Oudenarde. It was a brilliant summer for the arms of France and the prestige of King Louis XV.

After victory was certain, Maurice de Saxe threw himself on the ground and embraced the King's knees. "Sire," he said, "I have seen enough; I did not want to live today except to see Your Majesty victorious." Louis raised the great General and embraced him. Although the victory snatched from defeat was mainly due to the Marshal's brilliant tactics, the King's presence and bravery deserved recognition. He received it in full measure. "It is absolutely true and certain," wrote the Marquis d'Argenson to Voltaire, "that the King himself gained this battle by the firmness of his will."

Immediately after the battle the King and his son, using drums as desks, wrote to the anxious Queen. The letter of the King was impersonal: "From the field of battle of Fontenoy, May 11th, 2:30 P.M. The enemy attacked us this morning at five o'clock. They have been thoroughly beaten. I am safe, and my son also. I have no time to tell you more, it being wise, I think, to reassure Versailles and Paris. As soon as I can, I will send you more details."

The young Louis' letter rang with youthful pride. "My dear mamma, I compliment you with all my heart on the battle that the King has just won. He is all right, thank God, and I also, who have had the honor of being with him. I will write you more tonight or tomorrow, and I close by assuring you of my respect and love. *Louis*." Then a wistful postscript: "I beg you to kiss my wife and my sisters for me."

The King and Dauphin afterward rode over the battle-field on horseback. They reviewed the troops, who welcomed them with tumultuous acclaim and presented them with bullet-riddled flags captured from the enemy. Officers and men waved their hats on the end of their bayonets, shouting *Vive le roi!*

The King's first concern was for the wounded, and he ordered their immediate evacuation to the field hospitals which had been set up. The victory had been a costly one—the number of French killed and wounded was over 7,000, of whom more than 600 were officers. Some of the noblest names in France swelled the lists of the dead; but the casualty lists of the Allies exceeded 10,000.

The King, unlike Louis XIV, did not thirst for glory and believed that kings were answerable for the blood shed in their wars. Riding over the field of Fontenoy the evening after their battle, he pointed to the sprawled bodies of the slain and said to his son, "See the price of victory to a man of kindly heart. The blood of our enemies is, after all, the blood of our fellow men. The really glorious thing is to spare it."

Unfortunate for France that Louis XV did not follow more often the counsel of his own kind heart instead of the muddled advice of Ministers who had no hearts at all!

The couriers of the King carried the joyous news of Fontenoy not only to Paris and Versailles but to the new Favorite waiting at Étioles. The Royal victor's letters to the Marquise were longer in content and considerably more ardent in tone than those he wrote to the Queen. In the period of less than two months between the lovers' farewell at Versailles and July 1st the King's Mistress received eighty letters, all addressed *à la Marquise de Pompadour,* and sealed with the motto *Discret et fidèle.* This average of nearly two letters a day proved that the King's thoughts were not all devoted to the campaign.

This summer of Fontenoy was the happiest season of Madame de Pompadour's life. She had realized her ambition and did not yet know the toll it would exact. Her isolation at Étioles protected her from the malice of the Court. She was tasting the joys of future power without the burdens of responsibility, and knowing for the last time in her life the sweetness of complete peace of mind. Once presented at Court, her struggle would begin—the struggle to keep her foothold that would end only with her last breath.

But the days of reckoning lay ahead, invisible and unsuspected, and during the warm months of 1745 the Marquise de Pompadour's world was bathed in golden light. The King was in love with her, and she—was she in love with him? She thought she was. It was easy in the happiness of success for her to think so. The King's absence, the flood of love letters, kindled her imagination and she dreamed of Louis with romantic tenderness. She had all the privileges of his love without his incessant demands upon her frail body. At Étioles life was serene and quiet, affording the Marquise the rest she needed so desperately after the frenzied pace of the past winter.

Until she was formally presented at Court, Louis wished her seclusion to be almost complete. With the exception of M. de Tournehem, her family, and a few relatives, she received only three men. One of them was Voltaire. Before the King's departure he had sent her some of his verses, begging to see her. "I am," he wrote, "more interested in your happiness than you think, and perhaps there is no one in Paris who takes a more sensible interest in it. It is not as a gallant old flatterer of beautiful women that I address you, it is as a good citizen; and I ask your permission to come to talk to you a little at Étioles in May."

The ruler of French literature was quick to turn to the rising sun, seeing in the transformation of his little friend Madame d'Étioles the opportunity he had long awaited. As the King's Mistress, she would carry the ideas of the *philosophes* into the very citadel of the Monarchy. More important to Voltaire personally, she would become his protectress, the generous dispenser of honors and sinecures.

Voltaire's genius was undeniable and he was justifiably regarded as the first intellectual of his day. There was, however, a less attractive side to his nature. His avarice was exceeded by his vanity, his vanity only by his ambition. Of this, Marmontel wrote: "One passion only was fixed in him, and, as it were, inherent in his soul; it was an ardent love of fame, and, of all that flatters and feeds this passion, nothing to him was indifferent."

Voltaire hated to give in on any issue no matter how trivial; but he also hated injustice and bigotry and fought always for truth and the freedom to express it. In the realm of ideas he was a giant, but in small, material things he betrayed the petulance of a child, passing from one extreme to another in the passions that agitated him.

He turned on all his brilliance for the Marquise de Pompadour and displayed every facet of his genius. He impressed her with his knowledge, sometimes frightened her with his malice, and always flattered her unsparingly. When the King sent letters patent confirming her title as Marquise de Pompadour, Voltaire marked the occasion with a laudatory verse:

> Sincère et tendre Pompadour
> (Car je peux vous donner d'avance
> Ce nom qui rime avec l'amour
> Et qui sera bientôt le plus beau nom de France)

> Sincere and tender Pompadour
> (For I can give you in advance
> This name which rhymes with love
> And will soon be the finest name in France)

He did not restrict his pretty phrases to Madame de Pompadour's hearing but praised her wherever he could; especially wherever he thought word would get back to her. "She has read more at her age than any old woman of the country over which she is going to reign, and where it is so desirable that she reign."

Madame de Pompadour was as susceptible to flattery as any woman,—and it is easy to understand how she grew somewhat dizzy from Voltaire's adulation. A part of it was sincere; he was really impressed by her charm and her quick mind. But he would have said the same things to her if she had been as plain and dull as Marie Leczinska. In his frantic desire to advance himself he was more clever and ruthless than she who had once been Mademoiselle Poisson.

Madame de Pompadour might be stimulated by Voltaire's conversation and dazzled by his wit, but his unflagging self-exaltation occasionally grew wearying. Moreover, his attentions were motivated primarily by concern for himself rather than interest in her. She badly needed another friend, one who was sincerely disinterested and unselfishly attached to her. Such a friend she found in the Abbé de Bernis.

François Joachim Pierre de Bernis was born in 1715, the younger son of an impoverished noble family of Languedoc. Coming to Paris, he studied with the Jesuits at Louis-le-Grand and became an abbé, a status midway between that of priest and layman. By nature he was worldly, and he was honest enough to admit that he was unsuited to the priestly vocation. As a young man he applied to Cardinal Fleury, then Prime Minister, for a position that would relieve his dire poverty, but the old priest, having heard of Bernis' successes among the ladies of Paris, took a dislike to him and said that he could hope for nothing while the Cardinal was alive. "Very well, Monseigneur, I will wait," replied the Abbé. Since the Cardinal was nearly ninety, the remark was not without pertinence. Subsequently Bernis had no better luck with the sour Bishop of Mirepoix, who refused to grant a benefice to an abbé who wrote poetry.

Bernis was short and plump, in dress something of a dandy. He had a round pink face which wore an honest and cheerful expression. His noble birth and his gift for writing pretty if somewhat vapid verses made him welcome in the social world of the capital. He made no effort to hide his poverty but accepted it philosophically. Once he abruptly left a dinner before the meal was over and later explained to his hostess that he and the equally poor friend who shared his room had only one suit between them; the Abbé had suddenly remembered that his friend was also invited to a dinner and could not leave the house until Bernis returned with their clothes.

Because of the flowery nature of the Abbé's poetry Voltaire mockingly dubbed him *Babet,* the flower girl. Bernis accepted the nickname with his usual good humor and perhaps could afford to; after all he was already a member of the Academy, an eminence which even the great Voltaire had not succeeded in reaching.

The Abbé had met Madame de Pompadour when she was still Madame d'Étioles and was often invited to her house. He "had constantly resisted," he related rather smugly, "because the company they received was not what suited me." When the Comtesse d'Estrades told him that Madame d'Étioles had become the King's Mistress, he still hesitated to see her, pretending that such an association was not in keeping with his position. There is a false note here; Bernis, while not flagrantly immoral, was fully attuned to the standards of conduct of his time and could hardly have been shocked because the King had taken another Mistress. In fact, he later described the relationship between Louis and Madame de Pompadour as a pure, an ideal love. In spite of Bernis' good qualities, it is difficult to reject the suspicion that he was at first indifferent to Madame d'Étioles because he failed to foresee her rise to power.

Marmontel, who disliked Bernis, bluntly expressed such an opinion, writing that "when he learned that at the hunting parties in the Forest of Sénart the beautiful Madame d'Étioles had been the object of the King's attention, the Abbé immediately solicited permission to go and pay his court to this young engaging woman. . . . He arrived at Étioles by the public barge, his little packet under his arm. They engaged him to recite some of his verses; he amused, and exerted every effort to make himself agreeable; and with that superficial wit and varnish of poetry, which was his sole talent, he succeeded so well that in the absence of the King, he was admitted into the secrets of the letters passed between the two lovers."

This contemptuous appraisal is from an admittedly hostile source, but added weight is given to it by the Duc de Richelieu, who noted spitefully but probably with truth that "some time after . . . Madame d'Étioles became the King's Mistress . . . the Abbé was very sorry for having treated her lightly and thought himself obliged to compliment her, which could not bring him anything but gain."

It is only fair to quote Bernis himself on the beginnings of his long friendship with the Favorite: "I consulted the most honorable persons; they all agreed that having in no way contributed to the King's passion, I ought not to refuse my friendship to an old acquaintance nor the good which might result from my advice. I determined then to accept; they [the lovers] promised me and I promised them an eternal friendship. It will be seen that I kept my word.

Louis XV, from a pastel by Maurice-Quentin
de La Tour in the Louvre Museum, Paris.

Madame de Pompadour, from a painting by François
Boucher in The National Gallery of Scotland, Edinburg.

The King was to go to war in Flanders, and Madame d'Étioles was to pass the summer in the country. It was agreed, and approved by the Master, that I should see her often." Bernis' apologia is a shade too sanctimonious; it protests too much. Nevertheless it cannot obviate the fact that for thirteen years he gave Madame de Pompadour his loyal and perceptive friendship. He rose with her to become Ambassador, Foreign Minister, and Cardinal and when the break between them came, it was her doing, not his.

The King had good reason for wanting the Abbé to visit Madame de Pompadour during his absence. Her elegance, her wit, her manner of speaking—these were all charming, but they radiated the charm of Paris, not Versailles. She was indubitably stamped as a product of the middle class, and she reflected the tastes and mannerisms, even the language, of merchants, financiers, and literary men. That was perfectly permissible in those circles, but the world of the Court was different in every respect from the world of Paris. Perhaps it was not so intelligent a world, but it had its own rigid standards and these the new Marquise must learn. Louis knew the risk he ran in choosing a Mistress from the middle class, and he did not intend to be embarrassed by any bourgeois *faux pas*. Madame de Pompadour, he knew, was vulnerable enough in the hothouse atmosphere of Versailles without being subjected to additional jibes because of blunders in etiquette. There must be no blunders.

The Abbé de Bernis, with his quiet elegance of manner and complete self-possession, was a perfect instructor. Born to the nobility himself, he was at home in the rarefied atmosphere which Madame de Pompadour would soon breathe. Under his light, almost frivolous cheerfulness he hid an alert mind which soon perceived in Madame de Pompadour "a self-love too easily flattered as well as wounded, and in general an excess of distrust which was as easily aroused as calmed."

Bernis did not shower her with the outrageous flattery of Voltaire. "I always told her the truth," he modestly said. He added in her praise that for many years "she liked my sometimes harsh truths better than the flatteries of others." Yet Bernis was truly devoted to Madame de Pompadour, infinitely more so than the self-seeking Voltaire. The gay witty Abbé liked women, and he was still young enough to be genuinely impressed by the beauty and grace of his pupil. When he dedicated his pretty rhymes to her, they differed from Voltaire's in one important respect—they were sincere. But he was too clever to underrate the importance of support from the *philosophes* and advised her to "take the men of letters under your wing; it was they who bestowed the name of Great on Louis XIV."

The Abbé, occasionally assisted by the Marquis de Gontaut, became the preceptor of the new Mistress. Both these noblemen knew every detail, every intrigue, of Court life and out of loyalty to the King and gallant admiration for the Favorite they gladly gave her their knowledge. She studied the complicated rules of Court etiquette, learned by heart the genealogies of the nobility, and followed the involved pattern of personal loves and hates which were all-important at Versailles. She discovered that the Duchesse-of-this never spoke to the Comtesse-of-that because the Comte-of-that had become the lover of the Marquise-of-something-else. She memorized the names of those who were the King's friends and made a special note of those who amused him.

She was an apt pupil, being clever enough to realize the vital importance of appearing faultless when she made her debut at Court. Not a trace of Madame d'Étioles (much less Mademoiselle Poisson!) must show through the veneer which the Marquise de Pompadour was acquiring. From the wealthy world of mere fashion she moved into the elegant ritualistic existence of the hereditary nobility. She made the transition smoothly and learned so well the lessons of Bernis that the Prince de Ligne, visiting Versailles a few years later, could write: "After ... I was conducted to the individuals of the Royal Family, I was taken to a kind of second Queen, who had more the air of one than the first. ..."

As the summer neared its end a quickening air of excitement filled the rooms at Étioles. Everyone knew that Madame de Châteauroux's white and blue apartments in the Palace were being redecorated for a new occupant. The King's return was set for early September; after that, only one step remained to be taken before the Marquise de Pompadour was free to enter upon her new life. That step was her formal presentation to the Court of France.

VI

THE DEBUTANTE

*T*HE KING and the Dauphin returned from their victorious summer to a cheering Paris on September 7th, and three days later the Marquise de Pompadour unobtrusively drove in a closed carriage to Versailles. She went at once to the apartments which had been made ready for her and did not appear again until the details of her presentation were settled. (No woman had the right to appear in public at Court before her formal presentation to the King and Queen.)

It was with considerable difficulty that Louis found a lady of noble birth who was willing to demean herself by sponsoring the former Madame d'Étioles. The ladies of the Court, nettled at seeing the prize which should have gone to one of them snatched by a mere bourgeoise, stood aside in malicious uncooperation, relishing the embarrassment of the King. But money, vocal everywhere, was acutely so among the extravagant nobility and money solved the King's problem. He persuaded the old Princesse de Conti to introduce the new Favorite and agreed in return to pay her many debts. Before the bargain became known an indignant churchman remarked to the Princesse

86

that he could not imagine any noblewoman stooping so low, and the humorous old woman stopped him with a burst of laughter, begging him to "say no more, because it is I." She was not so honest, however, as the remark indicated, because at the same time she was confiding to the Queen that she had consented to perform the odious task only under great pressure from His Majesty.

The presentation was scheduled for six o'clock on the evening of Tuesday, September 14th. The *Salon de Conseil*, where the King received, was packed with a curious throng of courtiers, eager to witness the debut of the new Marquise. Few among them wished her well. Most of them prayed, if pray they could, that she would commit some *gaffe*, some breach of the stiff Court etiquette that would betray her middle-class origin and make her appear ridiculous.

Promptly on the hour Madame de Pompadour, accompanied by the Princesse de Conti, appeared at the door. A cousin of her husband, the Comtesse d'Estrades, and the Marquise de la Chau-Montauban, together with their ladies in waiting, completed the little group.

Madame de Pompadour, in spite of her innate poise, in spite of her endless rehearsals for this day, was nervous, but she did not reveal it. She was a dazzling picture as she entered the room, the fire of many diamonds flashing in her hair. Her beautiful arms and shoulders, exposed by the low-cut, formal dress of the Court, showed off to perfection the delicate pink tinge of her pearly complexion. Even her enemies admitted she was that rare being, a woman who was both pretty and beautiful.

Her enormous hooped petticoat of rich brocade weighed no less than forty pounds. Marshal Saxe once exclaimed in astonishment that these Court dresses weighed more than his breastplate and could not understand how the fragile ladies bore their burden for hours at a time. An even greater problem was the handling of the *bas-de-robe* or train. It was very narrow, excessively long, and presented a terrifying challenge to the most nimble-footed woman, especially when she had to withdraw backward from the King's presence. But the new Marquise seemed in complete possession of herself as she gracefully made the first curtsy at the door, advanced into the center of the room and made a second, and then approached the King, curtsying this time to the floor.

Louis, who stood awaiting her, seemed to have lost his ineffable dignity, and when the Marquise rose to her feet he muttered only a few embarrassed words. His nervousness communicated itself to her, although she managed to withdraw from the room flawlessly, kicking her long train out of her way as she moved backward.

The worst of the ordeal lay ahead—her presentation to Marie Leczinska. An even larger crowd waited with avid curiosity to witness the meeting of the Queen and the Mistress. Everyone speculated how the Queen would react to this new affront, and wondered with what cold words she would acknowledge the new Favorite.

As the Marquise approached the Queen she made a full curtsy, removing as she did so her right glove, and picked up the hem of the Queen's dress as if to kiss it. Marie Leczinska restrained her gently, and Madame de Pompa-

dour rose to face the wife of her lover for the first time.
As she looked into the kind and saddened face of the
neglected consort, she was seized with trembling and for
once in her life lost her composure. The Queen, dressed
in her fussy unstylish manner, prematurely aged and lacking the usual attractions of a woman, nevertheless had a
touching dignity that was matchless and a noble purity
that was unique at Versailles. Madame de Pompadour
waited for her to speak.

Although unworldly, the Queen was perceptive. She
knew what malice vibrated among the onlookers. She knew
that a curt nod, an inconsequential remark, would humili-
ate the lowborn woman before her and delight the aristocratic spectators. Marie's heart had already been irreparably
broken many years ago by Madame de Mailly, the first to
rob her of the King's love. No one could hurt her so much
again, least of all this middle-class woman who seemed
almost pathetically humble.

The Queen was moved by the gentleness of the Marquise's young face. Instead of murmuring an empty compliment, she leaned forward and kindly inquired after a
mutual friend, Madame de Saissac, who had befriended
Madame de Pompadour in Paris. The Favorite, more
overcome by the Queen's consideration than if she had
been snubbed, replied in a barely audible voice, "I have
a profound desire to please you, Madame." Marie Leczinska's kindness won her that instant a friend who never
betrayed her; even in the days of her greatest power,
Madame de Pompadour never wavered in her deferential
devotion to the Queen.

There remained her presentation to the Dauphin and Dauphine. Here the Marquise's reception was frankly insulting. The Dauphin hated, with all the prudery of his sixteen years, his father's successive Mistresses, and especially did he detest Madame de Pompadour, who was the friend of the Church's enemies. He greeted her coldly, and when he kissed her on the cheek as custom required, he stuck out his tongue at her. This amused the courtiers, but the Dauphin paid for his rashness; the King was furious when he heard of the rude gesture and sent him in disgrace to Meudon for a month.

As for the central figure of the trying day, the Marquise de Pompadour climbed the steps to her apartments in the attic, exhausted but triumphant. Her debut was accomplished; she was a Lady of the French Court and all obstacles to her success had been overcome. The rest was up to her.

A few days later the King and Madame de Pompadour retreated to Choisy, taking with them only a few chosen companions. As a special privilege, the Favorite was permitted to invite her literary friends Voltaire and Duclos, neither of whom Louis liked, and, of course, the chubby Bernis, of whom he had grown very fond.

Although the King was inclined to be stingy, he did not hesitate to honor the new Mistress by ordering a complete redecoration of Choisy, which he had originally bought for the ill-starred Madame de Vintimille. Nor did he limit the expense—the large drawing room was furnished in white satin embroidered with gold, and there was a smaller room done in flowered velvet. In this costly setting they lived quietly, mutually enchanted, and delighting in the reciprocal gratification which can be experienced only by those who are in love.

During these first weeks of her new position, now officially established, Madame de Pompadour's happiness was complete. Although incapable of sustained passion, she was sentimentally in love with Louis. She had not lived with him long enough to realize the countless complexities of his contradictory nature or to understand how arduous would prove the task which lay ahead—the unending task of beguiling the King's languid mind and filling his empty days. To all appearances the horizon that stretched before her was unbroken by clouds.

The King soon had an attack of illness which resembled the alarming symptoms he had shown at Metz. There was temporary consternation. Couriers galloped between Choisy and Versailles, and the Queen begged to be allowed to visit her husband. Although Louis quickly recovered from what was after all only a touch of jaundice, he consented with surprising thoughtfulness to the Queen's request. He received his wife with kindness and even escorted her himself on a tour of the newly decorated château. At dinner he was so friendly that the Queen was enraptured and "showed no desire to leave, but spoke graciously to Madame de Pompadour, who was respectful and not at all forward."

The Queen was not slow to understand that the Marquise was the impelling force behind this unusual display of attention, nor were the watchful courtiers. The Prince de Croÿ, himself virtuous and a man of scrupulous fairness, noted that the Favorite was "on good terms with the Queen, having persuaded the King to be nicer to her. . . ."

Shortly after the King and the Marquise returned to Versailles, the entire Court, following its annual schedule, moved to Fontainebleau for six weeks of hunting. These changes of residence were prodigiously expensive, although the distances covered were relatively short. The King had several principal palaces, and each time he moved from one to another it was necessary to transport hundreds of servants and endless wagonloads of supplies, sometimes even the furniture. On one trip to Chantilly, 700 people had to be fed, 200 of whom worked in the kitchen alone. Even the shortest journey, to Trianon, cost no less than 100,000 livres. Versailles, Choisy, Marly, Compiègne, Trianon, Fontainebleau—the Court moved in a fixed orbit from one to another, year after year.

At Fontainebleau, with the full Court in attendance, the Marquise for the first time played her new role of *maîtresse-en-titre* and presided with grace and ease over the small nightly suppers which the King gave. These informal gatherings, where Louis was relaxed and friendly, were attended only by his closest friends: the Duc de Richelieu, the Duc de Moras, the Duc d'Ayen; and among the ladies only those who were agreeable to the Mistress: the Princesse de Conti, the plump Duchesse de Lauraguais, who had resigned herself to losing the King and had prudently made friends with Madame de Pompadour, and the Favorite's cousin, Madame d'Estrades, who had already been awarded the coveted post of lady in waiting to Mesdames, the King's eldest daughters.

In contrast to the laughter and light conversation that rippled around the King's table, a mournful silence enveloped the dining of the lonely Queen. The sprightly Casanova, freshly escaped from imprisonment in his native Venice, visited Fontainebleau about this time, and described the unhilarious ritual of Marie Leczinska's mealtime.

I entered a superb room where I saw a dozen or so courtiers who were moving about, and a table big enough to seat at least twelve, but which had only one place set.

"Whom is that place for?"

"For the Queen. Here she comes now."

I saw the Queen of France, without rouge, simply dressed, her head covered with a big bonnet, her face devout and her bearing that of an old woman. When she drew near the table she graciously thanked two nuns who put a plate of fresh butter on the table. She seated herself, and immediately the twelve courtiers arranged themselves in a semicircle ten paces from the table. I hovered near them imitating their respectful silence.

Her Majesty began to eat without looking at anyone, keeping her eyes lowered on her plate. Finding one dish especially good, she took another helping and then glanced at the circle around her, no doubt to see if among the spectators there was not someone to whom she should make a remark.

She found one and called: "M. de Lowendahl."

A splendid-looking man, answering to this name, advanced with bowed head and answered,

"Madame."

"I think that this fine dish is chicken stew."

"I am of the same opinion, Madame."

After this response, made in the most serious tone, the Queen went on eating and the Marshal backed away to resume his place. The Queen finished her dinner without saying another word, and went back to her apartments the way she had come. I thought to myself that if the Queen of France ate all of her meals in that fashion, I would not want the honor of being her boarder.

When the King dined in public with the Queen, the intimate suppers could not be held in his apartments, and Madame de Pompadour gave tasteful little dinners in her own private suite. To the charm of her presence was added the surpassing skill of her own chef whom she had brought with her. At these small gatherings, in addition to the usual guests, Voltaire and Bernis were present. Everyone by now regarded the round and rosy Abbé as her unofficial counselor—as indeed he was.

At Fontainebleau Madame de Pompadour's suite of rooms was on the ground floor, those which had formerly belonged to Madame de Châteauroux. The King's rooms lay directly above and were connected with hers by a private staircase. With access for the enamored King so direct and private the poor Marquise had hardly a moment to herself. Louis came to see her as soon as he was dressed, stayed until it was time for Mass, then returned to eat some soup or perhaps a small cutlet. He was never a heavy eater, being always watchful of his trim physique, and the light meal served as breakfast and lunch. He remained throughout the long afternoon until five or six when he left to confer with the Ministers. On the days that he hunted he took the Marquise in his own carriage to the assembly point, where she and Louis' daughters mounted their horses and followed the Royal Chase through Fontaine-bleau's magnificent forest.

Obviously Madame de Pompadour had little time to herself. She rarely went out of her rooms alone except to pay her respects to the Queen. For one thing, during the rare periods when the King was away from her, the Marquise applied herself to further study of the usages of the Court. She had not entirely succeeded in sloughing off her middle-class mannerisms, and the courtiers, especially the women, made fun of her at every opportunity. If they could make her appear ridiculous and the King ashamed of her, she was lost.

Her father's presence did not lighten her task. M. Poisson, with his rough, almost bucolic, manner and his fondness for the bottle, was an easy mark for the heartless courtiers. To Madame de Pompadour's credit, she showed no embarrassment for her father's natural ways regardless of how much she suffered inwardly. She remained the affectionate daughter she had always been. In fact, typically middle class in the strength of her family ties, she often discussed her relatives and their affairs, frequently using expressions which were suitable in the drawing rooms of Paris but hardly appropriate in the chambers of a Royal Palace. She had an excessive fondness for nicknames and intimate terms of endearment. Bernis was her "feather-legged pidgeon," and Pâris-Duverney grew accustomed to being addressed by the Marquise as "dear blockhead." Louis, in spite of his infatuation, was often embarrassed by these expressions and these family details. He once remarked, half-amused, half-annoyed, that he would have to "educate her."

Already Madame de Pompadour was acquiring, and through no fault of her own, powerful enemies. The Marquis d'Argenson, rough and obscure in speech and slovenly in dress, called her "low born." This elder of the d'Argenson brothers was full of able ideas but was devoured by unconscious ambition; he was bitter, blunt, and tactless. His observation was chronically warped by wishful thinking, so much so that as early as 1745 he could solemnly write that "the Pompadour is about to be dismissed, and the King will live with his family." Until his pen was stilled by death the credulous Marquis continued to fill his journal with similar prophecies of ruin for the Favorite.

A far more dangerous foe was the Duc de Richelieu, fourteen years the King's senior and his evil genius for almost a lifetime. Louis François Armand du Plessis bore some of the characteristics as well as the name of his great-uncle the Cardinal. He was the gayest, greediest, and most unscrupulous of Louis' friends and had long wielded over the King an inordinate influence, especially in matters of pleasure. He was in charge of the entertainment, the suppers, and sometimes the celebrations of a more personal nature. It was he as much as anyone who had spurred the King on to marital infidelity. Richelieu hoped to increase his own influence through a grateful Royal Mistress. He had, indeed, been named First Gentleman of the King's Bedchamber as a reward for promoting his niece Madame de Châteauroux to the position of *maîtresse-en-titre;* after her death he had hoped to replace her with one of her sisters, Madame de Lauraguais or Madame de Flavacourt. When the little d'Étioles upset his plans he tried at first to hide his discomfiture and be friendly, but as it dawned on him that the new Mistress, though middle class, had come to stay, the Duc de Richelieu could not conceal his hatred.

Although he was vain and intellectually stupid, the Duc was a formidable enemy, principally because of his influence with the King. Louis had become so habituated to him that he refused to exclude him from the intimate circle; moreover, he found Richelieu's biting comments amusing. The Duc was vivacious and witty and had all the graceful airs of the class to which he was born. Yet even his politeness, flavored as it was with patronizing contempt, was intolerable to Madame de Pompadour.

He was a bad son, a faithless husband, an unfeeling father, and a treacherous friend, yet Madame de Pompadour had to put up with him and disarm him—if she could. His bright, observant little eyes surmounted by quizzical brows missed no blunder, and his wide mouth, thin as a crocodile's, was always eager to snap off the head of an unwary victim.

An adversary whose wit was more mordant and whose jealousy more intense was the King's favorite Minister, the Comte de Maurepas. Although only forty-four, he had been a Minister for over twenty years, since before Cardinal Fleury's rule began. During this long period the King had become thoroughly accustomed to him, a factor of no small importance in gaining Louis' favor. Maurepas was Minister of Marine and also of Paris, which latter post gave him the additional power of controlling the police. Louis was usually annoyed with details of government, but Maurepas was one Minister he was always glad to see. Maurepas ridiculed everything; his wit seemed unwearying, and he amused the bored King with endless gossip, jokes, and sometimes even with bawdy songs.

There was a feminine quality in Maurepas' jealousy. Some said that he was impotent; certainly he seemed to hate women, especially if the woman happened to be the King's Mistress. He had been the declared enemy of them all and yet had survived because Louis was fond of him. Even Madame de Châteauroux, in the brief hour of triumph before her death, had been unable to secure his dismissal.

Maurepas' jealousy of anyone else who lightened the King's tedious hours—he hated Richelieu for this reason—doubled when it was a question of a Mistress. He feared that a woman would give the King all he could give—amusement, distraction—and more. The Marquise de Pompadour soon felt the scalding satire of this frustrated man. Maurepas wielded a sharp pen, and the Favorite believed, probably with good reason, that he was the author of the anonymous verses against her, stinging in their venom, which began to appear mysteriously in Paris, and even at Court:

> Une petite bourgeoise,
> Élevée a la grivoise,
> Mesurant tout à sa toise,
> Fait de la cour un taudis-dis-dis.

Louis, malgré son scrupule,
Froidement pour elle brule,
Et son amour ridicule
A fait rire tout Paris-ris-ris.

A little bourgeoise,
Saucily bred,
Who reduces everything to her own measure,
Is turning the Court into a rat-trap.
Louis, in spite of his scruples,
Is frankly burning with love for her,
And his ridiculous passion
Makes all Paris laugh.

Poissonades such as these were to torment her throughout her reign, long after she had thrust Maurepas into oblivion, but she never ceased to believe that it had been he who had launched them.

One of her friends once upbraided Berryer, the Superintendent of Police, demanding to know why he had not exposed the authors of the scurrilous verses. Berryer, who was an honest official, significantly replied, "I know Paris, monsieur, *but I do not know Versailles*," his implication being that the secret author belonged to the Court.

In spite of this growing hostility—this increasing flow of poison which was never to slacken—there were some who paid just tribute to the Marquise. "The King seems to love her more than all the others," remarked Croÿ, "and he is right, she is the most lovable." The sincere M. de Luynes, probably reflecting the sentiments of his good friend the Queen, was generous with praise: "It seems that everybody finds Madame de Pompadour extremely polite; not only is she not malicious and speaks ill of no one, but she does not even permit anyone else to do so around her."

Such admirable qualities must have appeared singular at Court, but Madame de Pompadour's friendliness was genuine. It was instinctive with her to try to please those who surrounded her, and her long years of practice had developed the instinct into an art; but an unaffected desire to be agreeable lay beneath the artistry. Perhaps her exquisite courtesy and almost excessive desire to please were partly motivated by an initial sense of unsureness; nevertheless, she was tender and kind by nature, incapable at first of realizing that the depraved atmosphere of the Court turned all virtue into vice and all vice into virtue.

She was astute enough to understand that if she was to hold what she had won she would need as many friends as she could win. Her modest and respectful attitude to the Queen gained her the approbation of those few courtiers who were fair of judgment. The Marquise constantly inquired after Marie Leczinska, sent her bouquets of her favorite flowers, and was careful on one occasion, when illness prevented her from attending a charity function organized by the Queen, to contribute a large donation. Such tactfulness was in glowing contrast to the conduct of the previous mistresses. Madame de Mailly and Madame de Vintimille had ignored poor Marie, while Madame de Châteauroux had treated her with open disdain and had ordered holes bored in the walls of the Queen's rooms so that her spies could report what Marie said in private.

Madame de Pompadour persuaded the King—wonder of wonders!—to pay the Queen's debts, which had mounted, thanks to her many charities, to 40,000 livres. Also, while the Court was still at Fontainebleau, artisans were working feverishly at Versailles to redecorate the Queen's apartments, which had not been touched for years. When Marie returned to the Palace she was astounded to see the walls and mirrors radiant with new gilding, the furniture re-upholstered in lustrous white satin, and—something she had longed for—a new bed in the fashionable style *à la duchesse,* its headboard tufted with crimson damask, with hangings and valance of the same material. Probably appealing to the Queen's taste even more, the walls were covered with new tapestries representing scenes from the Scriptures. No wonder Marie Leczinska said of the Marquise, with a sigh of unqualified sincerity, "Since there has to be one, better she than another."

Madame de Pompadour was not satisfied to rest on her laurels, but sought in other ways to assure herself of the Queen's good will. "Day before yesterday," wrote the Duc de Luynes, "Madame de Pompadour said to Madame de Luynes that she was in the keenest anxiety and most bitter sorrow; that she knew somebody had frightfully aspersed her to the Queen; and, without explaining to what she referred, said she hoped that the Queen would not believe it, and that she begged her [Madame de Luynes] to speak about it to her."

After reporting this conversation to the Queen, Madame de Luynes, who was a simple soul, wrote reassuringly to the Marquise: "I have just spoken to the Queen, Madame, and I begged her to tell me frankly if she had anything against you; she answered in the kindliest way that she had not, and that she was very aware of your efforts to please her on all occasions; she even desired me to write and tell you so."

The Queen's amiable tolerance was not shared by the Dauphin. If he no longer stuck out his tongue at the Marquise, he nevertheless made no effort to conceal his dislike. When she was near he relapsed into sulky silence, scarcely bothering to acknowledge her presence. His rudeness deeply hurt Madame de Pompadour, but she did not openly complain. Her wounded feelings became known only through her friends.

The Dauphin's hostility was not only embarrassing, it was potentially menacing. Louis' life was all that stood between the Marquise and his son's hatred. Should dire mischance occur—a Royal fall while hunting or a straight shot from an assassin's pistol—he would become King within an instant, and then what fate might await her? The very least she could expect would be abrupt exile from Court, probably to the confines of some cheerless convent. Such a banishment would strike the Dauphin's over-developed religious sense as a fitting punishment.

It was primarily on religious grounds that his hatred rested. He was ruled by priests, and his thralldom to the Jesuits was especially abject. From childhood they had filled his ears with the King's sins, and the Dauphin had hated all the Mistresses, no matter who they were, for the transgressions which they shared with the King and for the blazing affront which their existence was to his mother the Queen. Now he was no longer a child; he was over sixteen and happily married. In fact, the serene respectability of his own marital life made the King's lapse seem all the more unbecoming. The Dauphin could hardly be expected, given his youth and his bigotry, to understand, much less to forgive, the love affair of his father. To him, Madame de Pompadour was, and would always remain, no better than a whore whose continued presence at Court degraded the Royal Family and the entire kingdom. The Mistress might charm or crush her other enemies, but the Dauphin's position made him invulnerable, and for the rest of her life the best she could elicit from him was a chill smile.

The Court was still at Fontainebleau when Madame de Pompadour received word that her mother had died on Christmas Eve at the early age of forty-six. Although Madame Poisson had been ill with cancer for months, her death deeply affected her daughter. What, then, was she doing at Court instead of spending the last hours of her mother's life at her side? Madame Poisson could have answered that question promptly and characteristically by pointing out the only logical explanation—Madame de Pompadour's first duty lay with the King. The ambitious mother, who had struggled so untiringly to transform her daughter into *une reine à la gauche,* would have been the last to suggest that family affection should take precedence over the demands of a Royal liaison. Not even death should upset the King's routine.

Madame de Pompadour's sorrow was nonetheless genuine. Although she probably loved her father more dearly, the ties which bound her to Madame Poisson were special ties, uniting two natures which understood each other perfectly. It was to her mother that she owed the skillful training which had done so much to lift her to her present position. If she lacked Madame Poisson's passion, at least she shared her fierce ambition. And it was from her mother that she absorbed her precise understanding of how to attract and hold the masculine heart.

Madame de Pompadour remained in her apartment for several days. The King, always helpless in the presence of feminine tears, consoled her as best he could and even volunteered to postpone the Court's scheduled visit to Marly. But the Marquise would not hear of any change in plans on her account. Wise as her mother would have been, she realized that in a few days Louis would be irritated that they had not gone to Marly and would blame her. So she dried her tears and insisted that everything go on as before. With her usual thoughtfulness she remarked that the ladies of the Court already had their wardrobes planned for the trip, and she saw no reason why her mother's death should inconvenience them.

A few days later Queen Marie Leczinska was the recipient of another pleasant surprise—a New Year's present from the King for the first time in years. It was a handsome snuff box of enamel and gold, with a tiny watch mounted in the center of the lid. Not only was the gift unexpected, it was unintended—having originally been ordered as a remembrance from Louis to the unfortunate Madame Poisson.

While Madame de Pompadour was weeping for her mother, Paris was raucously laughing at an epitaph—anonymous, of course—which in its own fashion saluted the dead woman:

> Ci-gît qui, sortant d'un fumier
> Pour faire sa fortune entière
> Vendit son honneur au fermier
> Et sa fille au propriétaire.

> Here lies one who, emerging from a dung-heap,
> In order to make her full fortune
> Sold her honor to the tenant
> And her daughter to his landlord.

Shortly after the Court returned to Versailles from Marly, the King grew restless again and searched for an excuse for another trip. As Madame de Pompadour had never been to the seacoast, he decided to take her on a state visit to Le Havre. Upon seeing the Archbishop of Rouen at Court, Louis informed him that on the way to Normandy he would do him the honor of being his guest. The Archbishop, appalled at the prospect of sheltering the King's Mistress under the episcopal roof, only bowed in reply.

The King, his irritation mounting, said more loudly, "Did you hear me say that I am coming to pay you a visit?" The embarrassed prelate, at a loss for words, bowed again in silence. The King was infuriated. "No, monsieur," he snapped, "I would rather be hanged than accept your hospitality."

In spite of such an inauspicious beginning, the trip to Le Havre proceeded merrily. Madame de Pompadour viewed the sea, and a mock naval battle was staged in her honor.

She assisted at the laying of the keel of a new ship, herself buckling the first bolt; perhaps it was fitting that the vessel was christened *Le Gracieux*.

When the journey was over the King was abashed to learn that it had cost almost a million livres. France was still at war and the Treasury was in no condition to support such prodigal waste. Louis decided, for the future, to limit his trips to the châteaux which lay in the neighborhood of Paris and Versailles; and so Madame de Pompadour, for the first time, had ample opportunity to settle down and adjust herself to life within the great Palace.

VII

THE GOLDEN CAGE

*W*HEN Madame de Pompadour first saw Versailles she must have been astonished at the vast bulk of the Palace rising from the plain, its endless width sprawled against the western sky. From the Paris approach the residence of the King, despite its titanic proportions, despite the gleaming gold which decorated the oval windows of the roof, presented a bewildering panorama of successive paved courtyards separated by gilded iron railings, almost encompassed by the long parallel wings which stretched forward from the central portion of the building. If in the excitement of the moment she thought about the Palace at all, she must have found her first impression disappointing—the crowded, confused entrance hinted only slightly at the splendor that lay within.

Her carriage halted in the inner courtyard, the Royal Court, which was surrounded on three sides by the Palace itself. Ahead of her, across the Marble Court, rose the brick walls of Louis XIII's small hunting château, the core of Versailles, which was all that had occupied the desolate, sandy plain before Louis XIV dreamed his imperial dream of transforming this wasteland into the most royal of residences. The room directly overhead, the tall windows of which opened on a balcony, was Louis XIV's State Bedchamber and the altar of this royal temple. Significantly, Louis XV never slept there now; he found it too cold and had deserted it for the charming series of rooms, the Little Cabinets, whose windows looked down upon her from the right side of the courtyard.

Not until the afternoon when she looked at the Palace from the vantage point of Le Nôtre's peerless gardens, rigid and formal in their classic purity of line, did she become fully aware that she was gazing upon one of the great glories of French architecture, Versailles—the abode of Kings—the most French thing in all France. Its immense western façade, as regular in its grandeur of design as the front was irregular in its sprawling confusion, loomed in solid majesty before her. The thousand windows of the Palace, transformed into sheets of molten gold by the reflection of the setting sun, could not have failed to send a thrill of exultation through the Marquise. This was indeed a fitting setting in which to embark upon her reign.

Versailles was certainly the most magnificent palace in Europe, but its comfort was not commensurate with its splendor. It housed some 10,000 people, and the crowded scurrying of courtiers along its lengthy corridors resembled the activity of a rabbit warren. Not only did it shelter the Royal Family, the Princes of the Blood, countless nobles, and innumerable priests, but even tradesmen from the town who did a thriving business on the ground floor, purveying stationery and perfume to the courtiers. High in the attics, beneath the raised roofs to which Mansart for-

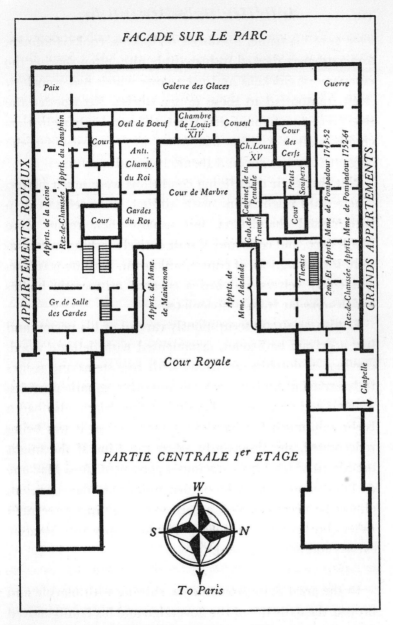

The Palace of Versailles

ever gave his name, hundreds of lackeys, cooks, footmen, and gardeners roosted in incredible filth, often sharing the company of chickens and even cows which had somehow been transported to these upper stories. No wonder the irreverent commented that when the wind was right they could smell Versailles five miles away—no wonder the elegant courtiers covered themselves with perfumes!

Not that their own living conditions were much better. Their walls might shine with gilding, their ceilings drip with crystal chandeliers, but usually their rooms were small, dark, and cold, and almost entirely lacking in sanitation. Plumbing was, of course, unknown. Bathing was rare, and costly velvets and satins covered aristocratic bodies which were far from immaculate.

Louis was always scrupulously careful of his person and had a private bathroom, ornamented with delicate wood-carvings of dolphins entwined with rose stems and scenes in bas-relief of fishing, bathing, and other aquatic pursuits. Marie Leczinska, on the far side of the Palace, also had a bathroom, much less handsome. Once, when it was being redecorated, she timorously asked the King if she might use his, to which Louis graciously consented. And Madame de Pompadour, dainty by nature and, in her new position, almost by necessity, took a bath every day in rose-scented water, brought to her in a portable copper tub ornately carved and heavily gilded.

In the great State Apartments, shining with marble and bronze, the daily life of the Sovereign and his family moved with unvarying precision, regulated by the clockwork of

Royal etiquette. Not even the King could change it, for the Monarch was a symbol, an institution as well as a man. Louis XV had to endure the same rigid routine which his great-grandfather had established and lived by. Louis XIV, the incarnation of Absolute Monarchy, gloried in it; Louis XV, lacking his ancestor's colossal egotism and essentially timid, sometimes found the lack of privacy almost insupportable.

The King's day began with the fixed and tedious ceremonial of the *lever*. Although he no longer slept in Louis XIV's great bed—that inert symbol of monarchy enshrined behind a gold railing, before which, even when empty, Princesses of the Blood curtsied—Louis XV climbed into it early every morning, hurrying in his dressing gown from Madame de Pompadour's apartments. When he was ready he nodded to his valet, who opened the doors into the *Oeil de Boeuf* where the courtiers stood waiting. Those who enjoyed the privilege of the "Familiar Entry" pushed into the overgilded chamber to gaze upon the King of France in his bed; after Louis had risen and put on his dressing gown, those who had the right of the "Grand Entry" crowded into the room. The "Entry of the Chamber" took place when the King had seated himself in front of his dressing table, after which the room was filled to overflowing by the "General Entry," consisting of those who had waited since dawn for this climactic moment.

After the King was dressed he proceeded in state, followed by the entire Court, through the Hall of Mirrors and the Grand Apartments to the Chapel where he heard Mass. His Majesty's day, launched with such a plenitude of protocol, unwound in the same prescribed manner. He always ate one meal in public, either alone or with the Queen. Often in the afternoon he managed to escape for a walk or, better still, the hunt, but he was almost never free from the company of others and the consequent burden of behaving as royalty must behave.

In the evening, when the intimate supper—or game of cards—or ball—or theater—or concert—was ended, the ceremonial reasserted itself, and the elaborate ritual of the *lever* was re-enacted in that of the *coucher,* the Court assembling once again in the State Bedchamber to see the King retire. Although everyone knew that he would slip from the huge bed as soon as the doors were closed and hasten upstairs to rejoin the Marquise, the fantastic ceremony was never omitted. And it never occurred to Louis that it should be. He was Lord of the Kingdom but he was still subject to the inexorable demands of his exalted station.

This stiff and unending formality consumed an inordinate amount of the King's time which might better have been spent in work. However, Louis did manage to see his Ministers every day and he held a reception for the Ambassadors every Wednesday. The hours of leisure which remained he devoted to his own amusements.

The existence of the Queen, without power or even influence, was still more tedious. By eleven o'clock she had heard Mass, exchanged a meaningless word or two with the King, and was waiting for her state *toilette,* which took place at noon. "Sometimes," says de Luynes, "I have seen

a dozen ladies together; none of them escapes her attention; she speaks to all of them . . . about personal matters,
the only things that flatter." At one o'clock she heard a
second Mass, then proceeded to dine in public. Although
the common people, if well-dressed, were admitted to the
Palace to witness this ceremony—and there was always a
crowd of them—their presence did not ruffle the Queen.
Like many people whose inner lives are empty, Marie
Leczinska ate a great deal, devoting herself to her meals
with unhurried thoroughness.

At six in the evening she took her place at the card table
to play her "sad cavagnole." If the King happened to be
present, Marie would not sit down until he had told her
to do so; usually she was embarrassed and he was irritated,
and they rarely said more than a few words to each other.
At ten the Queen retired to join her own circle of friends.

This harmless little group revolved entirely around her.
The most intelligent was Président Hénault, a clever and
witty conversationalist; another was Buffon, the famous
zoologist, who steadily resisted the attempts of Madame de
Pompadour to attach him to her own circle; de la Mothe,
an old soldier who longed, apparently in vain, to be made
a Marshal; Maurepas, the younger d'Argenson, and invariably the faithful Duc and Duchesse de Luynes, the latter
known affectionately as "The Hen." Of them all, the
Queen was fondest of the ducal pair. In the course of one
year she dined 198 times in the de Luynes' apartments and
while she ate the men stood respectfully, their meal being
served to them later in another room.

Sometimes the Queen went to the *Salon de la Paix* where

she held musicales; occasionally she even played herself (very badly) with some of the courtiers and musicians, but she always returned to Madame de Luynes' to resume her cards until late at night. From time to time she dozed, "in that delicious armchair near the fireplace," as she herself described it.

This group of loyal friends was virtuous without being sanctimonious. The Queen had a sense of humor and particularly enjoyed the racy witticisms of Maurepas. Sometimes she even permitted him to tell her a slightly risqué anecdote.

The Queen's existence, colorless as it appeared to be, filled an important need. While the King was losing the respect of the people, she was gaining it; the position she maintained at Court, not from pride but principle, was a bulwark of the Monarchy. At times her piety might border on dullness, but everyone respected it. People knew that Marie Leczinska went without luxuries and sometimes even necessities because of her unceasing gifts to the poor, and they loved her for it. Her successor, Marie Antoinette, far more dazzling and graceful, never occupied in the hearts of the people the place of Marie Leczinska; indeed, she failed in the task of being the kind of Queen that France demanded.

The Queen's son and daughters were ill trained and lacked their mother's goodness of heart. Their youth might be adduced in partial extenuation if their ill temper had not increased with their years. The Dauphin, haunted by his confessors and consumed with hatred of Madame de

The Palace of Versailles, from a woodcut in Guizot's *History of France.*

The Royal Chateau of Marly, from a woodcut in Guizot's *History of France*.

Pompadour, was "bored to death at Versailles for ten months of the year." He watched with bitterness while the King lavished gifts on the Marquise, while he had "only his ordinary allowance of money and was often very pinched and unhappy."

The astringent Marquis d'Argenson described the heir as "an unexampled compound of the most contradictory qualities; he had bigotry and no religion; impulses of a good heart, moved even to tears, and inhumanity; gentleness and harshness; traits of intelligence and stupidity, childishness and prudence, but above all, singularity; he goes about at night when others are in their beds."

The Dauphin was firmly dominated by his younger sister Madame Adélaïde. In order to flaunt her authority over him she overruled the few orders which the Dauphine ventured to give. Madame Adélaïde had a loud deep voice and abrupt masculine ways which amused but also startled the King. Even he seemed a little afraid of her.

She hated Madame de Pompadour venomously and frequently referred to her as "Mama Whore." Since Madame Adélaïde was the strongest willed of the royal children, she ruled them all and was constantly inciting her brother and sisters to rudeness against the Marquise. "The Royal Family is beginning to conspire against Madame de Pompadour," d'Argenson related with satisfaction. "At the last hunt she was in the calèche of the Dauphin, the Dauphine, and Mesdames, who all agreed to say nothing to her, no matter what she said to them." Such childish cruelty was deeply hurtful to the Marquise who, whatever her faults, did not possess a mean spirit. The poor woman found it extremely painful to bear these insults coolly, but her exquisite tact rescued her; she pretended to overlook the slights, and continued to exert herself to be agreeable to the King's spiteful children.

At the age of twelve, the King's eldest child Elizabeth had married Don Philip, a son of Philip V of Spain. *Madame l'Infante,* as she was called, was her father's favorite. She resembled him physically and, in many ways, mentally. His other children may have had intelligence but she was the only one who showed it. When she returned for a visit she followed Louis about "like the most ardent courtier." Unlike the King, Madame l'Infante was ambitious and had little use for concerts and gambling. Instead she would send for the Ministers or shut herself up "for three or four hours to write." She had an even disposition which her successful marriage had strengthened. (All of her discontented sisters lived out their lives as old maids.) Unlike them, Madame l'Infante always showed courtesy and graciousness to her father's Mistress, and Madame de Pompadour was profoundly thankful.

On one of Madame l'Infante's visits she was described as being "fresh and very tall in comparison with her sisters, who are not so. She is very badly off for clothes, and even for linen; they say that her wardrobe has not been renewed since she [first] left France." Not content with this observation, the critic irrelevantly added: "Her Chevalier of Honor is a horrid toad, very dirty."

Madame Henriette, the twin of Madame Elizabeth, was the most gentle and likeable of the Royal daughters; Madame Victoire was quiet and shared the Queen's fondness for eating, while Madame Sophie was so timid that she could never look anyone directly in the face but glanced at them sideways like a hare. Madame Sophie was really ugly, but Madame de Pompadour, charitably trying to conceal the fact, wrote to Abel Poisson that "Madame Sophie is almost as tall as I, very pretty and plump with a beautiful skin and throat; her profile and the King's are as alike as two drops of water; full-view *not as pretty* because she has a disagreeable mouth."

The youngest of the Princesses, Madame Louise, was rather plain but very vivacious and a spirited horsewoman. In her later life she became profoundly affected by piety and entered the Carmelite Order as a nun in order to pray for the King's salvation.

In the first years of Madame de Pompadour's life at Versailles, the Dauphin and Mesdames were scarcely beyond childhood. When the Queen bore her last child (Madame Louise), the King was only twenty-seven. Being relatively few years older than his children he was on excellent terms with them, especially his daughters who, in spite of the rank and privileges which surrounded them, were little more than gorgeously dressed dolls. Louis visited them every day and remained for long talks. "Really," said the Marquise, "nothing is more touching than these interviews; the tenderness of the King for his children is unbelievable, and they respond with all their heart."

Certainly Louis' paternal affection was one of his warmest and most human traits; the Prince de Croÿ said that it was a joy to see him surrounded by his family. "The King," he wrote, "hugged them all a long time, looking at them with an air of charming tenderness. One must admit that the King is the best of fathers. . . ." The gloomy d'Argenson struck a different note in describing the life of Mesdames when the King was absent. "The Dauphin and Mesdames," he noted, "are becoming melancholy and are giving way to their personal tastes without constraint; they dislike seeing anyone, and never speak to others; their talk is of death and catafalques; they amuse themselves by playing quadrille in their dark antechamber by the light of one yellow wax candle and saying to one another with delight, 'We are dead.' "

No wonder! Brought up in the embalmed atmosphere of the Court, fettered from babyhood by ritual and ceremony, these royal puppets never knew the meaning of a normal childhood. They learned too early the details of their adored father's private life, and as they were powerless to interfere, they could only withdraw in aching frustration. Mesdames were useless to France unless they contracted advantageous marriage alliances; as for the Dauphin, he was consigned to the hapless position of waiting for the King to die before he could become of any importance in his own right. The devout at Court might pray for that untimely event, but to the Dauphin's credit he loved Louis and never wished for his death.

The hothouse atmosphere of Versailles was filled with a mushroom growth of inefficiency, graft, and vested interests. To Madame de Pompadour, brought up with a bourgeois respect for money and a nice ability to keep her personal accounts in order, such financial irregularity was appalling. Louis XV was no reformer; he naturally followed the line of least resistance and was content to leave things as he found them. During his long reign there was no serious attempt at economy, no effort to curtail the selfish waste, and when he died the annual expenses of the Court amounted to 40,000,000 livres.

France was the richest country in Europe and could easily have supported this burden and more had the taxes been fairly distributed. But the clergy and the nobility, still enjoying the privileges of feudalism in the Age of Enlightenment, paid no taxes. The Church owned one fifth of the usable land, and enjoyed an annual income averaging 400,000,000 livres, yet it stoutly disclaimed any obligation to share a part of the cost of government. From time to time the clergy voted a "free-will" offering to the Treasury, amounting to a hundredth of its annual income. It refused to give more.

Since the days of Louis XIV the great nobles had deserted their large estates for the splendors of Versailles. Extravagant, vain, and parasitical, the nobles looked upon work as demeaning; except for seizing the plums of government, army, and Church, and scrambling for sinecures at Court, they did nothing. The vast revenues they derived from their estates were never sufficient for their fancied needs; their prodigality kept them on the edge of bankruptcy; and they resorted to questionable practices to refill their pockets.

The ladies in waiting of the Queen made the rounds of her apartments every night, collecting the candles which had been lighted only once and selling them for their own profit. Every three years Marie Leczinska's enormous supply of dresses and linen was renewed, regardless of need, in order that her Lady of Honor might exercise her traditional right to dispose of them as she pleased. The King's First Gentleman of the Bedchamber numbered, among his perquisites, the right to supply powder and pomade to the Court, while the Grand Equerry furnished the uniforms of the Swiss Guards at a handsome profit.

Naturally there was an unending jealous struggle to occupy these profitable positions, all of which were at the sole disposal of the King. They were an essential part of the system of absolute monarchy which Louis XIV had erected, aimed at reducing the French nobility to the status of mere ornamental satellites.

When the Queen married, over 400 new posts were created for her household; when the Dauphin was only seven, more than 100 people were considered necessary to care for his needs. The distribution of such exalted positions as Governess, First Valet, and Lady in Waiting assumed more importance in the eyes of noble aspirants than the victory or defeat of French arms—and in the awarding of these coveted posts the favor of the King's Mistress was essential. Madame de Pompadour did not long delay in taking advantage of that fact.

In addition to the graft they furnished, most of these useless offices paid handsome salaries, increasing the drain on the Treasury. Such waste exacted its inevitable toll. D'Argenson, always painting in darkest colors, lamented that "poverty is beginning to attack the Royal Treasury in such a way that the household of the King lacks absolutely everything. The King's grooms ask for charity, and their wives beg in the streets of Versailles after dark; yet the expenses of the household are increasing; there is no longer any order or regularity."

But the *ancien régime* pursued its course apparently untroubled. Decay gnawed at its foundations while on the glittering surface all remained as it was, had been, and presumably would be—the same names, the same faces, the same ranks, circling monotonously in the same orbit, playing to the end their appointed roles in the congealed farce of Court etiquette.

While Louis was too conscious of his Bourbon ancestors to neglect his central role in the ceremony, the tedious routine unutterably wearied him. Louis XIV never once thought of escaping it, but Louis XV, summoning his feeble will power, constructed for himself a retreat where he could while away his leisure hours in undisturbed privacy. There, high above the ritualistic gyrations of his courtiers, he spent his happiest hours with Madame de Pompadour—and there she skilfully spun the threads of habitual companionship which bound the King to her for life.

VIII

LOVE'S WAYS ARE HARD AND STEEP

*I*N *1737-38,* after Louis had irrevocably separated from the Queen, he redecorated for himself the series of rooms on the north side of the Marble Court which are known as the Little Cabinets. Here he could, in some small measure, escape from the stifling atmosphere of the State Apartments and enjoy a modicum of privacy.

These rooms of Louis XV may still be visited; with a little imagination, their appearance in their days of glory can be recalled. Unlike the rooms of Louis XIV they were not heavy with bronze and marble and stucco but were of a wonderful elegance, representative of the faultless crafts-manship of the eighteenth century. Here the sun streamed in through the tall windows, turning the pendants of the chandeliers to drops of fire and imparting an airy lightness which was in striking contrast to the cheerless magnificence of the State Apartments.

The bedroom—indeed, all these rooms—was embellished with marvelous woodcarvings of shells, flowers, and many dimpled cupids, the fitting emblem of Louis XV's reign. White paneled walls were edged with delicate gilding and gracefully carved gold frames held Venetian mirrors which

reflected endlessly the soft luxury of the furnishings. Over
the doors hung two of the finest portraits in the Royal
collection—Francis the First by Titian, and Marie de
Medici by Van Dyck.

Adjoining the bedroom was the *Salle de la Pendule,* with
its carved mantel of violet marble surmounted by large
mirrors. The medallions which were centered in the panels
of the wall each portrayed a group of children—blowing
soap bubbles, seesawing, gathering grapes, weaving gar-
lands of flowers, playing with a dolphin or a small dog.
Beyond lay the bright corner room, the *Cabinet de Travail,*
whose tall eastern windows faced the highway that led to
Paris. There was also a dining room, bathroom, and a
cabinet des perruques, where the King powdered himself.
Even those who possessed the entrée to the Little Cabinets
were not allowed to enter here.

The King soon discovered that the Little Cabinets,
charming as they were, did not furnish the privacy he
craved. "An odd thing just happened to me," he said one
day, coming into Madame de Pompadour's room. "Would
you believe that as I went into my bedroom I found myself
face to face with a strange man?"

"My God, Sire!" exclaimed the Marquise, thoroughly
startled.

"It was nothing," the King answered. "But I admit that
it gave me quite a shock. 'What are you doing here?', I
asked him politely. He threw himself to his knees, saying,
'Forgive me, Sire, and have me searched.' He was almost
inarticulate with fright and emptied his pockets to show
that he had taken nothing; at last he managed to stammer

that he worked in the kitchen, that he had taken the wrong stair, and all the doors being open, had arrived in my bedroom." The King spoke calmly of this unnerving intrusion, but he was obviously holding himself in and had been much upset.

As for Madame de Pompadour, she was greatly alarmed, agreeing with her brother "that the King could have been assassinated in his room without anyone knowing it and without anyone being able to tell who did it."

The vast palace was always filled with strangers who wandered almost at will wherever they pleased, and sometimes they were not as innocent as the inadvertent intruder into Louis' bedroom. A witness reported that "four thieves were caught in the Hall of Mirrors itself, two of whom were behind the Dauphin when they were seen to pick his pockets. A new law condemns such thieves to be hanged for even the simple theft of a pocket handkerchief, if they ply their trade in a Royal house."

And so Louis, seeking a sanctuary where he would be absolutely undisturbed, retreated farther, building that incredible series of hidden rooms nearer the roof—the Little Apartments. Rising two or three stories in height, a maze of winding corridors and secret staircases, they were hidden from outside view by the steep slope of the mansard roof. These Little Apartments looked out on an inner courtyard which provided them with light—the *Cour des Cerfs*.

Here the King lived in a world so far removed from the teeming Court below that it might have been in the sky. Here he kept the treasures that were closest to his heart—his geographical maps, his secret correspondence, his library and even, on an upper terrace open to the sky, a dovecot, a poultry run, an aviary of rare birds, and luxuriant shrubs which transformed the roof into a miniature hanging garden.

The Little Apartments, small and low-ceilinged, lacked the gilding of the spacious rooms below. Instead they were decorated in that delicate shade of translucent green called *vernis Martin* or sometimes in pale gray. The furnishings were costly but of restrained simplicity, fitting for the luxurious hideaway of a very rich man who could indulge every whim. Only a selected few were invited to these "delicious retreats"; those who were not, like the Marquis d'Argenson, sneered at the "rats' nests," and complained that their sumptuousness had cost the Treasury 600,000 livres.

In the little dining room Louis gave the intimate suppers of which he was so fond, those friendly unceremonious gatherings where almost, but not quite, he descended to the level of a private gentleman. The Prince de Croÿ left an interesting description of one of them:

Having climbed to the Little Apartments by the small staircase, we waited for supper in the tiny salon. The King did not enter until it was time to seat himself at the table with the ladies. The dining room was charming and the supper went very pleasantly, without embarrassment. We were served by only two or three valets, who disappeared after having put before each one of us the course we were supposed to have. . . .

The King was gay and relaxed, but always with an air of grandeur that could not be ignored. He did not seem

in the least timid, but on the contrary spoke well and often
... he seemed very much in love with Madame de Pompadour and not embarrassed to show it. ...

He seemed well informed about little things and small
details without being upset by them, and without commit-
ting himself on important matters. He was born with discretion. However, everyone thinks that in private he tells
almost everything to the Marquise. ...

I noticed that he spoke jokingly to her about the campaign, and how he really wanted to leave for it. It seemed
to me that he spoke too freely to his adored Mistress, but
above all he wanted to amuse himself, and for him *there
was nothing more important than that*. As for her, she
conducted herself very well, and has much influence, but
the King wishes to be absolute Master, and is firm on that
point. ...

Marshal Saxe was also there, but he did not sit down as
he does not eat but one meal a day; however, he is very
fond of food and nibbled constantly at various dishes. The
King ... seemed to love and admire him a great deal and
talked to him in a frank and pertinent way. Madame de
Pompadour is devoted to the Marshal.

We were two hours at the table, and there was plenty of
relaxation but no license. Afterward the King went into
the little salon; he heated and poured the coffee himself,
as the servants had gone and we all had to help ourselves.

The King played Comète, a little game which he loves,
with Madame de Pompadour, Coigny, Madame de Brancas
and the Comte de Noailles; Madame de Pompadour hates
it and seemed to be looking for an excuse to get away. ...
The King asked everyone to sit down, even those who were
not playing. I leaned against the screen in order to see the
game; Madame de Pompadour insisting that the King
retire and go to sleep, he got up at one o'clock and said
gaily, "Let's go! Let's all go to bed!"

The ladies made their curtsys and left, the King bowed
in reply and withdrew into the Little Cabinets, and all of

us went down Madame de Pompadour's little stair and appeared, as usual, at the King's public *coucher,* which took place at once.

During the long reign of Madame de Pompadour there were hundreds of evenings such as this, informal but always decorous and well bred. These were the suppers twisted by the pamphleteers of Paris into Lucullan "orgies," where the King and his Mistress and their friends were accused of indulging in every kind of depravity—as if Louis XV could lose his natural dignity and the Marquise play false her own impeccable taste!

Not far from the Little Apartments, under the very roof of the northern façade of Versailles, were the three rooms which the Marquise occupied during her first years at Court. They are empty now, and the primitive elevator, or flying chair, which spared her weary body so many steps is gone; but the rooms are still accessible by climbing a hundred or more stairs.

If the ghost of Madame de Pompadour, attired in some pastel shade—blue, pink, or rose—sometimes returns to haunt these rooms, she no doubt smiles gently as she stands by the tall windows and looks across the unaltered green carpet of the *Parterre du Nord.* Perhaps she is searching the horizon for the outlines of the Forest of Marly, or perhaps she is only gazing reminiscently at the fountains playing in the *Bassin de Neptune.*

Her suite consisted of an anteroom, a bedroom, and a dining room, which had a small pantry where dishes were kept warm. The shell motif of Verberckt's woodcarving was simple and elegant, and the mantels, which are still there, were of marble. Long pier glasses, placed on one side of the room, reflected the Beauvais tapestries which ornamented the opposite wall.

Her spacious bed, silken-sheeted and bedecked with lace, stood in an alcove whose rounded arch bore the carved three towers of the Pompadour crest. Her furniture was in the incomparably graceful style of the period—wide chairs (to accommodate the panniered dresses) of satinwood or rosewood, upholstered in blue or striped velvet or in brocaded silk; a desk with plaques of enamel adorned with painted flowers; a regiment of tables of all kinds—tea tables, card tables, bedside tables, a writing table, and a dressing table.

"The triumphal piece of furniture," de Goncourt wrote, "is this table with its mirror; it is adorned with laces like an altar, swathed in foaming muslin like a cradle, encumbered with philtres and fineries, paints, pastes, scents, vermilion rouge, vegetable rouge, mineral rouge, chemical white, blue for veins, Maille vinegar for wrinkles; and ribbons and tresses and aigrettes; a bewitching little world of coquetries, of a century fragrant with amber in a cloud of powder!"

These cosmetics which the Marquise so assiduously applied to her porcelain complexion were dangerous to her fragile health. They contained poisonous red lead and mercury, and the carmine with which she rouged herself caused itching and headaches. The itching she could alleviate with an ivory scratcher, but the headaches remained chronic.

Every morning, charmingly disordered in a loose negligée, she sat at the dressing table and strove to repair the ravages of the night before. And every evening, after the little supper was over and she had climbed the narrow stairs, she retreated again to the altar of beauty to make herself alluring for the King's pleasure.

She was allowed no respite. Louis' love for her was at first entirely physical, and the Marquise was hardly equal to his incessant demands. In a desperate attempt to stimulate her frigid nature she went on a diet of celery soup, truffles, and chocolate (then considered an aphrodisiac), but the rich food gravely impaired her health and in the end was futile.

"I have acquired a cold sea-bird," complained the disappointed Louis. Sometimes he left her without a parting kiss, and one night pretending that the weather was too hot, he deserted her bed for a solitary couch across the room. Madame de Pompadour burst into tears as she recounted this crowning humiliation to her friend Madame de Brancas. That sensible woman consoled the distraught Marquise, and pointed out the ruinous folly of her strenuous regime. "Make your company more and more delightful to the King by your gentleness," she advised. "Do not repulse him at those other moments, and leave the rest to time. The chains of habit will bind him to you permanently."

The advice of Madame de Brancas was sound. Louis might find the Marquise lacking in ardor and her charms inadequate during the nocturnal hours, but for him the hours of the day were longer—and it was then that Madame de Pompadour regained the hold which might have slipped the night before.

When Louis spent the day with her, time glided by unnoticed. Remembering with confidence her mother's admonition that physical ties alone never hold a man, the Marquise studied the King's varying moods and imperceptibly adapted herself to them. She learned the meaning of every intonation of his voice, every glance from his large and lusterless eyes, every change of expression on his beautiful, satiated face. She amused him; more remarkable, she understood him—and thus she became indispensable to the King who was habit's slave.

It was during these hours of daily contact that the value of Madame de Pompadour's education became apparent. She told Louis droll stories of Paris, a world he knew little of, and opened for him a door of understanding into the lives of his intelligent, thrifty bourgeois subjects. Sometimes she sang a poignant air of Lulli or Rameau, accompanying herself skillfully on her harpsichord.

She possessed to a consummate degree the faculty of never indulging too long in any diversion; when her sensitive intuition warned her that Louis was about to relapse into boredom, she turned to a new mode of entertainment. She might be aching with weariness, suffering from fever or a cold, but she was always cheerful and pleasing—the same woman and yet not quite the same.

For the King never knew when he entered her apartment, what new vision would greet him—an oriental sultana garbed in a Turkish negligée—a fresh simple shepherdess—a rosy young woman dressed for gardening—or a cultivated woman of the world, dainty and affecting in a low-cut taffeta dress.

If the King wanted to talk, the Marquise listened with an interested air even though she had heard him tell the same story a hundred times. Louis was not an easy conversationalist, and his topics were few—the hunt, how many stags he had killed; his health; who was ill, and who had died. Although terrified of illness and death, funereal subjects held an irresistible fascination for him. He once asked a courtier where he wished to be buried, and the keen reply, reminding Louis of his own mortality, came quickly: "At Your Majesty's feet."

In spite of the splendor and comfort with which the Marquise was surrounded, in spite of her triumph, or more likely because of it, the strain told. To walk the tightrope of Versailles, where nearly everyone schemed for her downfall, would have overwhelmed a woman more robust than she. The late hours, the rich foods, the mental and above all the psychic strain wore her out before her time. To appear enchanting whenever Louis visited her, be it day or night, to conceal her own worries and infirmities, and possibly her occasional boredom with him, proved an almost crushing task. Her life, she sighed, was "like that of an early Christian, a perpetual struggle." She did not add that the struggle was self-imposed.

"It's terrible, the life I lead," she wrote to a friend. "I've hardly a moment alone . . . twice a week, invariably, journeys to the Petit Château or la Muette. Furthermore there are my Court duties, as exasperating as they are necessary

... Queen, Dauphine, Daughters, Infantas! Just ask yourself whether it gives me time to breathe. Pity me, and don't be too hard on me."

Even her enemy the saturnine Marquis d'Argenson was moved to grudging admiration at her endurance and observed with astonishment that "she is forced to keep up with the King and go about with him who goes so much; they make her drink milk when she is with him in the country, but she has no rest when he is with her. She must hurry about, and drink and eat ... certainly there must be in this beauty some mysterious strength which keeps her fresh and beautiful in the midst of such fatigue. ...."

Occasionally Madame de Pompadour had to contend with ill will from an unexpected quarter—the Queen. Marie Leczinska, usually so benign, sometimes showed a flurry of feminine spitefulness toward the King's Mistress. One day the Marquise entered the Queen's Apartments carrying a large basket of flowers, her exquisite arms and hands gloveless as a sign of respect. Marie, trying to embarrass her, praised her beauty in a patronizing way, exaggeratedly calling attention to her glorious eyes and ravishing complexion. Although the Queen's remarks were flattering, her tone of voice was unpleasant and superior. Madame de Pompadour blushed and attempted to withdraw, but the Queen, seeking to disconcert her still more, remarked that she had been told so often of her beautiful voice that she desired to hear it. Although Madame de Pompadour demurred, the Queen flatly ordered her to choose a song and sing it with the mass of flowers still in her arms.

The Marquise, seeing that there was no escape, regained

her poise and sang, in her light sweet voice, the exultant solo from *Armide:* "Enfin il est en ma Puissance." The chamber turned silent before this strange duel—the radiant Mistress, vernal and fresh as the flowers she carried, singing her song of love's triumph in the face of the aging faded wife. The Marquise had turned the tables on the Queen and victory was hers—but such victories exacted their price in strained nerves, and Madame de Pompadour must have surrendered herself to tears of disillusionment when she regained the seclusion of her attic retreat.

Like countless women before and since, Madame de Pompadour was fortunate enough to have a personal maid who was a fountain of measureless solace and strength. To Madame du Haussay, courteous, faithful, and devoted, the Marquise turned with relief, finding in her the intimate confidante so indispensable to a woman in her vulnerable position. Madame du Haussay knew all the secrets of Madame de Pompadour, and, being tactful and discreet, she kept them.

Madame du Haussay was by no means an ordinary servant. She had been brought up in the country, of a good family, and was a respectable widow with a son. She was not in the least ashamed of her position, and being with Madame de Pompadour more intimately than anyone else, enjoying the unique relationship of maid to mistress, she knew her better than anyone else, even the King. Madame du Haussay saw the Marquise in the hours when her defenses were down, when she was no longer the powerful Favorite, the charming witty enchantress who bewitched the King, but merely a woman—a woman who was often tired, ill, and unhappy.

"I pity you, Madame," she exclaimed to the Marquise, "although everyone else envies you."

Perhaps the greatest tribute that could be paid to Madame de Pompadour as a human being was the absolute, the unswerving adoration she received from her maid. She never *had* to be charming to Madame du Haussay, who loved her simply for herself.

Madame du Haussay was not pretty, but her appearance was neat and pleasing. She dressed in a uniform of colored linen, and her auburn hair was framed in a quaint high cap whose frills played around her honest face. She had a fresh mouth and pretty white teeth; her hands were well kept and rather large. It was those capable hands which tied and untied the myriad knots and ribbons of dresses and negligées, which brushed and powdered Madame de Pompadour's fine light hair, and which ministered to her needs when she was ill, smoothing the ruffled pillow and straightening the disordered covers of the bed. Many times Madame du Haussay mixed the chicory water which the King liked to drink. Louis trusted her and was never embarrassed by her presence, particularly after the alarming incident which occurred during the Marquise's early days at Versailles.

In spite of her modestly lowered eyes, Madame du Haussay was a close observer, missing nothing. A frank and unmalicious recorder, her charming memoirs (everyone wrote them in the eighteenth century) reveal a wealth of information about Louis and Madame de Pompadour. Let her paint from life a midnight scene in the bedroom of the Marquise:

An event which made Madame and myself tremble gained me the King's good will. In the middle of the night Madame came into my room dressed in her chemise and in a state of despair. "Come," she said, "the King is dying!" One can imagine my fright. I put on my petticoat and found the King in bed, gasping. . . .

It was an acute attack of indigestion. We threw water on him and he revived. I made him swallow some Hoffman's Drops, and he said to me: "Don't make any noise; go to Dr. Quesnay and tell him it is Madame who is ill, and warn his servants not to talk about it."

Quesnay was quartered near by; he came at once and was astounded to see the King in such a condition. He took his pulse and said, "The crisis is over, but if the King were sixty years old this would have been more serious." He went to get a drug, soon returned, and began to rub the King with perfumed water. I have forgotten the remedy which the Doctor used, but the effect of it was marvelous. It seems to me that it was General la Motte's Drops.

I woke up a wardrobe girl to make some tea, pretending it was for me. The King took three cups of it, put on his dressing gown, his socks, and, supported by the Doctor, succeeded in reaching his own apartment. What a sight to see all three of us half-naked!

Madame got into a dress as soon as possible, and so did I; the King had changed behind the curtains, which were decently closed. He chatted about his short illness and showed considerable appreciation for the attention we had given him.

More than an hour afterward, I still felt terrified by the realization that the King could have died in our midst. Luckily he returned at once to his own rooms and none of the servants knew what had happened. I told the wardrobe girl to straighten up the room, and she thought that Madame had been sick. . . .

How many times Madame and I have said to each other, "Suppose he had died here? What an embarrassment! What a scandal!"

After smoothing over so mortifying a situation, it is not astonishing that Louis, usually so suspicious, came to like and trust Madame du Haussay or that the Marquise confided to her that "the King and I rely so much on you that we consider you like a dog or a cat, and go on talking as we please."

And so Madame de Pompadour's life unwound in the hidden recesses of the upstairs apartments, every minute of her time occupied with duties at Court, exercise of her growing influence, and—most essential of all—unceasing analysis of the King's strange character.

IX

PORTRAIT OF A KING

*A*N ENGLISH WOMAN who saw Louis XV in 1745 said that to judge by his face he must have all the perfections of heart and mind and that it would be impossible for anyone not to love him. Certainly his graceful legs and his slim figure would have attracted women even if he had not been King of France.

But it was his beautiful face which captured and held the admiration of all who saw him. His most striking feature was his large velvety black eyes which were crowned by dark brows, the right one quizzically arched, the left smooth and regular. His Roman nose, although large, was not fleshy and bulbous as were so many Bourbon noses. His mouth curved upward at the corners, and both the upper and lower lips were pleasingly full and sensuous. That soft mouth might indicate weakness, but it was not the mouth of a cruel man.

The same Master of the Hunt who so well described Madame de Pompadour has left an equally pictorial description of the King. "A very notable air of nobility was engraven on his countenance," wrote Le Roy, "and this was still further enhanced by the way in which he carried his head. His expression was stately, but unaffected, and although the King was naturally shy, he had succeeded in obtaining sufficient command over his feelings to ensure that his expression should always be firm, but without the least suspicion of displeasure. In public he bore himself with an air of assurance, with perhaps just a tinge of severity, but that was all. In private, especially when he was talking to anyone with whom he wished to be friendly, his eyes would light up with kindness and he seemed to be trying to conciliate the affections of those with whom he was conversing."

The character which lay beneath this elegant mask was not a simple one. It was incredibly complex and almost completely contradictory, baffling so astute a woman as Madame de Tencin. "One might as well talk to the rocks," she wrote to Richelieu. "I cannot conceive of a man who is able to be everything and who prefers to remain a cipher. ... He pays not the least attention to what is passing in his Kingdom. Nothing seems to interest him. In the Council he shows the most absolute indifference, and signs everything that is put before him. In truth, to have anything to do with such a person is enough to drive one to despair. It is noticed that in every case he inclines to the course which promises the least amount of trouble, and that is generally the worst one."

Madame de Tencin's contemptuous appraisal was only superficially correct. Had she been able to probe into the King's hidden nature, she would have found anything but indifference to what went on around him. His seeming unconcern was but a defense thrown up to conceal the defect which colored his whole nature—an appalling inferiority complex.

Naturally its roots lay deep in Louis' childhood, beginning when the orphaned boy of five was delivered into the resolute hands of Fleury. The child-King's tutor deliberately fostered Louis' feeling of dependence, encouraging him to shirk decisions and to leave everything to Fleury. Even after the King married and became a grown man, he retained his uneasy sense of inferiority and his belief that no idea of his own could possibly be of value. Such modesty could be charming in a private citizen but was hardly a desirable trait in an Absolute Monarch in whose hands lay all the threads of the Kingdom.

Aware of his inertia and lack of force, Louis usually followed the advice of others in order to avoid a scene. He, the Master of France, hesitated to suggest a course of action for fear it might encounter resistance in the Council —he knew too well that his tragic feebleness of will would betray him into acquiescence. He was accused of duplicity because he would be gracious to a Minister one day and send him a curt note of dismissal the next. It was not duplicity, however, but simply a constitutional inability to endure any unpleasantness, any argument.

And yet at times he could be firm, even immovable. Against the advice of his Ministers, contrary to the stormy objections of the public, and even counter to the wishes of Madame de Pompadour, he stood adamant in his determination to exile Charles Edward Stuart, the Young Pretender, after the signing of the Treaty of Aix-la-Chapelle. On other occasions, especially in his controversies with the

Parlement of Paris, he showed astonishing resolution, sharply reminding that fractious body of quarreling lawyers that "in my person alone is the supreme authority—legislative power belongs to me alone—public order emanates from me; I am its supreme guardian."

Contrary to the traditional estimate of him Louis did not have an inferior education, and his interests were wide, especially in the sciences. Not only did he have his private observatory on the roofs of the Little Apartments, but he sent astronomers as far as Peru and Mexico to measure the shape of the earth. He was passionately interested in geography and covered the walls of his study with maps. Dr. Quesnay, himself an eminent scientist and founder of the Physiocrats, openly admired the King's manifold interests. Louis was fascinated by botany, and, like his Mistress, could converse for hours with Croÿ about trees and shrubs.

In the realm of literature he was intellectually incurious and at times actively hostile to the great writers of his reign. In a sense this was because Louis was naturally devout and regarded the *philosophes* as little better than atheists. But there was another reason—the King was extraordinarily perceptive and not easy to deceive. He recognized intuitively that the shafts of Voltaire and his followers were aimed not only at the Church but inevitably at the Monarchy as well.

Although the King was indifferent and sometimes antagonistic to the literature of his reign, he was not insensitive to other forms of art. He knew nothing of the technical details of painting, sculpture, and music, but that did not mean that he was unappreciative of their beauty. Like many a wealthy man he surrounded himself with the finest and most costly examples of eighteenth-century genius, and the details of his rooms confirm that he could appreciate beauty and grace. Louis XV cannot be termed uncultured, and certainly not boorish. That description fits better his grandson, Louis XVI.

Contrary to the impression of most of his contemporaries, Louis XV understood the principles of government very well; but its details bored him, and his opinions, sound though they might be, were undermined by an inherent sense of pessimism. Once when a Minister spoke of plans to strengthen the Navy the King shrugged sadly: "I have heard that talk twenty times. I think France will *never* have a Navy."

And yet Louis did not sit idly by during his long reign. He was primarily responsible for creating the bureaucracy, and under his rule the senior clerks of the Departments became more efficient. Unhappily, his choice of Ministers was not equally fortunate. Under Louis XIV the Ministers of the Crown were given a free hand in their respective departments, subject only to the King's supervision, and they discharged their duties with zeal and competence. Under Louis XV the Ministers were of inferior caliber, jealous of one another, and always fearful of the Court and especially of the Mistresses. Madame de Pompadour they came to fear above all others, and in time she came to be the unofficial Prime Minister, tolerating in the government no one who disagreed with her views.

It is customary to compare Louis XV unfavorably with

the more spectacular Louis XIV. Admittedly Louis XV was not an astute organizer and administrator, but on the other hand he did not love war and conquest or seek personal glory at the expense of other men's lives. His government spent less on war than Louis XIV's, taxes were no greater and poverty no worse. The privileges of the nobles did not increase, and immorality, if equally widespread, was at least free of hypocrisy. Many of Louis XV's ideas were sounder than those of Louis XIV, but he lacked the colossal ego of that ruler, the self-assurance necessary to put them into effect.

Theodore Lavallée, no admirer of the King, wrote that "the secret correspondence of Louis XV shows that this prince had the sentiment of national grandeur as if by royal instinct and family tradition; it is full of good sense, dignity, and loyalty. No one can read it without regretting that this noble policy should have been rendered sterile by lack of will."

The comment was all too true. Louis spent part of each morning at his correspondence, writing letters which reveal a keen political judgment and an instinctive knowledge of what was best for France. He expounded these ideas to the King of Spain, to his son-in-law Don Philip, and sometimes to people who were completely obscure.

Nowhere do the King's principles shine more favorably than in that almost incredible diplomatic correspondence known as *Le Secret,* which he conducted for years unknown to his Ministers. The King had private agents in every European capital, and often knew long before the Foreign Ministry what was going on in Madrid, Vienna, or London.

At meetings of the Council he delighted in asking for information on some recent development abroad, and if the embarrassed Foreign Minister replied that he had not yet received a report, the King would quietly proceed to tell him the latest political news from the capital in question. The Minister had no recourse but to conceal his chagrin as best he could.

Although *Le Secret* extended into every part of Europe, its principal concern was Poland. Louis was profoundly anxious to revive French influence in Warsaw and if possible to secure the election of a French Prince to the throne when it should become vacant. His candidate was the Prince de Conti who assisted him in the secret correspondence and was the only one at Versailles who knew of its existence.

Madame de Pompadour suspected some intrigue, and not the least of the reasons why she disliked Conti was her jealousy of his work with the King. Try though she did, she was never able to learn the details of *Le Secret,* and as for the Foreign Ministry, it operated in a maze of bewilderment. *Le Secret* actually constituted the King's own Foreign Office, and more often than not the orders which Louis drafted to his private agents flatly contradicted the government's official foreign policy.

Why this strange dual activity? Why did Louis the Man spend so much of his time thwarting and contradicting Louis the King? Boutaric indicated the answer in discussing the King's "obscure intrigues to satisfy his will, which he is afraid to assert, yet which is often right. He likes to conspire because he hates open resistance, that is, scenes."

Boutaric might have added that Louis chose this method as a sly way of hitting back at the tiresome people who surrounded and badgered him—Ministers, family, and—yes, sometimes Madame de Pompadour herself. Thus did his strange inward nature turn and avenge itself upon them, and the greatest tragedy of all was that his hidden and devious policy was often more high-minded than theirs.

It would be wrong to suppose that the King's penchant for intrigue was merely a whim, a childish attempt to confuse others and amuse himself. Louis dissimulated because he felt that he *had* to—his deep distrust of people drove him to it as a measure of defense. He was suspicious of everyone, even—at first—of Madame de Pompadour. One day while horseback-riding with M. de Brige, who had known the Marquise when she was Madame d'Étioles, the King tried to trap him into a confession of intimacy with her. "Confess to me that you have been her lover—she has admitted it, and I ask the proof of your sincerity." M. de Brige refused, replying truthfully that it was not so.

Oddly enough this sense of distrust was not directed toward the ordinary people of France but only the courtiers who surrounded him at Versailles. Absolute Monarch though he was, he had an almost touching faith in his subjects' affection, and when he lost it in later years he was deeply hurt; characteristically, however, he masked his feelings and assumed an air of indifference. "Things as they are will last as long as I; let those who follow me do the best they can."

In spite of the incomparable composure which the King

showed in public, he found it hard to conceal his dislike of crowds and especially of strangers. Even when seeing close friends for the first time after an absence he was embarrassed and at a loss for words. Only after several meetings did Louis relax and resume his normal manner.

It must have been a staggering task even for the clever Madame de Pompadour to fathom such a nature. She had never before known anyone like the King—her associates had been lively, talkative, and witty, but Louis was none of these. Sometimes he seemed to find it almost painful to laugh and, begging the Marquise to discontinue an amusing story, would lapse into morose silence.

When Madame de Pompadour first knew Louis he was inclined to be stingy, especially with cash. To him a draft on the Treasury for 1,000,000 livres meant less than parting with 5 gold louis. And yet in this too he could be inconsistent. One day, meeting Bernis on the Marquise's little stairway, he asked the purpose of the bolt of cloth he was carrying. The round little Abbé answered with some embarrassment that Madame de Pompadour had given him a roll of chintz with which to decorate his apartment. "Well, then," said the King gaily, handing the astounded Abbé a stack of gold pieces, "she's given you the cloth, here's for the nails."

One of the King's most appealing traits was his love of animals, and the only thing that could make him really angry was for someone to mistreat one of his pets. He was fond of dogs and horses, but he especially loved his huge white angora cat. This enormous tom was unusually gentle and affectionate and would lie for hours on a crimson damask cushion in front of the fire.

One night when the King was upstairs with Madame de Pompadour, the *valets-de-chambre* amused themselves by pouring cologne on the cat's paws and watching its frenzied antics as the alcohol penetrated the skin. "It leaped down, emitting a series of alarming reports from its rear, and ran about yowling, skipping and prancing like a ballerina. In the middle of it all the King arrived like a bolt from the blue. 'What is going on here?' he demanded icily. 'What are you doing to my cat? I mean to get to the bottom of this.'"

The attendants sheepishly confessed their prank, and watched anxiously to see if the King was taking it as a joke. Decidedly he was not. His face was stern, and as he turned on his heel he said, "I leave you here, but if you want to amuse yourselves, I am going to see that it won't be at the expense of my cat." His remark was uttered, wrote one of the chastened participants, "in such a tone of voice that no one has ever made the cat dance since."

The King liked a kind heart, and although he was himself accused of ingratitude and duplicity, actually he detested those traits. When Madame de Pompadour succeeded in forcing the Comte d'Argenson's dismissal, a former sycophant of the disgraced Minister approached Louis and smirkingly remarked that he had "just seen M. d'Argenson's trunks leaving." The King turned his back on the courtier in disgust and said witheringly, "and the cock crew!"

Usually the King was kind and, like many timid people,

especially considerate to inferiors. He was always thoughtful of his servants, who adored him. Once he refused to reproach a lackey who had brought him two shoes for the same foot, explaining that "he who made the mistake feels worse about it than I do." Many times on winter mornings he rose early in the cold bedroom and lighted the fire himself rather than disturb the sleep of his valet.

Dufort de Cheverny, who introduced the Ambassadors into the King's presence, wrote: "I have often been more at home with him than many other people I know . . . the kindness with which he treated me is written deep on my heart." A moving tribute, and one which bears the ring of truth rather than flattery.

And yet there is inconsistency here too, for Louis could also be selfishly inconsiderate. Sometimes during a hunt, after riding hard all day and changing horses several times, he would inquire anxiously if the horses were tired. It never occurred to him to ask about the men.

Often he seemed deliberately callous toward those whom he loved most. One evening at Choisy, when his infatuation for Madame de Pompadour was at its height, she sent word that she was ill and begged to be excused from dinner. Louis frowned. "Has Madame fever?" he asked. "No, Sire," the messenger answered. "Very well, then, let her come down!" And the Marquise, her skull splitting with one of her violent headaches, came down.

Like most of his line the King did not know the meaning of physical fear. When the Dauphin was dangerously ill with smallpox the doctors begged Louis not to expose himself; nevertheless he insisted on spending long hours at his son's bedside. In his passion for hunting he showed himself fearless, indeed almost reckless. No mount could be too spirited, no chase too long, no cornered boar too ferocious to daunt the King.

His love of hunting was not only a passion, it was a veritable need, physical and mental. If Louis went more than a day or two without violent exercise, his body became sluggish and he suffered touches of jaundice or gout on the knee. But perhaps the greater therapy of his strenuous sport was psychological—it took his thoughts off himself and dissipated his congenital melancholy. He returned from the chase fresh when everyone else was exhausted, and, what was more important to the Marquise, he returned gay and in good humor.

Although she detested the hunts she followed them, sometimes on horseback, sometimes in a carriage, in order to please Louis. Later, as her health declined, she gave this up, no doubt agreeing, for once, with d'Argenson, that "at Court there is nothing but hunting and laying waste the fields. . . ."

More than any other vice or defect of character, more than incurable boredom and feebleness of will, Louis XV's detractors have branded him with the stigma of sensuality, even concupiscence. The well-disposed Prince de Croÿ admits that Louis was too fond of women, and the scribblers of the Revolution have bequeathed to posterity their lurid and scurrilous tales of vice in the *Parc aux Cerfs*.

It is impossible to deny that Louis XV had five principal Mistresses and an incalculable number of liaisons, to say nothing of a number of natural children (twenty would be a reasonably conservative estimate). A formidable record— and yet is it sufficient to conclude therefrom that the King was beset by uncontrollable passions, the slave of an over-sexed nature? That is the verdict handed down by his enemies—but it fails signally to take into account the King's intrinsic nature.

A diametrically opposed view, hinted at by some, is that Louis was inclined to homosexuality and, in order to con-ceal it, feigned a passion for women. If so, he was incredibly skilled at playing the male role for half a century.

These accusers point to the youthful infatuation of the King, then fourteen, for the Duc de la Trémouille, an elaborately effeminate youth a year or two older. Cardinal Fleury and Madame de Prie, having no desire to foster another Henry III on the throne, summarily dismissed the willowy Duc from Court and Louis saw him no more. This hypothesis is absurd, depending as it does upon what was for a boy of fourteen a perfectly normal affection for an older companion. Nothing in the King's subsequent life indicates in the slightest degree any homosexual tendency.

The answer, then, to the King's rococo private life lies in neither of these extreme versions. When he married he was somewhat timid—not surprising for a boy of fifteen— and he remained faithful to the Queen for seven years. What drove him to take his first Mistress was curiosity more than passion. The King's unimaginative mind was easily bored; he demanded new interests, and Marie Leczinska, with her unending pregnancies and prayers, was hardly the person to supply them.

Although Madame de Mailly was anything but a beauty, she held Louis' interest by her selfless devotion and by being "different." In time she gave way to Mesdames de Vintimille and de Chatêauroux, mainly because her younger sisters offered the blasé King the promise of something new. A thousand women could not have satisfied Louis because what he sought was not the fulfillment of a physical need but a complement to his own lack of inner resources.

This is the real reason for his crushing boredom. He did not know what to do with himself and was too inert mentally to try to find out. He depended on others, especially women, to point out new paths of distraction and diversion. Like Don Juan, he was driven down the road of promiscuity not by passion but by an incurable restlessness and an unending search for mystery. Every woman with whom he became infatuated—for Louis was incapable of *love* except in the selfish sense—seemed to him the repository of a thousand mysteries, and none more so than the Marquise de Pompadour. She freed him, as much as anyone could free him, from the terrible bonds of loneliness, and to Louis her endless talent for inventing new diversions offered as sure an escape from ennui as he would ever find.

X

AN ACTRESS IS MANY WOMEN

EFORE THE Marquise rounded out her first year as Mistress to the King, she had introduced him to a novel diversion. During the Lenten season of 1746, in order to deflect Louis' mind from the implications of the season of penance, she arranged a series of small musical concerts. The enthusiasm with which the King responded gave her an even happier idea, a plan which would serve the double purpose of providing a new interest and strengthening her own hold on him. The disquieting fact that the King's attention was already wandering had not escaped her unceasing vigilance. He still climbed the stairs every night to her apartments and he still devoted much attention to her in public, but the Marquise acknowledged in her secret thoughts that he was disappointed by her lack of ardor, and she sensed the deadly danger of rivals who confidently hoped to displace her.

Louis showed more than a passing interest in the young and beautiful Madame de Périgord, and the surprising fact that his interest was not returned only increased his curiosity. To the astonishment of Madame de Pompadour and the Court, Madame de Périgord was truly virtuous, withdrawing voluntarily to her estates in order to escape the Monarch's attentions. But Madame de Périgord was an exceptional woman at Versailles and there were others whose presence made the Marquise tremble.

The coarse Comtesse de la Mark flaunted her hopes before everyone, and the nobly born Princesse de Rohan, who had once hoped to succeed Madame de Châtearoux, renewed her efforts. Most dangerous of all, from the viewpoint of the Marquise, was the Princess de Robecque, who coupled unusual physical beauty with a cool intelligence equal to that of the Favorite herself. It was imperative to launch a counteroffensive at once.

What more ingenious, then, than to inaugurate a theater, in which the Mistress herself would be the star performer? Madame de Pompadour not only loved the stage and had enjoyed considerable experience on the boards of her own playhouse at Étioles, but she was a born actress. Indeed, a large part of her success up to now stemmed from her highly volatile nature, her incomparable ability to adapt herself to the varying moods of different people.

She well knew that actresses arouse the frustrated jealousy of women and exert an equally powerful fascination on men, principally because an actress is one woman and yet many women, appearing reassuringly familiar and yet enchantingly different in every new role. The Marquise had already experimented with a variety of brilliant costumes in the privacy of her own apartments. What could be more logical than for her to step forward into the bright glare of the footlights and recapture the King's waning interest?

And so the *Théâtre des Petits Appartements* came into being. With the unstinted cooperation of Le Normant de Tournehem, now Director-General of the King's Buildings, a small theater was constructed near the Medal Room, complete in every detail. The scenery was painted by Pérot, and the costumes designed by Perronet, the most fashionable *couturier* of the day. The Director-General furnished a highly varied assortment of props, including artificial jewelry and flowers, masks of every conceivable sort, dancing shoes and silk stockings, spangles of gold and silver, crowns of laurel, a magician's wand, a thunderbolt, and a perfuming pan.

Far more difficult was the task of organizing the company and recruiting the cast. The Duc de la Vallière was appointed manager; Moncrif, friend of the Queen (who piously disapproved of such goings-on), assistant manager; and the Abbé de la Garde, Librarian to the Marquise, secretary and prompter. Among the chief actors were the Vicomte de Rohan, the Duc de Chartres, the Duc d'Ayen, the Duc de Chaulnes, and the Duc de Nivernois, with whom Madame de Pompadour had acted before. The actresses included Madame de Brancas, Madame de Sassenage, and the witty Madame de Marchais, all devoted friends of the Marquise.

The King was charmed by the new project and assisted the Marquise in drawing up the rules which were supposed to govern so haughty a cast. Reflecting as they do the gallantry of the eighteenth century toward the feminine sex, the regulations are worth quoting:

1. To become a member of the company, the candidate must prove that he has acted before since novices are not desired.

2. Each member will choose the part he wishes to play.

3. No member may play a different type of part from that which has been agreed upon without the consent of all the cast.

4. If a member is absent, he may not select his understudy; only the company has this right and will take a vote on the question.

5. When the absent member returns he must resume his role.

6. No member may refuse to play a role of his chosen type on the pretext that it is too difficult. These first six articles apply to actresses as well as actors.

7. Only the actresses have the right to choose the selections which the company will perform.

8. They also have the right to select the date of performance, and to decide on the number of rehearsals and their time.

9. Every actor must be present on time for the rehearsal, or subject to a fine which the actresses shall fix among themselves.

10. Actresses are allowed a leeway of half an hour, after which their fine shall be set by themselves only.

The Theater of the Little Apartments opened its doors

with a performance of Molière's *Tartuffe*. The cast consisted of fourteen persons; the audience numbered only
nine. In addition to the King, for whom all this effort had
been expended, there were present M. de Tournehem,
Marshal Saxe, Abel Poisson, and the King's valet Champ-
cenetz. All of them were avowed followers of the Marquise
—she alone controlled the distribution of the tickets of
admission, and such enemies of hers as the Prince de Conti
were conspicuously absent.

Madame de Pompadour performed the role of Dorine
the maid, and as she had foreseen, her acting eclipsed the
rest of the cast. She knew she had scored a signal success
when Louis, after the performance, complimented her.
"You are," he said in his husky voice, "the most charming
woman in France."

The success of the company was instantaneous. *Tartuffe*
was followed by lighter comedies such as *Le Mariage fait
et rompu* (not inappropriate) and *Préjugé à la mode,*
which the Marquise felt were more suited to her delicate
charm. The comedies were frequently followed by ballets
in which she displayed her graceful dancing or operettas
which provided a vehicle for her pleasing voice.

The Court buzzed with excitement at the Mistress's
latest triumph, and since the Marquise kept her small
hands tightly on the reins of the theater her power was
greater than ever. Everyone hoped for one of the coveted
invitations and, even more, for the chance to fill one of the
parts, however small. It became more important to be a
member of the cast than to ride in the King's hunting

parties, and the Duc de Nivernois, who had never been invited to the little suppers, now dined often with the King by virtue of his position in the theater.

An anecdote which Madame du Haussay recounts in her memoirs shows to what lengths the courtiers would go to snare a role.

During the time when the Little Theater was playing, [she wrote], I was able to obtain a lieutenancy for one of my relatives by an unusual circumstance, which shows how much value the highest persons set on even the most trivial means of access to Court circles.

Madame did not like to ask anything of M. d'Argenson [Minister of War]; and pressed by my family, who could not imagine that I would have any difficulties in getting a minor post for a junior officer, I went myself to M. d'Argenson. He received me coldly and put me off with some vague remarks. I went out, and his son, the Marquis de Voyer, who had been in the room, followed me.

"You wish," he said to me, "a certain position. There is one vacant which has been promised to me for one of my friends, but if you will do me a favor I will let you have it. I want to be a *policeman,* and you are in a position to make me one."

I told him I could not imagine what kind of joke he was pulling.

"This is what it is," he said. "They are going to give *Tartuffe* in the Apartments, and in it there is a policeman's part which consists of only a few words. Get that role from the Marquise for me, and the appointment you want is yours."

I did not promise anything, but related the entire incident to Madame, who promised to take care of it. The thing was done, I obtained the post for my relative, and M. de Voyer thanked Madame as if she had made him a Duke.

The Marquise was gratified by the applause of the courtiers and delighted by the approval of the King, but, womanlike, she wanted more. She wanted nothing less than the Queen's presence to grace her bewitching appearances on the stage. Nothing could appeal less to Marie Leczinska's sense of propriety than the theater, especially when it was the triumphal setting of the Favorite.

Madame de Pompadour, however, was clever enough to choose a sure way to gain her point. She knew that the Queen desired a marshalship for M. de la Mothe, and the Marquise persuaded the King to give him the honor. The Queen learned of her old friend's promotion at the King's *lever*, and as she bent to kiss his hand in gratitude, Louis raised her up and—of all things—embraced her!

He had not, he explained, cared to invite her to the theater because the plays had been somewhat broad and he feared they might offend her. But, the King went on to say, the next offering would be more to her taste, and she would please him very much by attending it. When the poor Queen witnessed the performance she must have wondered what Louis thought her tastes were, for the comedy, *Préjugé à la mode*, made fun of conjugal fidelity! But Madame de Pompadour had had her way, and Marie Leczinska's presence halted the clucking disapproval of the devout at Court.

As the Queen, seated with her daughters and the Dauphin, watched the star of the play she kept her thoughts to herself, but the Duc de Luynes noted soberly that "the ridicule which one saw applied to married love has given rise to some reflections on the Queen's presence at a per-

formance where Madame de Pompadour acts with so much
expression and grace."

A light operetta, *Érigone,* followed, in which the Marquise, dressed in a bodice of white taffeta covered with
silver designs, showed that she could dance and sing as
well as act. "Her voice is not strong," de Luynes added,
"but it is very agreeable, and she sings with much expression. The dances were charming, but no one danced so
gracefully as Madame de Pompadour."

In spite of the success of the first season, the original
theater had serious disadvantages—there was not enough
room for the musicians and the audience was too far from
the stage to understand the actors' lines. And so it was
decided to build a larger theater in the space occupied by
the Ambassadors' Staircase, the only space in the Palace
large enough to fulfill the Marquise's requirements. The
magnificent stairway of Louis XIV, one of the glories of
Versailles, was demolished, and in its place rose the New
Theater of Madame de Pompadour.

Wishing to surprise the King, the Marquise extracted
from him a promise not to visit the work while it was in
progress. Although Louis was almost overcome with curiosity, not once during the two years required for the theater's construction did he break his word. When the New
Theater opened in November 1748 its appearance of
delicate luxury surprised as well as delighted him.

The theater had accommodations for an audience of
forty and as many musicians. The comfortable chairs were
upholstered in blue and silver, and the rest of the decora-

tions, supervised by François Boucher, were carried out
in the same harmonious color scheme. Because it was sometimes necessary to use the hall for state functions, the entire
theater was mobile, equipped with ingenious machinery
for rapid dismantling. This could be done in seventeen
hours, and the theater reassembled in twenty-four.

Cochin's memorable engraving of the performance of
Acis et Galathée, presented on January 23, 1749, leaves
an unforgettable impression of how the New Theater
looked in its full tide of success. The King and Queen
are seated in the center of the balcony, directly facing the
stage. Marie Leczinska, in her plain black dress and with
the inevitable black lace shawl covering her head, might
be the mother of the slim and elegant Louis who sits beside her. The King wears a short, carefully powdered
white wig and diagonally across his chest, from right to
left, the Blue Ribbon, the badge of the Order of the Holy
Ghost.

The King and Mesdames Henriette, Adélaïde, and Victoire, dressed in handsome Court gowns, hold copies of
the libretto of the Opera which is being sung before them.
The balcony along the side of the theater, to the right
of the Royal Family, is filled with thirteen gentlemen of
high rank. The pit is completely occupied by the musicians
and the rest of the audience, all men. Among them are
great lords, painters, and men of letters, mostly personal
friends of the Marquise.

She, of course, in the role of the sea nymph Galathea,
occupies the center of the stage, which depicts a rocky
green coast. Her lover Acis, played by the Vicomte de

Rohan, is costumed in a tight coat of cherry trimmed with gold; his skirt, of the same material, is more like that of a ballerina than a shepherd.

It is Galathea, however, who draws the attention of the audience. She stands with her arms widespread in despair and her head lowered, singing a haunting aria which bewails the lovers' fate. Her enormous skirt of white taffeta is "painted with reeds, foam, and shells," and her bodice of pale rose is decorated with pearls. In this bewitching blend of pastel sea colors she appeared to the enraptured King not as the woman he knows so well but as an infinitely alluring daughter of Neptune. Captivated by the illusion, Louis feels a surge of tenderness in his heart for the Marquise and believes himself more in love than ever.

In spite of the enhancement of her charms which the stage provided, in spite of the new triumphs it produced, the Marquise could hardly expect her theater always to run smoothly. Her numerous enemies were too piqued to permit her the undiluted pleasure of success. Parisians muttered at the expense of the New Theater, and rumors circulated that its cost had exceeded two million livres. Such fantastic exaggerations infuriated the Marquise, and one day at her *toilette,* surrounded by courtiers, she burst out: "What is all this talk about the New Theater costing two million? I want everyone to know that it cost no more than twenty thousand *écus,* and why shouldn't the King spend that amount on his pleasure?" "And," she went on as an afterthought, "it's the same way with the houses he builds for me!" Actually the theater had cost seventy-five thousand livres for its construction alone. The Duc de la Vallière admitted that disbursements for the year 1749 exceeded half a million, not including the equipment and furnishings provided by the Royal storerooms.

The added physical strain which the theater imposed on the frail Mistress was tremendous. The season usually began in the autumn, when the Court returned from Fontainebleau, continued until the beginning of Lent, and then resumed after Easter until late in the summer. There was a regular schedule of performances—comedy on Mondays, opera on Wednesdays, and sometimes additional offerings. To take part in all the performances, much less the endless rehearsals, would have tired a professional actress, and meanwhile Madame de Pompadour's other duties at Court continued as exacting as ever.

Nevertheless the indefatigable Marquise stuck to her self-appointed task and only serious illness could induce her to miss a performance. "I have had a headache today," she wrote to her brother, "and I have dragged around for three days, but it did not keep me from playing *Le Prince de Noisy* yesterday and tomorrow again to finish."

There were other troubles too, inevitable accidents, backbiting, and outbursts of temperament. The sensitive Madame de Brancas was so wounded by a sneering remark she overheard, reflecting on the ability and taste of the company, that she resigned for a whole year. In the beginning of 1749, shortly after the debut of the New Theater, one of the stagehands was killed in an accident and the superstitious began to murmur.

Although most of the courtiers dared not openly attack

the theater, the harsh Marquis d'Argenson, who blamed the Marquise for his dismissal from the Foreign Ministry, could not repress his bitterness: "There has just been printed an absurd collection of the plays at His Majesty's Cabinets or Little Apartments—nonsensical selections— pitiful puerile things. In it one may read the list of dancers and singers, officials and buffoons, great Court ladies and theater-girls. As a matter of fact, the King spends all his time watching the Marquise and the rest of them being trained by professional actors, who are familiar with the monarch to an extent that is scandalous and sacrilegious."

D'Argenson cannot be taken very seriously. His thoughts swung like a weather vane, veering in all directions from the force of his desires. Because he hoped for the fall of Madame de Pompadour he was always prophesying it, from month to month and year to year. Since his removal from office he quoted others at Court (often his younger brother, the Minister of War): "Persons who see clearly and who stand well at Court declare that Madame de Pompadour will soon be dismissed, the cause being the King's shame at his fetters and at the love he has placed so low."

Not that d'Argenson, although inclined to prudery, objected to a royal mistress—what he wanted for the King was a mistress whom *he* could control. "Some other beauty, well-chosen, gentle, and in no way attached to the Pârises. ... Let her have a fine bust, fine arms, and be well set-up; let her be a *brunette,* in better health, not given to music and theatricals, and not meddlesome in affairs of the State. ..."

The gravest crisis in the Pompadour theater was precipitated by the bitter quarrel between the Marquise and the Duc de Richelieu. The resentful Duc, returning from the siege of Genoa early in 1749, promptly placed himself at the fore of Madame de Pompadour's enemies. He was consumed by envy of her paramount influence with the King, and he determined to strike the Mistress where it would most wound her feminine vanity—in her own special province, the theater.

In his position as First Gentleman of the King's Bedchamber Richelieu commenced his needling campaign. Although the rigid protocol of Versailles decreed that all entertainments come under the supervision of the Gentlemen of the Bedchamber, the Marquise and her theater manager, de la Vallière, had consistently ignored this rule. Whenever anything from the storerooms was needed for the theater—chandeliers, girandoles, furnishings, carriages —the Gentlemen of the Bedchamber were summarily bypassed.

The Duc d'Aumont, who was First Gentleman during Richelieu's absence, had timidly protested to the King of this offensive treatment, but the Marquise's resolution had blocked any action. "Wait until His Excellency [Richelieu] comes back," said Louis, who well knew the Duc's nature, "and you will see something different."

The King was right. Immediately after entering upon his duties, Richelieu issued an order that nothing was to be taken from the storerooms without his written permission and that no musician of the Court was to play in any performance without his express authorization. This struck the theater a double blow, and Madame de Pompadour was beside herself with rage. When the Duc de la Vallière remonstrated with Richelieu, the latter, with characteristic insolence, called him a fool and snapped his fingers in his face.

"He thought nothing of thwarting little Pompadour," d'Argenson wrote gleefully, "and treating her like an opera-girl, having had a great deal of experience with that sort of woman." And then another of Monsieur d'Argenson's inevitable prophecies: "Mistress as she is of the King he [Richelieu] will torment and tire her out."

But Richelieu underestimated his adversary. The Marquise rushed to the King trembling with fury, and precipitated such a scene that Louis was appalled. When to her tears and sighs she added the pointed remark that in striking at the theater Richelieu was also interfering with the King's own pleasure, her battle was won. The next time the King's boots were being removed after the hunt, Louis asked casually: "Your Excellency, how many times have you been in the Bastille?" "Three times, Sire," answered the Duc, forcing a smile. But the hint was enough; Richelieu realized that he had gone too far, and that the best he could do was to execute a face-saving retreat.

Since he had continued during this fierce struggle to attend the little suppers, the Duc could plead, with some semblance of plausibility, that he had never intended to offend the Marquise. He spoke to the Duc de la Vallière as though nothing had happened and instructed the storerooms and musicians to consider themselves always at the command of Madame de Pompadour.

Actually Richelieu had suffered a serious reverse. From

then on he avoided direct conflict with the Favorite and pretended to be her devoted friend. The Duc's concealment of his feelings was convincing, at least to the naïve de Luynes, who wrote that "M. de Richelieu has shown so much artistry and feeling, so much politeness and even gallantry for Madame de Pompadour in all this affair that neither his friendship for her nor for M. de la Vallière has been affected for one minute." Everyone seemed happy, including the Duc de la Vallière, who was rewarded with the *Cordon Bleu*.

Performances at Versailles went on for another year, until 1750, when the King, alarmed by the terrible expense and the mounting chorus of disapproval from the public, ordered them halted. In the spring of 1751 plays were resumed at the Marquise's Château de Bellevue, which had just been finished.

But the change seemed to destroy the original enthusiasm of the company. The Bellevue theater was too small, and the cast gradually lost interest. Perhaps the real reason for the eventual disbanding of the troupe was Louis' loss of interest. The last performance was Rousseau's *Le Devin du Village*, in which the Marquise played her only male role. The Theater of the Little Apartments came to an end in the spring of 1753, but while it lasted it had furthered enormously the power and influence of Madame de Pompadour.

XI

POWER IS MADE TO BE USED

*A*LTHOUGH the position of Mistress to the King was semiofficial, its occupant, at least during the reign of Louis XV, held more potential power than the most influential Ministers. The Mistress saw more of the King than any one else and, if so inclined, could take advantage of his supine nature to advance her own interests. Madame de Mailly was interested in nothing but the King's love, and Madame de Vintimille's day of glory was too brief to have any decisive effect, but Madame de Châteauroux had never hesitated to influence Louis, whether it be on questions of war, politics, or merely the distribution of sinecures to her favorites.

When Madame de Pompadour became Louis' Mistress her supreme concern was to maintain her ascendancy over him and to consolidate her position. It was not long before she realized that neither her beauty—nor her brains—would suffice to keep her powerful enemies at bay. She needed strong allies, friends in the most important posts at Court, and to obtain them she reached out, first hesitantly and then with growing confidence, toward the fascinating, dangerous threads of power.

Her first move was to conclude an alliance—in the circumstances, a most natural alliance—with her old friends the Brothers Pâris. The assistance of these four men—Pâris-Antoine, Lord of the Treasury, Pâris-Claude, Paymaster of the Army of Flanders, Pâris-Montmartel, Banker to the Court, and Pâris-Duverney, financial dictator after the failure of John Law—was essential to the government which depended upon them to pour large quantities of cash into its depleted coffers.

Shortly after Madame de Pompadour's rise to power, however, the Pârises were in anything but a lending mood. Orry, the dour Comptroller-General, was inclined to scrutinize too closely the accounts they submitted for payment and recently had flatly refused to approve one of their contracts. The Pârises informed the Marquise that no more funds would be forthcoming to the government while Orry remained in office.

Madame de Pompadour had reasons of her own for disliking Orry—the taciturn Comptroller looked with a gloomy eye on the Court's increasing extravagance—and she agreed to use her influence. Her influence was enough. The King protested mildly that Orry was honest and efficient but in the end he gave way to the Marquise's entreaties. Orry was dismissed and his place was filled by Machault, the Intendant of Valenciennes. Machault, like Orry, was grave and austere, with a vast knowledge of finance and a strong sense of duty. It was understood, however, that he would approve without question all the Pâris accounts as well as the expenditures of the Court.

The King liked him despite his curtness and severity,

because he found him easy to work with; but in the future Machault was to be regarded—and justly so—as a faithful adherent of Madame de Pompadour. The office of Director-General of the King's Buildings, which had been joined to that of Comptroller-General, was separated and given to Le Normant de Tournehem. And so the Marquise's first venture into politics turned out well for everyone—herself, the Pârises, Machault, and de Tournehem—everyone, that is, except Orry and the taxpayers of France.

In July 1746 the Dauphine, that grave Spanish bride whose marriage festivities had furnished Madame d'Étioles her opportunity to meet the King, gave birth to a Princess and quietly died. The King, who had returned from the Army to witness the *accouchement,* remained for the elaborate and almost interminable obsequies which Court etiquette prescribed. After the magnificent gloomy rites the entire Royal Family, including the Marquise, retired to Choisy to spend their grief.

The only person whose mourning for the red-haired Dauphine would never end was the Dauphin himself. A widower at seventeen, smug and cold, he had nevertheless deeply loved his wife, and although reasons of state would demand his remarriage, he could never truly give his heart again. On his deathbed twenty years later, his last wish was that his heart be buried at Saint-Denis near that of her who had been his first love.

His sorrow, however, must not be allowed to endanger the dynasty. He must marry again in order to secure the succession. Louis the Dauphin was apathetic to the problem of choosing a second wife, but the courtiers speculated endlessly on the identity of the next Dauphine. Would she be a sister of the late Maria-Rafaela? Madrid always had a plentiful supply of Infantas ready to be pushed across the Pyrenees into advantageous foreign marriages. It turned out, however, that Spain was ignored, for in the delicate choice of the next Dauphine Marshal Saxe—and Madame de Pompadour—took a hand.

Maurice de Saxe had set his heart on obtaining the coveted prize for his own niece, Marie-Josèphe of Saxony. In his scheme he enlisted the decisive aid of the Marquise, who was genuinely attached to him. Writing to his half brother the Elector of Saxony and King of Poland, Marshal Saxe had good news to report: "The King is inclined to favor the Princess Marie-Josèphe for private reasons, health and fecundity being more important to him than political considerations. . . . I take the liberty of enclosing a letter from Madame de Pompadour, from which Your Majesty can judge that I stand high in the Little Apartments."

The Marquise made rapid headway in her campaign for the Saxon Princess. Only the Queen was opposed to the choice; Marie Leczinska shrank from the prospect of accepting as a daughter-in-law the child of Augustus III, who had replaced her own father on the Polish throne. Amiable ex-King Stanislaus was less troubled, and later magnanimously congratulated his successor on Marie-Josèphe's good fortune.

Madame de Pompadour, capitalizing on the Queen's good will toward her, added her persuasions, and Marie

Leczinska yielded with a sigh. After all, what difference did one more sacrifice make? Besides, she too was fond of Maurice, the victor of Fontenoy.

After the affair was settled and the Duc de Richelieu had departed for Dresden as Ambassador Extraordinary to claim the Princess, Marshal Saxe, again writing to Augustus III, attributed the credit where it was due: "Sire, I received yesterday a letter from His Most Christian Majesty in which he sent me all the objections of the Queen, which it was necessary to overcome, and in which Madame de Pompadour has served us well, for she is on the best of terms with her." He added that the Pârises had also helped to wear down Marie Leczinska, noting that "they are intimate friends of the Favorite and furthermore it was they who financed the Queen's own marriage, so they have a great deal of influence over her."

The King was filled with happiness over the coming wedding and took an active interest in the details of the arrangements, which the Marquise had promptly gathered into her own hands. This was the sort of power which her feminine nature fitted her to exercise with grace and charm —deciding what kind of decorations would brighten the capital and choosing the color of the costumes for the balls which would be given. In such matters her exquisite taste was infallible—and she knew it. She frankly enjoyed the social power which she now possessed, and managed everything with gaiety, lightness, and infinite grace.

She who had, in the days when she was Mademoiselle Poisson, endured the snubs of aristocratic Paris, now had her turn and reveled in the inexpressible joy of being absolute mistress of the invitation lists. She scanned with a sharp eye the names of those who were to be invited, and if she wished to add one of her friends the King permitted her to have her way.

Her sister-in-law, Madame Baschi, was not sufficiently highborn to receive an invitation to the Royal reception for the new Dauphine at Choisy, but the Marquise was undaunted. Not without a touch of *arriviste* boastfulness she exclaimed, "I can be considered included among the great officials, therefore my sister-in-law can be put on my list!" The King, with an indulgent smile, made no further objection and added the name of Madame Baschi in his own handwriting.

The Dauphin's second marriage, which he endured with very little grace, took place on February 9, 1747, almost exactly two years after his first one. The celebrations were a repetition of those which had occurred two years before —the same impressive ceremony in the Royal Chapel, the same enthusiastic revelry in Paris, and the same carefree ball at Versailles, during which the King, masked, sat at the feet of the Marquise. The only new performer was the Dauphine Marie-Josèphe, "well-made, with a beautiful skin and eyes which were charming when they were animated." She looked very German, as indeed she was, and her expression was placid and almost heavy. This youn bride of fifteen was destined to be the mother of thre Kings of France; looking at her portrait it is easy to see where two of them, Louis XVI and Louis XVIII, acquired their stolid expression and lethargic physique. Marie-Josèphe had a thick nose and a feminine but enticing mouth. Nevertheless her evident desire to be agreeable and her friendly manner, so different from the haughty bearing of her predecessor, won the esteem of all who came near her.

The only person who was indifferent to the marriage was the Dauphin himself. Indelicate, even coarse as it may seem, etiquette demanded that the entire Court witness the putting-to-bed of the bridal couple. When the two, hardly more than adolescent, were installed in the great bed the King, wishing to ease the Dauphine's embarrassment, sent her uncle Marshal Saxe within the railing to talk to her. Marie-Josèphe, however, appeared perfectly composed and chatted calmly with the Marshal, but the Dauphin hid his head under the covers. Some observers ascribed this action to his distaste for the marriage or to his sulky disposition, but others, more understanding, said it was to hide the tears he was shedding for his first bride.

A month before the Dauphin's remarriage, but directly caused by it, occurred the dismissal of the Marquis d'Argenson as Minister of Foreign Affairs. This sad-faced noble, always confiding his complaints and frustrations to his diary, was nevertheless in many ways an able Minister, loyal to the King and ambitious to restore France to her place of glory in Europe. His fall was not entirely the fault of the Marquise, although he blamed her for it. The Court of Madrid was angered that the choice of Dauphine had not again fallen upon a Spanish Princess, and the French Ambassador to Madrid, the Duc de Noailles, wrote Madame de Pompadour that the Spanish government would be satisfied with nothing less than the dismissal of d'Argenson, whom it held responsible for the fancied insult.

No one, of course, least of all the Duc de Noailles, bothered to inform Madrid that the Marquise was far more responsible for the Saxon marriage than d'Argenson. Her role in the Minister's fall was passive rather than active—she lifted not a finger to save him, mainly because she desired to fill his place with the Marquis de Puisieux, an incompetent friend of herself and Pâris-Montmartel.

Louis, although reluctant to sacrifice d'Argenson, bowed to Spanish pressure and dismissed him in January 1747. The frivolous courtiers, who detested the Marquis d'Argenson for his crude manners and cruder speech, were delighted, but Madame de Pompadour later came to appreciate d'Argenson's worth and regretted his fall. It was too late; the dismissed Minister, convinced that she alone had been responsible for his disgrace, became her undying enemy, and for the misinformation of posterity devoted pages of his journal to the defamation of her character.

As the months and then the years slipped by, those who had so hopefully predicted the early downfall of the Marquise were forced to revise their strategy. Her hold on the King seemed stronger than ever, her influence increased with every new day, and the prudent course was to pay her homage.

Every afternoon at one o'clock a throng of courtiers, seeking favors of all kinds, crowded up her little staircase to attend her *toilette*. Even the respectable Prince de Croÿ, who was never to so much as nod to Madame Du Barry (Madame de Pompadour's successor), did not hesitate to press his requests upon Madame de Pompadour. He was wise to do so, for through her hands flowed the vast number of lucrative appointments, pensions, and honors which oiled the machinery of Court life. The King almost invariably followed her advice, whether it concerned the guest list for supper or an appointment to an ambassador-ship. "The Mistress," declared one of the courtiers, "has declared that she wishes twelve Farmers-General of her own choosing, and two hundred subfarmers. She has a cabinet full of petitions for these places, and everybody now addresses her openly."

The Marquise would not have been human if she had remained entirely unaffected by her growing power. Although her natural desire to be agreeable was too in-grained to be repressed, her composure and awareness of importance inevitably contrasted with the sense of in-security she had experienced during her first days at Ver-sailles. Croÿ perceived this change in 1747, shortly after d'Argenson's dismissal:

"Madame de Pompadour was heavier and her figure better than ever. She interested herself in many things without having the air of doing so or of appearing busy. On the contrary, she seemed, either by nature or design, to be more occupied with her little comedies and other hobbies. She sets her cap for the King in many little ways, and uses the most skillful wiles of bewitchment to hold him. In the beginning she tried to please everyone . . . but now being stronger and knowing everyone, she is a little more decided and less obliging, but still polite enough and at least giving the appearance of trying to please."

It is pleasant to evoke this picture of Woman Triumphant—the radiant Mistress, seated before her dressing table in her jewels and magnificent clothes, exchanging a risqué joke with Marshal Saxe, smiling affectionately at wise-eyed Doctor Quesnay, or gently tapping her brother on the arm, while the place-seekers, pushing and crowding into the small room and occupying every available inch, hoped for a word or even a friendly glance from this fragile dispenser of all power.

In his *Memoirs,* Marmontel describes his first visit, as a poor unknown, at the *lever* of the Marquise. "She received us informally, although with obvious shades of distinction. To one she said, speaking shortly and with a light air, 'How do you do, Duclos'; to Bernis, in a more friendly tone, 'Abbé,' giving him occasionally a little pat on the cheek, and to me more seriously and in a lower voice, 'How do you do, Marmontel?' "

Marmontel was discouraged over his poverty and the failure of his writing and asked Madame de Pompadour to give him a quiet sinecure. She remarked with quick sympathy that he was "born to write" and encouraged him to persevere. Her interest was so unaffected and sincere that Marmontel left the manuscript of *Les Funérailles de Sésostris* for her to read; in returning for it some days later he inadvertently discovered the value placed by the courtiers on the Marquise's slightest sign of favor.

"I presented myself one morning at her *toilette,* when the room was crowded by an assemblage of courtiers, who had just been at the King's *lever.* She was surrounded by them, and whether she was displeased with someone near her or wished to escape the weariness that this circle occasioned her, as soon as she saw me she whispered, 'I want to speak to you,' and leaving her *toilette* went into her cabinet, where I followed her. She only wanted to return my manuscript, on which she had penciled her notes. She showed me the passages she had marked and explained her criticisms for five or six minutes, during which interval the whole circle of courtiers stood around waiting for her. She reappeared and I, concealing my manuscript, went modestly to resume my place. I expected that this occurrence would produce an effect, but the impression it made on the whole company far exceeded my expectation—all eyes were turned on me, on every side I was greeted by little nods and friendly smiles, and before I left the room I had received enough dinner invitations to last the whole week."

The Marquise's establishment in the Palace was almost royal. Collin, a former official of the Paris Law Court and an old friend of M. Poisson, became her major-domo, was permitted to wear the Cross of St. Louis, and stood behind her chair while she dined. The equerry who walked beside her sedan chair was an impoverished nobleman, the Chevalier d'Hénin. In the Palace alone her employees numbered between fifty and sixty, including a physician, a steward, a *maître d'hôtel,* an overseer, a butler, four footmen, a chef and his assistant, two assistant cooks, a pastry cook, a doorkeeper, two head porters, a concierge, a housekeeper, a wardrobe woman, three personal maids, three seamstresses, two accountants, two Negroes, an assistant clerk, three coachmen, three postilions, four grooms, a huntsman, and a torchbearer.

The Marquise's kindness and generosity were occasionally marred by flashes of arrogance. There were times when she seemed to have lost her sense of proportion, and she gave herself airs that were ludicrous, considering her origin. At her *lever* there was only one armchair in her boudoir, the one which she herself occupied. Everyone else was expected to stand, as if in the presence of Royalty.

One day the Prince de Conti, always scornful of the Favorite, grew tired of standing and flopped on her bed, exclaiming mockingly, "My, what a comfortable bed!" Madame de Pompadour bit her lips with fury, but since Conti was a Prince of the Blood, she could only repress her anger. Shortly afterward, however, her turn came when the Marquis de Souvré, a nobleman known for his flippancy, sat on the arm of her chair and continued his chatter without paying the least attention to her rising anger.

She hastened to complain to the King, and Louis summoned Souvré for a reprimand. "But Sire," the insolent Marquis replied, "I was very tired and as I saw nowhere else to sit down, I sat down where I could." The King burst out laughing at Souvré's droll expression, and let the matter drop. In spite of himself he could be amused at his Favorite's pretensions.

"The Marquise," confessed Bernis, "had none of the serious vices of ambitious women, but she had all the little pettiness and frivolity of those whose beauty and superior brains have filled them with an overweening vanity. She did evil without intent, and good because the fancy took her; her friendship was as jealous as love, as light, as inconstant, and as precarious." His last words were to prove truer than the cheerful Abbé realized—and to his own ruin.

The Marquise gradually grew more overbearing in managing every moment of the King's time. She intruded into his conferences with the Ministers, not because she was hungry for political power but merely to distract Louis and take his mind off vexing problems. Louis, unfortunately, was more than willing to be interrupted during a tedious report, and appeared almost grateful when the Marquise dispersed a burdensome conference. "Go away, M. de Maurepas," she would say, "you are upsetting the King!"—and the Minister, throwing an angry look in her direction, would reluctantly bow himself out.

In response to a question concerning an important appointment, "We will see," she replied, referring to herself and the King. Even Ambassadors discovered that it was no longer possible to have a private audience with Louis; the Prussian envoy wrote to Frederick II that every time he conferred with Louis XV, Madame de Pompadour was present.

During the supper parties in the Little Apartments the servants were given orders not to disturb the King in any circumstances. Every message, no matter how urgent, was

Madame de Pompadour, from a pastel by Maurice-
Quentin de La Tour in the Louvre Museum, Paris.

Madame de Pompadour's Chateau de Bellevue.

first referred to the Marquise, and the King was interrupted only if she decided it was necessary. Once when
Maurepas was discussing naval affairs, the Marquise cut
him short to demand that he appoint one of her friends
to a vacancy. "It is necessary that His Majesty order it,
Madame," protested Maurepas coldly. Louis shrugged.
"Do as Madame wishes," he said wearily. And the appointment was made.

Madame de Pompadour ventured into politics on the
highest level during the negotiations preceding the Treaty
of Aix-la-Chapelle. France, sometimes assisted by her unreliable Prussian ally, had been at war for eight years
against Austria, Holland, and Great Britain. The French
delegates to the peace conference were the inept Foreign
Minister, Puisieux, and an Italian adventurer, Comte de
Saint-Severin, to whom the Marquise had given his final
instructions: "At least remember not to return without
peace, the King wishes it *at all costs.*"

Despite the brilliant victories of Marshals Saxe and
Lowendahl in the Austrian Netherlands, France gained
nothing from the Treaty and even humiliatingly agreed
to dismantle the sea defenses of Dunkerque. Louis XV's
son-in-law Don Philip gained from Austria the three
Italian duchies of Parma, Piacenza, and Guastella, but of
what benefit was that to the people of France?

When the terms of Aix-la-Chapelle were published the
people were furious, and Parisian fishwives expressed their
contempt for anyone by saying, "You are as filthy as the
Peace." Marshal Saxe snorted his disgust: "I don't under-

stand your damned politics, but I know that the King of Prussia took Silesia and kept it, and I wish we might imitate him."

Most galling of all was the clause which bound Louis XV to expel the Young Pretender, Charles Edward Stuart, from France. Paris, ardently Jacobite, mistakenly blamed Madame de Pompadour for this craven capitulation to English arrogance, and when Bonnie Prince Charlie was arrested at the *Opéra*, bound with silken ropes, and hustled off to the fortress of Vincennes, the fury of the people could hardly be controlled. The Young Pretender, with French blood in his veins, indignantly demanded of his captors, "Is this then the land of courtesy?", and departed from France only under strongest protest.

On December 18, 1748, a few days after his arrest, the streets of Paris were scattered with handbills which reflected the cynical state of public opinion:

We, George of Brunswick, by the Grace of God, King of England, Ireland, Scotland and France, order and enjoin Louis de Bourbon, our Regent in France, to arrest Charles-Edward, so-called Prince of Wales, and to have him taken, hands tied, to Rome, where we desire that he shall live; and we command him, as soon as this is done, to present himself to us to render account. Given at London, December 1, 1748.

GEORGE

The arrest of the Young Pretender had an epilogue which, curiously enough, rid the Marquise of her most implacable enemy, Maurepas. The *Poissonades* reappeared in the streets of the capital and the halls of Versailles, and one evening at Marly the Marquise, removing her napkin, uncovered a verse which surpassed, in its scurrility, any that had previously appeared.

> Par vos façons nobles et franches
> Iris, vous enchantez les coeurs,
> Sous vos pas vous semez des fleurs,
> Mais ce ne sont que des fleurs blanches.

> By your noble and free manners
> Iris, you enchant all hearts,
> Under your feet you scatter flowers
> But they are only white flowers.

This cruel reference to the Marquise's menstrual difficulties and to her repeated miscarriages was more than she could bear. Although she lacked proof, she was convinced that the malevolent Minister of Marine was the anonymous author, and she rushed to confront him.

"I won't let it be said that I send for the King's Ministers. I go to them. When will you discover the author of these verses?"

"When I discover them, Madame," Maurepas answered, "I will tell the King."

"You think very little, Monsieur, of the King's Mistresses," said the Marquise, trembling with passion.

Maurepas smiled insolently. "I have always respected them, Madame, *no matter what kind they are.*"

Maurepas' insulting self-assurance was understandable. He, the declared enemy of all the Mistresses, believed himself to be their nemesis. Madame de Mailly had come to see him two days before her dismissal; Madame de

Châteauroux had died a horrible death shortly after he had carried to her the King's letter of recall; now it was the turn of the Marquise, whom he hated more than any of her predecessors. But Maurepas underrated her feminine resources and overestimated the value of his favor with the Queen and the Dauphin. The King appreciated his sparkling imagination and lively wit and refused to consider his dismissal, but Madame de Pompadour, feeling for the first time real hatred stirring within her heart, determined to ruin him.

Reviving the ill-founded slanders that Maurepas had poisoned Madame de Châteauroux, she affected an intense fear of being poisoned herself. At the Little Suppers she ostentatiously refused to touch her food until someone had tasted it, and she ordered Quesnay to sleep near her, supplied with every conceivable type of antidote. She appeared feverish and ill, wept constantly, and implored Louis to dismiss Maurepas.

Although it was only a few weeks since her bitter quarrel with Richelieu over the theater, she now found in him an unanticipated ally. The Duc had long hated Maurepas and immediately seized this chance to bring about his fall. He wrote and gave to the Marquise a long memorandum attacking Maurepas' administration of the Navy; she promptly showed it to the King who, by now thoroughly exasperated, made up his mind to end the tiresome struggle.

Characteristically, however, he refrained from the slightest indication of his displeasure to the doomed Minister. The first that Maurepas knew of his destruction was his receipt, in the hours of early morning, of a letter written the night before from the Marquise's estate of La Celle. Its words were brief—and brutal.

I promised you that I would warn you. I keep my word. I no longer require your services and you must hand in your resignation to M. de St. Florentin. You will go to Bourges. Pontchartrain is too near. I give you the remainder of the week to make your plans for departure. You must see no one except your family. Do not answer this.

LOUIS

The flippant Maurepas, his glittering satire withered within him, was so unhinged by the abrupt disgrace that for more than twenty-four hours he could not retain even water on his stomach. He withdrew entirely from public affairs, not to be recalled until after the death of Louis XV a quarter of a century later.

In the years immediately following the Treaty of Aix-la-Chapelle, a wave of prosperity swept over France. The country was rich, and the Comptroller-General, Machault, made a heroic effort to correct the glaring inequalities of the unfair tax system by introducing an income tax. The *vingtième,* or twentieth, was supposed to be paid on the incomes of everyone—nobles and clergy as well as *bourgeoisie* and peasant. But the clergy refused to surrender their ancient exemption and succeeded in influencing the King through his family, while the nobles, although legally obligated to pay, delayed and improvised so shamelessly that only a fraction of their assessed taxes ever trickled into the Treasury. The financial burdens of the nation continued to be borne by the middle class and the peasants.

With the failure of financial reform, popular bitterness increased. Menacing threats echoed through the streets of Paris—"Down with the King, hang Pompadour, break Machault on the wheel!" The wildest tales of Court extravagance—and worse—were circulated and believed in Paris. It was said that Louis had contracted leprosy and must be bathed in the blood of children to arrest his loathsome disease; consequently, when the police were ordered, as a routine duty, to clear the streets of depraved homeless children, a series of fierce riots ensued, during which a policeman's body, mutilated by the mob, was dragged through the streets by a rope attached to his neck.

The King was so outraged when he heard of the lynching that he refused for some time afterward to visit Paris, saying, "Shall I show myself to those vile people who say I am a Herod?" His temper was hardly soothed when he found, on his mantelpiece at Versailles, an anonymous note on which was written: "You travel to Choisy and Crécy—why don't you go to Saint-Denis?" (Saint-Denis was the burial church of the Kings of France.)

Nor was Madame de Pompadour spared the people's execration, which exceeded that shown to the King. One day in 1750 she went into Paris to see the apartment which had been prepared for her daughter's use at the Convent of the Assumption, intending to dine later with the Marquis de Gontaut. When she reached his house the frightened nobleman met her at the door and begged her to go back to Versailles at once, pointing as he spoke to a threatening crowd which had gathered on the walls of his garden. Madame de Pompadour, thoroughly chastened, hurried away unable to comprehend the loathing she inspired.

With the terrifying specter of the people's hatred added to the backbiting of the courtiers and the interminable struggle with her enemies at Versailles, it is hardly surprising that the gray hands of disillusionment seized the fragile Marquise before she was out of her twenties.

"It is necessary to be friendly to everybody," she wrote to her brother, "for if we limited ourselves to those we esteemed we would be detested by almost the entire human race. . . . Do not think that because I am young I cannot give good advice; I have seen so much during the four and a half years I have been here that I know more than a woman of forty."

There is inevitable sadness in watching the toll which the strain of her life exacted from the Marquise—not only a growing cynicism but an unmistakable deterioration of her ethereal beauty. She acquired the habit of biting her pale lips, in order, her critics said, to bring color into them; but more likely she began the practice not from vanity but as an unconscious attempt to repress her tortured nerves. Dark circles of fatigue shadowed her beautiful eyes and faint wrinkles appeared in their corners. Powder could still hide the wrinkles during her public appearances, but what about the endless hours of the night when she must still appear alluring to her insatiable Master?

The rich foods and lack of proper exercise induced a costive condition which was responsible for chronic headaches and occasional blemishes which marred her translucent skin. These she could conceal, in the fashion of the day, with beauty spots of all shapes and sizes, but nothing short of a radical change of régime could reestablish the delicate balance of her health—and that was a price Madame de Pompadour was unable, and unwilling, to pay. She who had once seized her destiny was now its captive, and she would play out her role to the very end. Meanwhile, there were still joys to be experienced, still pleasures to be extracted from her position, and she proceeded to enjoy them to the fullest.

XII

PLEASURES AND PALACES

EROI, the author of *Curiosités Historiques*, speaks of an account book belonging to the Marquise which was copied from her own notes. Its first page was entitled: "List of expenses incurred during the reign of Madame la Marquise de Pompadour, from September 9, 1745 to April 15, 1764."

Since the Marquise herself took the time to supervise these accounts, it is unlikely that they were exaggerated; the figures, therefore, may be accepted as a conservative estimate of her cost to the French people during the nineteen years she dominated at Versailles. The total amounted to the staggering sum of 36,827,268 livres or more than $73,000,000. No wonder the overtaxed Parisians hooted her in the streets and linked her name forever with the financial ruin of France!

The natural question was, where did she spend the money? Surely, they reasoned, she was insuring herself against an uncertain future by depositing heavily in foreign banks. They were wrong, however; the truth was that the Marquise was usually in debt, and when she died her executors found in cash only 37 gold louis. Her account book shows that while her living expenses were enormous, the greater part of her resources was swallowed in building, that most princely of pastimes.

Writing to her father she explained: "I am much less rich than when I was in Paris; that which I have, has been given to me without my asking for it; and the expenses of my houses have weighed heavily upon me. That has been the pleasure of the Master, and there is nothing to say about it, but if I had desired riches all the sums spent would have given me a handsome income." Somewhat disingenuously she added, "I have never wanted anything . . . at least I have the consolation that the public knows this and accords justice to me. . . ."

The Marquise at various times owned more than seventeen estates, not including houses which she bought merely for investment. Her passion for altering, redecorating, and building rapidly grew into a mania, providing an outlet for her creative urge and at the same time satisfying her bourgeois instinct of possessiveness. She was not thinking entirely of herself, however—she could never afford that luxury. Louis entered into every plan she conceived, every action she performed, and as she said, it was to divert him as much as to please herself that she embarked on an orgy of construction.

It was mainly for him that she installed at Trianon the menagerie and famous botanical garden complete with a conservatory to shelter the plants which had been brought from all over the world. There was also a kitchen garden in which the King could observe the first strawberries grown in France (he was excessively fond of them), and supervise experiments in the sowing of corn. A farmyard and a fine dairy, stocked with blooded Dutch cows, completed this expensive gesture to the King's interest in scientific farming.

Gabriel designed a tiny pavilion where Louis and the Marquise could sit in comfort and gaze out upon the rows of orange, lemon, olive, and oleander trees which lined the paths. Verberckt carved a frieze of pigeons, peacocks, hens, and ducks, but the rural motif became enchantingly incongruous when he added an inevitable cupid, playing with farm baskets and implements.

Although Madame de Pompadour's buildings consumed vast sums, the money was not entirely unproductive. She provided work for the greatest artists in France—the architects Lassurance and Gabriel, the painters Boucher and Van Loo, the woodcarver Verberckt, and the sculptor Pigalle, whose creative efforts added to and enriched the artistic treasures of the kingdom. Her constructions were beneficial even in the realm of economics, creating a ceaseless demand for building materials and providing work for hundreds of laborers. Finally, inasmuch as many of the Marquise's major properties were bequeathed to the King or reverted to the Crown at her death, it is hardly fair to accuse her of bankrupting France solely for her own gratification.

The first property which Madame de Pompadour acquired for her own was the Château of Crécy, near Dreux. She paid 650,000 livres for it in 1746, and spent nearly five times that amount in extensive alterations of the house and gardens. The glory of Crécy was its octagonal room for which Boucher painted his enchanting panels of children engaged in adult occupations—among them music, dancing, painting, gardening, and sculpting.

The Marquise was happy at Crécy and—more important—so was the King. He soon learned to like the country life and enjoyed the simple games of blind man's buff and prisoners' base no less than the inevitable shooting. Louis himself designed the Crécy household uniform—a lace-trimmed green coat with gold buttons.

The Marquise played the kind great lady to the neighborhood, not from affectation but because she was truly generous and enjoyed money only to spend it. She contributed dowries to poor young brides of the near-by village, built a house for the priest, and even sold some of her magnificent diamonds in order to provide funds for a hospital.

Imbued with consideration for others, she was a gracious hostess and several times received the Court at Crécy. After 1755, however, the King was trying to reduce expenses—one six-day visit to Crécy had cost 100,000 livres— and the Marquise saw less and less of her estate, finally selling it in 1760.

Crécy was the first of her properties, and it sharpened her desire for more. She soon bought the two pavilions of Montretout and La Celle, situated between Paris and Versailles. Although La Celle had twenty guest rooms, the Marquise referred to it as the "little château" and used it only rarely, principally as a spot where she could dine during the hot summer months. She tired of it within three years and disposed of it in 1750.

The smaller Château of Montretout she liked even less, although it was the scene of one of her happiest memories. Louis, surprisingly thinking of her pleasure before his own, gave the Marquise a party in the summer of 1748. In the middle of dinner four little girls and fourteen musicians, dressed as shepherds and shepherdesses, filed into the dining room. One of the shepherdesses presented a huge bouquet to the guest of honor, the shepherds played light airs on their instruments, and as dinner was ending a spectacular display of fireworks was set off in honor of St. Jean, patron of the Marquise. Louis was so enthralled with his own party that he changed his mind about returning to Versailles and remained overnight at Montretout.

He was not always so amiable. When the Marquise reciprocated two months later with a fête at La Celle he was gloomy and depressed, made no effort to hide his boredom, and sullenly refused to dance. Even Marie Leczinska, when she heard of his rudeness, remarked that she felt sorry for Madame de Pompadour "who deserved better treatment."

The Marquise owned a large house in the town of Versailles, almost next to the Palace and connected to it by a secret passage. This residence, still standing as the Hôtel des Réservoirs, was handsomely furnished, and the King often stopped there on his way home from hunting.

The Marquise's stables at her Versailles hôtel contained twenty-six carriage horses and six saddle horses as well as vehicles of all kinds; among them a sedan chair and traveling carriage, both lined with flowered red silk, and a two-wheeled chair known as a *vinaigrette,* used by the Marquise in going to and from the Palace and pulled, like a rickshaw, by one man.

For the convenience of Madame de Pompadour on her visits to Paris, the King furnished a suite on the ground floor of the Hôtel de Pontchartrain, usually reserved for Ambassadors. The Marquise complained that it was not spacious enough, and proceeded to purchase, in 1753, the Hôtel d'Evreux, which is now the Elyseé Palace, the residence of the President of France. Its price was 650,000 livres, and another 100,000 was spent to add a dining room, dressing room, and several closets. The Marquise's bedroom was hung with magnificent Gobelins, each of which displayed in the middle two intertwined L's surmounted by a crown.

The Marquise intended to appropriate part of the adjoining Champs Elysées for use as a vegetable garden, but the indignant Parisians protested so violently that she abandoned her plan. Even without this addition her grounds were extensive and protected from intruders by a *saut de loup* or ditch, on the inner side of which stood a green iron fence.

Although Madame de Pompadour became very fond of the Hôtel d'Evreux, she could afford little time there. The headquarters, office, and workshop of her busy life were naturally her apartments at Versailles, and she dared not face the risk of long absences from the King—some rival might worm her way into the routine of Louis' existence and teach him that the Marquise de Pompadour was not indispensable. And so she seldom went to her beautiful Paris house, although she probably thought of it as a future home if she should survive the King.

Of all the buildings dear to Madame de Pompadour's heart, Bellevue was the one on which she lavished the most attention and care and which, in the end, proved the most disappointing. She wanted this mansion to be hers from its first foundation stone, its first planted shrub. She spent unwearied hours going over the plans with Lassurance, and was so pleased with his designs that she obtained for him the Cross of St. Michael.

Bellevue, begun in 1748, stood on a slope overlooking the Seine between Sèvres and Meudon. Eight hundred workers were employed in the construction of the château, and although their progress was slowed by the sandy nature of the soil, Bellevue was finished within two years. Its construction alone cost more than 2,500,000 livres and within three more years the Marquise distributed an equal sum to painters and sculptors who embellished the mansion.

Bellevue was a casket of precious treasures, crammed with furniture and exotic *objets d'art* ... tables of marquetry and ormolu; desks of buhl, lacquer, and satinwood, gracefully curved in that style now known as *Louis Quinze* or sometimes called *le style Pompadour;* an immense array of bronzes, vases, glass, porcelain, statues, books, and intricate *bibelots;* a gold birdcage filled with enameled birds; Venetian lanterns framed in bronze and ormolu; girandoles and chandeliers of silver; and toilet sets of silver, gold, or lapis.

Boucher, who designed much of her furniture, had a passion for amethysts, crystals, corals, and shells, and the Marquise, sharing his taste, added collections of these to her store of riches. Surrounded by such luxury, it is somewhat astonishing to find Madame de Pompadour casually writing that "the house, though not very large, is charming, without any pretense at magnificence."

Rumors of the enormous cost of the Marquise's new mansion spread to Paris, and for once the sum she had sucked from the Treasury was not exaggerated. Another *Poissonade* duly appeared:

> Fille d'une sangsue et sangsue elle-même
> Poisson, d'une insolence extrême
> Étale en ce château, sans honte et sans effroi,
> La substance du peuple et la honte du Roi.

> Daughter of a leech and leech herself,
> Poisson, extremely insolent
> Displays in this chateau, shamelessly
> And without fear,
> The resources of the people
> And the shame of the King.

The Marquise had scheduled a lavish show of fireworks to celebrate the King's first visit to Bellevue, but frightened by warnings that a hostile crowd intended to watch, she cancelled the ostentatious display. Other unlucky occurrences that evening caused Louis' visit to be less than successful. He and his gentlemen appeared in the newly designed Bellevue uniform, purple velvet trimmed with gold lace, but everyone had neglected to foresee the hideous clash of purple with the green uniforms of the lackeys. Although the evening was cold, fires could not be lighted because the chimneys proved defective and the handsome rooms filled with smoke. The guests, choking and gasping, were forced to leave; the King was bored and angry; and the Marquise so vexed that she burst into tears.

Bellevue knew happier moments, however. A few weeks later the King came to attend a performance in the theater there and was enchanted both by the play and the mansion. A short time later the Marquise gave a spectacular fête to celebrate the Dauphin's recovery from smallpox. Everyone agreed that the entertainment was unusually beautiful, although the Dauphin, still nursing his hatred of the Marquise, refused to appear.

Madame de Pompadour was at first delighted with her new house, as another letter to her brother reveals: "I shall see Bellevue on Wednesday, and I am like a child with joy at seeing it again." In the next few years Bellevue was the scene of weddings, fireworks, and fêtes Champêtres, but gradually the Marquise lost interest in what she had planned as her dream palace. The theatricals ceased in 1753, and after four more years of increasing indifference to Bellevue, Madame de Pompadour sold it to the King for less than a seventh of its cost. After the death of Louis XV in 1774, Bellevue became the residence of Mesdames. It was destroyed during the Revolution.

These residences were only the most important or best known of Madame de Pompadour's properties. There were many more: a hôtel and Hermitage at both Fontainebleau and Compiègne, châteaux at St. Ouen, Ménars, and Anvilliers, and a house at Passy, which she later exchanged with the King for more land to add to her marquisat of Ménars. Faced with the staggering task of furnishing this array of residences, no wonder the Marquise became the best customer of French tradesmen, not only for luxuries but for necessities as well. An item in the inventory of her estate lists 11 leather boxes and wicker baskets, crammed with 112 pairs of sheets, 160 tablecloths, 1600 napkins and dish cloths, and 388 kitchen aprons. It is a wonder there were not more!

It is hardly surprising that Madame de Pompadour, endowed with discerning taste and unlimited means with which to indulge it, should have reigned undisputed in that kingdom dearest to a woman's heart—the realm of style and fashion. A beguiling assortment of objects were inspired by her and named for her—Pompadour carriages, chairs, sofas, mirrors, and mantels; there was even a toothpick *à la Pompadour*. Her manner of brushing her hair straight back from her brow added a new word to the vocabulary of the *coiffeur*. Boucher designed her fans, which were treated with *vernis Martin* and painted with the cupids and nymphs he loved so well.

It was inevitable that the slender well-proportioned Marquise, far more chic than the aristocracy and possessing the flair for dress of the native Parisienne, should become the unquestioned Queen of Fashion. It was she who introduced gowns of broad stripes, skirts of dainty flowered silk, and negligées of English calico. She designed a negligée which was named for her, shaped like a Turkish jacket, tight at the neck and wrists, fitted to the shape of her superb bust, and close at the hips—a boudoir garment styled to reveal rather than to conceal the form beneath.

Her wardrobe exceeded in size and cost that of the Queen or any of the other ladies at Court. Expense was never a consideration, at least for the Marquise, and as her natural beauty began to fade her toilette grew ever more magnificent. One evening at Marly she appeared in a dress trimmed with English lace worth 22,500 livres, almost as much as the price of one of her small estates. Her jewelry was incomparable in the number and purity of its dazzling gems—she owned a necklace of white diamonds consisting of 547 stones, and 42 rings of great value, which was only a small part of her collection.

Saint-Beuve paid eloquent tribute to her influence on style:

In any study of the eighteenth century Madame de Pompadour is inevitable. We must not fear to call things and epochs by their name; and the name by which the eighteenth century may most appropriately be called, for the taste, the style universally reigning in the arts of design, in the fashions and usages of life, in poetry even—is it not that coquettish and decorative name which seems to be made expressly for the beautiful Marquise and to rhyme so well with *amour?* All the arts of that period bear her seal.

The great painter Watteau, who came before her time and who created a magic pastoral world, seems to have decorated and embellished it expressly so that she might take possession of it to bloom and reign there. The successors of Watteau delighted unanimously in recognizing the scepter of their natural protectress ... the *style Pompadour* unquestionably existed before the advent of the beautiful Marquise, but she sums it up; in herself she crowns and personifies it.

However appropriate it may seem to link the graceful curved and fragile style known as *Louis Quinze* to the name of Pompadour, her personal preference inclined to the simpler, more classical style that began about 1750, with which the name of Louis Seize is linked. Much of the furniture which she owned at her death was of this later period, but neither her taste nor her preference could separate her name from the soft and feminine style which was fashionable when she became the King's Mistress.

One glory which is permanently bound to the name of Madame de Pompadour, from which her bitterest enemies cannot rob her, was the establishment of the Royal Porcelain Factory at Sèvres. She had always loved beautiful porcelains and resented that France produced none to equal the fine products of China and Saxony. In 1749 she persuaded the King to turn over to her the small porcelain manufactory at Vincennes which had been established eight years earlier and which through neglect had almost ceased production.

The Marquise, assisted by friendly financiers and Machault, organized a new company capitalized at 250,000 livres, plus the gift of an additional 100,000 from the King. A few years later the establishment was transferred to the tiny village of Sèvres, and the glory of French porcelain had begun.

The factory at Sèvres employed 500 skilled workers, sixty of whom were painters. These artisans were so skillful that anyone presuming to hire one of them away from Sèvres was fined 3,000 livres. The establishment was directed by Jacques Boileau; the models for the products were made by the goldsmith Duplessis; and their decoration superintended by Bachelier, the landscape painter.

At that time all French porcelain was made of soft paste rather than of the hard paste used in Dresden. The beautiful array of colors developed by the French artists became one of the superlative attributes of Sèvres china—bright yellow, violet, and three shades of green. But the most famous were the favorite blues and pinks of the fragile woman who had called all this into being—*bleu de roi*, a deep royal blue, *bleu turquoise*, a lighter blue, and the Marquise's favorite, a pale raspberry shading into pink, which was named *rose pompadour*.

The popularity of the new porcelain was immediate. The King and the Marquise often visited the factory to encourage the workers and bought lavishly—dinner services, vases, and figurines. Every year the Marquise sponsored a display of the porcelains at Versailles, where she herself acted as saleswoman and encouraged the nobles to buy generously. A vase was priced at 25 livres, a plate at 50, and a coffee cup at 2. "An exorbitant price," complained d'Argenson. "Dresden porcelain is cheaper and better." But the verdict of the world was otherwise and acknowledged that the early porcelain of Sèvres surpassed that of Dresden in shape and beauty. Louis XV had the exquisite satisfaction of sending to Augustus III a Sèvres dinner service that evoked groans of envy from the artisans of Saxony. Demand for Sèvres china became so great that in 1760 the King bought the factory for the Crown, and it has since belonged to the government of France.

The porcelain of Sèvres was fashioned into almost every imaginable article of utility or ornament, from six *pôts-de-chambre* for the bedroom of the Marquise to the unbelievably delicate flowers planted in vases of Meissen. Louis, seeing for the first time at Bellevue a vase of Sèvres roses and lilies, was so deceived by their natural appearance that he wanted to cut them, and only when he touched their glazed surface did he realize they were artificial and that their scent was simulated by atomizers concealed in the room. He was so charmed by these flowers that he ordered additional ones created for all his country houses.

The Marquise had given to France a priceless industry, born out of her love of beauty and her bourgeois sense of profit. Unfortunately that middle-class trait, employed in this enterprise to the advantage of France, showed itself in other ways which drained rather than replenished the ailing Treasury.

XIII

LA BOURGEOISE

NE OF THE most serious accusations leveled
at Madame de Pompadour is the charge that she sold
high offices of state, commands in the Army, and even pass-
ports for her own enrichment. Although not one shred
of evidence has been produced to support this charge,
it continues to shadow her reputation, largely because of
the discrepancy between her income and expenditures—a
discrepancy more apparent than real.

After her separation from her husband, the new Marquise de Pompadour, possessing 3,000 livres in cash and
a house in the rue St. Marc, was well-to-do but hardly
wealthy. The King granted her a monthly allowance of
24,000 livres or approximately $50,000 a year. During the
next four years the allowance varied, sometimes reaching
the sum of 30,000 livres a month, and in addition Louis
gave her large sums as New Year's presents and continually
showered her with estates and jewels. After 1749, however, the King's passion began to cool, and her allowance
was reduced to a mere 4,000 livres a month, obviously
insufficient to support her extravagant scale of living.
How, then, did she make up the difference? It is this

question which has led so many to assume that the Favorite resorted to the sale of her influence.

The answer to the riddle lies in her carefully kept account books and in the inventory of her estate. Brought up in the financial circles of the upper middle class, the Marquise early acquired an acute sense of money, and she brought to the extravagant world of Versailles a bourgeois sense of order in fiscal affairs. Regardless of the gruelling task of holding the King's interest—of her unending struggle to outwit and crush rivals and enemies—of time consumed by theatricals, balls, hunts, suppers, and illnesses, she managed to find time to devote to her business affairs. It was France's loss that she did not apply her shrewd head with equal fervor to the financial problems of the kingdom. Assisted by her manager, the capable an intelligent Collin, she kept exact records of her income, including her astute investments.

Of the first importance were her receipts in rents. In addition to the house in the rue St. Marc which had formed part of her dowry, she owned other houses at St. Ouen, Choisy, Compiègne, and in the rue St. Honoré. All these she regarded as rental properties which were expected to produce an income.

Then there were her receipts from the sale of wine and crops from her various lands, carefully collected and recorded by Collin. The King made over to her contracts which brought in an annuity of 90,000 livres, and from the sale of Crécy she received another annuity of 100,000. At the time of her death her annuities amounted to 230,000 livres, a far from trifling sum.

But that was by no means all. She bought shares in privateers which were fitted out to prey upon English commerce, and she shared heavily in their prize money. We find that the supposedly frivolous Marquise was part owner of such privateers as *Louis le Bien-Aimé, L'Américaine, La Rose, La Bohémienne,* and *La Diane,* whose graceful names could mitigate only slightly the grim nature of the business upon which they sailed.

One of Madame de Pompadour's most successful fields of investment was in industry. Quite apart from the factory at Sèvres, which reverted to the Crown, she owned (under a dummy name) a glassworks which produced crystal, bottles, carafes, and enamels. Her inventory lists its utensils and other assets and shows a profit of 120,000 livres for the years 1755-1764. There were other industrial undertakings as well, most of which Collin ran for her benefit.

The existence of this additional income seems to clear the Marquise of the charge of venality and to explain satisfactorily how she was able to spend such vast sums even when she no longer received great amounts from Louis. Nevertheless, from the accounts it is apparent that she was always up to her ears in debt, and sometimes she turned to gambling in order to provide herself with cash. Although too level-headed to enjoy it, she won more than she lost, gaining over 37,000 livres in May 1752. But she was always short of ready money—during her last illness Collin was forced to borrow 70,000 livres to meet her immediate needs.

A principal reason for this chronic financial strain was the Marquise's generosity. Her first impulse, from the beginning of her triumph, was to share her marvelous fortune with her friends and her family. She arranged for the impecunious Bernis to occupy an apartment in the Louvre, and in similar harmless ways did favors for the friends of her youth.

But it was to her family that she devoted her greatest efforts—and what could be more natural? The Marquise remained at heart a bourgeoise, strongly aware of her family and bound to them by a naturally affectionate disposition. If she felt a certain pride in using her position for their benefit, even perhaps a temptation to show off, was she not obeying the instincts of normal human nature?

Madame Poisson had died before she could enjoy the material rewards of her daughter's success, but François Poisson prospered—and unashamedly—from her association with the King. In 1750 the King bought for him the estate of Marigny-en-Orxois, and the weaver's son blossomed forth as the Sieur de Marigny. But he never pretended to alter his bourgeois viewpoint in which money played so dominant a part.

He did not scruple to ask incessant favors from the Marquise, who, though she loved him dearly, was embarrassed by his lack of tact and understanding. Her letters, written to him on small notepaper with gilt edges and decorated with blue and red flowers, speak for themselves: "I am very much embarrassed, *mon cher père,* that you desire Vincennes for M. de Malvoisin [her first cousin]. How can you get the idea of placing a man of 25, no matter how smart he is, who has served only six years? Really, he will have to be satisfied with his position.

There are many people who do not obtain such a position until they have served twenty years. What is sure is that I cannot ask a thing so unjust."

And again: "I know, *mon cher père,* that several *cordons rouges* are promised, but I strongly doubt if it is possible to obtain one for M. de Petit. It has never been a question of the provostship of Paris for my brother; neither he nor I has the money to afford it. . . ." Sometimes M. Poisson asked outright for money, as this answer of the patient Marquise indicated: ". . . you may always have access to my funds which M. de Montmartel has, but there is not much now, because I have lent almost all of it. . . ."

Happily, not all the Marquise's letters to her father dealt with mercenary matters; there are many, written in a sensible, almost abrupt but always affectionate tone which are full of bourgeois sentiments, and which show that Poisson adored his grandchild, Alexandrine d'Étioles. "It is not fair of you, *mon cher père,* to have given me no sign of life for so long. I have had fever six days, the King has given me the honors of a Duchess, and all this has not affected you at all. . . . I well see that little Alexandrine has chased Reinette from your heart; it is not fair, and I must love her a great deal to pardon her."

Like any other indulgent grandfather, M. Poisson spoiled Alexandrine, for the sensible Marquise protests: "You should reproach yourself for having given her indigestion. Why is it that grandpapas always spoil their grandchildren? I find that she is getting very ugly, but if she is not shockingly so I shall be satisfied, because I do not insist that she be very beautiful. That only makes all women your enemies. . . ."

The Marquise adored her daughter, and in reality spoiled Alexandrine far more than M. Poisson ever did. In 1750 she had the child brought for a time to Versailles, where Madame du Haussay looked after her and the elderly Crébillon tutored her as he had done the Marquise not so many years before. Alexandrine was a lovely little girl, fortunately resembling her mother rather than the forgotten M. d'Étioles. The proud Marquise showed her off to everyone and permitted her, on one special occasion, to play a small part in one of the performances of the Little Theater.

It was hardly surprising that the attention Alexandrine received turned her small head. At the Convent of the Assumption in Paris, where she went to school, she was addressed as *Madame* Alexandrine, a salutation usually reserved for a Princess of the Blood. She grew willful and haughty and quarreled violently with the little Princesse de Soubise over who should take precedence in passing through the door. *"Elle a manqué de politesse,"* noted the Marquise with succinct disapproval in describing her daughter's ill behavior.

Just as Madame Poisson had dreamed of a great future for the Marquise, so Madame de Pompadour built her hopes around Alexandrine. To marry her to one of the great names of France became an obsession; not only would such an alliance provide a brilliant future for Alexandrine but it might be useful in strengthening the

Marquise's own position at Court. One could never have too many powerful friends.

Her first desire was to marry Alexandrine to the young Comte du Luc, *le demi-louis,* the King's son by Madame de Vintimille. The Marquise confided to Madame du Haussay that this was the dearest wish of her heart in order that "her grandchildren might blend the resemblance of their grandfather and grandmother." There were tears in the Marquise's eyes as she said this, but the King regarded her plan coldly. One day at Bellevue she contrived to bring the children together in the King's presence; Louis, when he learned that the handsome boy was his son, was embarrassed and, although he treated Alexandrine affectionately, paid no attention to the wistful Comte de Luc. Nothing further came of the Marquise's dream.

Her next candidate was the Duc de Fronsac, the son of the Duc de Richelieu. Her former adversary, resigned to the continuance of Madame de Pompadour's reign, was anxious not to offend her, but he was equally averse to mingling the blood of his House with that of Poisson. He replied that while he deeply appreciated the honor and was profoundly grateful, he could not give an answer until he had consulted the House of Lorraine to which his son was related on his mother's side. The Marquise understood the tactful refusal and let the matter drop.

At last she succeeded in arranging for Alexandrine's betrothal to the Duc de Picquigny, son of the bankrupt Duc de Chaulnes. In return for their consent, the Marquise agreed that the Duc and Duchesse de Chaulnes were to be appointed governor and governess to the children of the

Dauphin. The betrothal was to occur formally when Alexandrine reached the age of thirteen, but before then fate intervened.

Next to Alexandrine, Madame de Pompadour's chief family concern was for the future of her brother Abel, who had already received the title Marquis de Vandières. Quiet in taste and refined in manner, he was not much like M. Poisson, but then neither was the Marquise. The King was fond of him and referred to him affectionately as *Frerot* —Little Brother. In 1749 Louis promised the young man the post of Director-General of the King's Buildings when Le Normant de Tournehem should die, and in order that he might be better qualified for his future position, Abel set out, accompanied by Cochin the engraver and Soufflot the architect, on a two-year tour of Italy.

At that time the Marquis de Vandières was twenty-three, pleasing and agreeable in appearance. Although plump of body, he had not yet acquired an *embonpoint* or double chin. His forehead was broad, his nose small and delicate, and his mouth rather effeminate. His appearance gave the impression of a sensitive and cultured young aristocrat.

Madame de Pompadour loved her brother dearly, with all the affectionate possessiveness of an older sister, and planned for him a brilliant future. It was she who insisted that he make the tour of Italy, the cradle of all the arts, and her letters to him are among the most human she ever wrote. The first one reached the young traveler at Lyons:

"You were right, little brother, not to say good-by to me, because in spite of the usefulness of this trip for you and the desire that I have had for it for a long time for your good, I would have suffered in parting from you. I do not recommend that you write to me often, for I am sure you will not fail to do so, but what I do urge upon you above all is the greatest politeness. . . ."

Five days later, in a hurried afterthought, she cautioned him to be careful what he wrote to her, and when it was confidential not to "send it unless there are couriers. It is ridiculous that I forgot to warn you about something so essential. Send me your exact route so that my letters will not go astray again."

The sister at Versailles, with enough activities to fill the time of five men, still worried, womanlike, about the small details of her brother's comfort: "Find out what clothes you will need and send the list to me; I will take care of it, as I wish you to be presentable in every way. Also let me know if you have clean laces. . . ."

As a matter of course the Marquis de Vandières paid his respects to the Pope, and in commenting on his letters Madame de Pompadour revealed a respectful but eminently practical attitude toward His Holiness and the Church in general: "I don't doubt that you had great satisfaction in kissing the toe of St. Peter, and that you have gained a number of indulgences. By the way [she goes on in the same breath] give your letters for me to M. de Nivernois so I will receive them quicker." And a few days later: "I am delighted at the benedictions that the Holy Father gave you . . . the consideration that one has for me does not astonish me in France where everybody has or can have need of my services; but I was astonished that it was true in Rome. In spite of this situation, which one must accept since it exists, my head is not turned, and except for the happiness of being loved by the one you love, which is the best of all conditions, a solitary and less brilliant life is much to be preferred. . . . It seems that my father wants a chaplet, so you ought to give him the preference over me." She added archly, "I make the sacrifice for him without regret."

The Marquise referred recurrently to the King, always in terms which radiated serene affection: "The older I get, my dear little brother, the more philosophical my thoughts become . . . except for the happiness of being with the King, which assuredly consoles me for everything, the rest is nothing but a tissue of malice. . . ."

Her first consideration was for Louis' health, while she continued to neglect her own. Admittedly self-interest partly explains her concern for the King's well-being, since she was lost without him, but still her sincere love for Louis was too evident to be denied. "We are supposed to go tomorrow to Crécy but I have canceled the trip, there being in the country many sore throats like there were in Paris a year ago. I am too much attached to the King to risk even the lightest discomfort to his person." But on the other hand: "I have a terrible cold that has given me fever for 24 hours; it is a little better. I am going down to the salon this evening, which incidentally is devilish for colds."

Two months after her brother returned to France, Le Normant de Tournehem, who had played so important a role in the destiny of the Poisson family, died and the Marquis de Vandières duly succeeded him. He became

Madame de Pompadour and her daughter, from a painting by François Guérin from the collection of the late Baron Edmond de Rothschild.

Madame de Pompadour, from a painting by
François-Hubert Drouais. Reproduced by permission of the Earl of Rosebery.

Marquis de Marigny upon the death of M. Poisson three years later, and it was as bearer of that title that he achieved his greatest importance during Madame de Pompadour's lifetime.

It soon became evident that Marigny's trip, during which he had lovingly studied the masterpieces of Italian painting and architecture, had been a wise investment. Like the Marquise he had natural good taste, and as Director-General of the King's Buildings he was in a position to give French artists the support they needed so badly. In a less spectacular fashion, Marigny did more for them than the Marquise herself. French art was languishing, the nobility rarely ordered paintings, and the Court, which ordered them by the dozen, rarely paid for them. Marigny, quietly and with characteristic modesty, changed all that. He increased the prices paid to artists, and placed sizable orders at Gobelins for the decoration of the buildings under his supervision.

"That is a man but little known," said Dr. Quesnay of him. "No one speaks of his spirit and his knowledge, nor of what he has done to advance the arts; no one, since Colbert, has done as much in his place. He is a very honest man, but no one sees in him anything except the brother of the Favorite, and because he is fat everyone thinks he is heavy and dull witted."

Marigny, by far the most honorable of his family, was acutely conscious of his comparatively low origin and suffered from a feeling of inferiority. Although he ably discharged his duties, he was timid about advancing his own interests and was morbidly sensitive of his sister's position, indeed far more sensitive than she. Marmontel, who was his secretary for a time, preserved Marigny's feelings on this point: "On one occasion, on his return from the theater, he told me that he had been very embarrassed. As he sat in the balcony, thinking only of enjoying the comedy, he heard one of the actors, playing the part of a drunken soldier, exclaim, 'What! Shall I have a pretty sister and get nothing out of her, when so many others raise a fortune . . . ?' 'Imagine,' he said, 'my confusion and embarrassment! Fortunately the audience did not notice that I was there.' "

Marigny was at times genuinely reluctant to accept his sister's affectionate nepotism, wisely pointing out that it would only increase ill will toward her. He refused to become Minister of Marine, and when Louis appointed him secretary to the Order of the Holy Ghost, permitting him to wear the Blue Ribbon, he protested to Marmontel that he was not worthy of it. Marmontel, understanding perfectly well that Marigny secretly wanted reassurance from someone he trusted, replied diplomatically that "his nobility was in his soul, which was fully equivalent to that of blood."

Like many who rise socially, Marigny took himself seriously, especially in public. Although he sometimes joked rather crudely in private, he was essentially humorless, heavy where the Marquise was light, and could not stand the slightest levity directed at himself. His uneasy temper and his constant fear that others were ridiculing him often led to outbursts of rudeness which flawed a nature that was basically amiable and kind.

It was characteristic of the Marquise's ambitious and dominating nature to desire a brilliant marriage for her brother, with herself choosing the bride. Although Marigny was deferential to the Marquise, he refused in this instance to bow to her wishes, insisting—extraordinary man—that he would marry only for love. Sometimes in order to appease his sister's growing impatience, he pretended to consider the matter, but not even the promise of a dukedom and the Hôtel d'Evreux as a wedding present could bring him to a decision.

One day, reading a letter from Marigny (who had not dared face her), the exasperated Marquise burst out furiously to Madame du Haussay: "I had arranged a marriage for him with the daughter of a nobleman, he pretended to agree, and I pledged my word. Today he tells me that he has heard that her parents are unendurably haughty and that the girl herself is badly brought up and has expressed the greatest contempt at marrying him, and he begs me to call the whole thing off! But he has let me go too far, and now I have made irreconcilable enemies. The trouble is that his friends have given him these ideas; they do not want him to change his life, fearing that they will not be acceptable to his wife."

Madame du Haussay attempted to calm her angry mistress, while reflecting to herself that Marigny was right. The next time he appeared the Marquise treated him very coldly, and he said nothing and seemed ill at ease. Madame de Pompadour made amends to the jilted bride by arranging for her another advantageous marriage at Court; two months after the wedding the young girl's conduct was so flagrant that the chastened Marquise had to confess that her brother's information had been correct.

Madame de Pompadour's concern for her relatives was not confined entirely to her immediate family. Her dead mother's brother, Jean-Louis de la Motte, became a Farmer-General (and a millionaire); her cousin Poisson de Malvoisin, who had begun his career as a drummer in the Piedmont Regiment, was catapulted into a commission—to the inevitable envy and hatred of his colleagues; and when M. de Malvoisin's daughter married, the Marquise insisted that the ceremony he performed in the chapel at Bellevue and gave a handsome dowry to the bride.

Madame du Haussay gives an account, obviously truthful, of a plea for assistance which the Marquise received from one of her poor relatives:

She was in the last stages of misery, and I discovered that Madame had started out by giving her 6 louis meanwhile waiting for more information. Collin took charge of the affair, and went to M. de Malvoisin . . . the story was found to be true. Madame then sent the woman 100 louis, and guaranteed her a pension of 1,500 francs. All of this was done very quickly, and Madame was thanked as soon as her relative could dress herself a little more cleanly.

The day that she came to pay her thanks, the King, who ordinarily did not come at that hour, saw the woman leave and asked who she was. "She is one of my poorest relatives," answered Madame.

"Did she come to ask you for anything?" demanded the King suspiciously.

"No."

"And why not?"

"Because she came to thank me for a little favor I did

her," answered Madame, blushing for fear that she would seem boastful.

"Well, if that is it," said the King, "and since it is your relative, let me help, too. I will give her 50 louis from my purse, and you know that she can send tomorrow for the first installment."

Madame burst into tears, and kissed the King's hand again and again. She told me this herself three nights later, when she had a little fever.

Madame de Pompadour's solicitude for those who needed her aid was one of her best qualities, and if she was guilty of flagrant nepotism, so was everyone else at Versailles who had the opportunity—courtiers, Ministers, and Royalty. The practice was considered not only normal but respectable, and anyone in power who declined to advance his relatives and friends would have been considered either base or insane. At least Madame de Pompadour took real joy in helping others, and she gave with an open heart—not only to relatives but to needy men of genius whose careers were of inestimable worth to France. Upon this fact rests one of her chief claims to fame.

XIV

THE LADY MAECENAS

HE MARQUISE'S interest in all forms of art, while usually that of the sensitive observer, occasionally took a more active form. She executed a series of engravings copied from Jacques Guay's original work on stones, and on rare occasions, under Guay's professional guidance, attempted the precise and difficult art of engraving on stones. The results, frankly amateurish, were none too happy, and it was in the role of patroness rather than artist that the Marquise shone.

To painters Madame de Pompadour appeared as a prodigal goddess, a benefactress whose generosity knew no limits. In order to support them she commissioned frequent portraits and paid promptly and well. Her interest, however, was not that of an expert but of a fashionable woman eager to keep abreast of the latest trends, and her collection contained no old masters but only contemporary works, mostly portraits of herself or Louis, or allegorical subjects such as Boucher captured in "Le Lever du Soleil" and "Le Coucher du Soleil."

François Boucher was the Marquise's friend as well as her favorite painter, and she followed his advice on almost

every question of fashion. Boucher was clever and dissipated, spending most of his time with opera girls who
served him in the dual role of model and mistress. He once
painted for the devout Queen a portrait of the Holy Family, and the enraptured Marie Leczinska never knew that
the divine face of the model who had posed for the Virgin
was that of the artist's current *amour.*

Boucher's "Marquise sur la Chaise Longue" is one of his
most pleasing portraits, and shows, perhaps better than any
other, the coiffure and style of dress that Madame de
Pompadour made famous. Her short hair is simply dressed,
adorned with a spray of flowers, and brushed straight back
from her forehead; her wide satin dress is a garden of ribbons, flowers, and laces. This portrait was painted during
her early years at Versailles and shows her face still fresh
and young, unmarked by strain and fatigue—it is her face
as she looked when she won the King's heart.

The lovely pastel by Maurice-Quentin de La Tour,
which hangs in the Louvre, has been incomparably described by Sainte-Beuve:

She is represented seated in an armchair, holding in her
hand a sheet of music; her left arm rests upon a marble
table on which there is a globe and several books. The
thickest of these volumes, which touches the globe, is
Volume IV of the *Encyclopédie;* next to it stand *L'Esprit
des Lois, L'Henriade,* and *Le Pasteur Fido,* evidence of
the tastes, both serious and romantic, of the queen of this
place.

On the table, at the foot of the globe, is a blue volume
turned face down, inscribed on its back *Pierres Gravées—*
this is her own work. One engraving is loose and hangs over
the side of the table; it represents an engraver at work and

bears the words *Pompadour sculpsit.* On the floor, leaning against the table, is a portfolio full of engravings and designs, embossed with her arms. Farther back, between the legs of the table, stands a Japanese vase, while behind her chair is another chair on which lies a guitar.

But it is the woman herself—marvelous in her elegance, gentle dignity, and exquisite beauty—who compels our attention. Holding the sheet of music lightly and carelessly, her attention is suddenly attracted—she seems to hear a sound, and turns her head. Is it the King who comes and is about to enter? She appears to be expecting someone, and she listens with a smile.

Her head, thus turned so slightly, shows the outline of her neck in all its grace and reveals her hair, very short and deliciously waved, its blond tints just visible through the light film of powder which barely covers it. The head floats in a pale blue background which is, in general, the prevailing color of the picture as a whole. There is nothing in this fairy boudoir that does not seem to pay homage to the goddess, nothing, not even *L'Esprit des Lois* or the *Encyclopédie.*

Her flowered satin gown yields at the curve of the bosom to several rows of those ribbon-knots which were called *échelle de rubans,* and which are here the color of very pale lilac. She herself has the flesh and tints of a white lilac, slightly azured. This bosom, those ribbons, that gown—the whole ensemble blends harmoniously, even voluptuously. It is beauty shining in all the glow of triumphant maturity.

The face is still young, the temples have kept their youth and freshness, and the lips are equally fresh and have not yet withered, as it is said they later did from her habit of biting them to repress her anger. Everything in the face and the attitude expresses grace, supreme taste, affability and dignity rather than gentleness; she has the air of a queen, acquired, it is true, but which, after all, seems natural to her and is sustained without much effort. . . .

The Marquise had great difficulty in persuading de La Tour to render this portrait, and he consented only with the express condition that no one be allowed in the room while he was working. He was a small man, physically weak, with very bright eyes and immaculate clothes. When he arrived for the first sitting, he asked permission to change into his "work clothes"; the Marquise consenting, de La Tour took off his coat and suspenders, unbuckled his shoes, hung his wig on the chandelier, and placed an old silk cap on his head.

Within a few minutes the King came into the room, and the artist flew into a rage. "You absolutely promised, Madame," he sputtered, "that no one would be admitted." Louis raised his eyebrows with amusement at the irascible little man's refreshing lack of respect and urged him to continue his work.

De La Tour flatly refused, remarking, "It is impossible for me to obey Your Majesty. I will return when Madame is free." And he picked up his colors, gathered his scattered apparel, and departed, muttering to himself from time to time, "I do not like to be interrupted!"

After this unfortunate beginning, Madame de Pompadour had a hard time persuading him to return. De la Tour did not like her anyway; his preliminary sketch of her head (which mercifully she never saw) shows an avaricious and calculating woman of the middle class and is replete with the artist's contempt. The famous portrait was completed in 1757, when the Marquise was thirty-six years old, and de La Tour received 24,000 livres for his work.

De La Tour's portrait of Madame de Pompadour represents her in one of her more sincere roles—the gracious intelligent bourgeoise of the Age of Enlightenment, the reader of books and admirer of authors. She possessed a splendid library, which was for reading rather than display. Most of its volumes were in French, although the Marquise knew some Spanish and Italian and had copies of romances in those languages. She was, like most women, an admirer of fiction, especially English novels; she also read law, political science, philosophy, and European history.

The finest section of her library was the magnificent collection of dramatic works, and ballets of the *Opéra, Théâtre Italien,* and *Opéra Comique.* There were also translations of Greek and Roman authors, and theological works were not entirely omitted—there was a copy of Massillon's sermons, which Louis used to read to her when seized with religious remorse, and two blue morocco volumes of the Office of the Virgin Mary, illustrated with eight drawings by Boucher and fastened with a gold clasp.

The Abbé de Bernis had advised the Marquise to cultivate literary men, and she followed his suggestion gladly. Her taste for literature had already been formed; not only did she have the eager interest of the educated middle class in intellectual pursuits, but she found the conversation of thinkers and writers a welcome and stimulating change from the repetitious stories of the King and the vapid chatter of the courtiers. Most of the writers praised her, and she, conscious of posterity, was grateful for this form of recognition, but the *philosophes* needed her far more than she needed them.

Writing, or at least publishing what one had written, was no simple affair in France under the Old Regime. In the absence of copyright laws, literary piracy flourished, and an author could expect only small financial returns from even the greatest success; without the patronage of a person of wealth, his career was almost impossible. Even if a Maecenas were found, there still remained the twin hurdles of ecclesiastical and political censorship. A writer having the temerity to criticize the Church, the government, or an official of either would likely find himself consigned to the Bastille for an indefinite stay.

With such handicaps it is amazing that so many literary giants prospered. That they did so was due in no small measure to the protection which Madame de Pompadour extended to them. She provided the *philosophes* with lodgings and pensions, saved them from the Bastille, and sometimes started them on the road which led to the Academy. In her endeavors she met with stubborn opposition not only from the conservatives at Court but from Louis himself, who never acquired a taste for the *philosophes*.

Sainte-Beuve was not flattering the Marquise when he admiringly wrote that "she was the Mistress who was fitted for this reign, the only one who could have succeeded in making something of it in the line of opinion, the only one who could have diminished the crying discord between the least literary of Kings and the most literary of epochs."

The *philosophes*, while divided by rivalries and personal dislikes, and ranging from the ambivalent Catholicism of Voltaire to the frank atheism of Diderot, nevertheless were united in their hatred of medievalism and tradition. They stood for enlightenment and progress, for the separation of Church and State, and for free enterprise instead of government control of the economy. They did not desire an outright revolution and they were not republicans, but they hoped for a constitutional instead of an absolute monarchy. While Madame de Pompadour had no desire to curb the King's power, she would not have been sorry to clip the wings of the Church.

Since the *philosophes* found their strongest adherents among the *bourgeoisie,* the Marquise's sympathy for most of their views was logical. The middle class was still Christian and loyal to the Crown in the person of Louis XV, but its members, growing in numbers and wealth, hated the old feudal laws which strangled commerce. Because they paid a heavy share of the taxes, they desired—quite reasonably—a voice in determining how their money was spent; above all, they wanted a status comparable to that of the middle class in England.

There was a sizable group among the *bourgeoisie* and even the nobility which was liberal and violently Anglophile. They shared the English concept of government which Voltaire had acquired during his exile in London, and their strength was especially evident in the *Parlement* of Paris. Reduced by Louis XIV to the status of a Law Court, the *Parlement* had had its power of "remonstrance" restored by the Regent—unwisely. And in the years of intellectual ferment after the Treaty of Aix-la-Chapelle, the growing struggle between *Parlement* and Crown proved the greatest trial of Louis XV, who considered the parliamentary leaders his chief enemies. Since the *philosophes—*

and *Parlement*—were anti-Church, or at least anti-Jesuit, Catholic rigorists agreed with the King.

Very little of this tumult reached the more than fifteen million peasants who continued to be the backbone of the Kingdom. Although they owned only one fifth of the land, their careful farming reaped rich harvests; but the ruinous taxation, taking more than half their income, almost destroyed them. They paid taxes of all kinds to the nobles, for the use of ovens, wine presses, and bridges; they paid income tax and land tax to the King, to say nothing of the salt tax and being forced to labor on the roads—no wonder the patient peasant was left with a slim margin of survival!

And yet he did not complain. Clinging to his simple faith in God, he was the strongest support of the Monarchy; with him its power and prestige still stood high, and he would continue loyal as long as hope was left to him. The day that the *philosophes* succeeded in destroying the faith of the peasant, that day would spell the doom of the throne in France.

One day the King and the Marquise received identical letters, which though respectful nevertheless contained a startling number of alarming predictions: "The *philosophes,* under the pretext of enlightening men, are sapping the foundations of religion. All sorts of liberty depend upon each other—they [the *philosophes*] and the Protestants tend to republicanism as well as the Jansenists. The *philosophes* attack the trunk of the tree, the others some of its branches, but their efforts, although not concerted, will some day bring it down. Add to these the Economists, whose object is political liberty, as that of the others is liberty of worship, and the Government may find itself in twenty or thirty years undermined throughout and falling tumultuously into ruins."

Louis fully agreed with the sentiments of the anonymous letter-writer, but the Marquise, after lapsing silent for a few moments, dismissed the matter from her mind. Less perceptive than the King in such matters, she could see no serious danger in the brilliant thoughts which the *philosophes* tossed back and forth while dining in the Palace in the cramped quarters of her own physician, Dr. Quesnay.

Generally the guests at Quesnay's dinners were Marmontel, Buffon, Turgot, d'Alembert, Duclos, Helvétius, and sometimes Voltaire, but he was too much of an egotist to get along with his colleagues. The Marquise could not induce the group to meet in her salon, but if the King was engaged elsewhere she frequently managed to slip away and join them around the table for coffee and conversation. Surely, she thought, there was no subversion here under the King's own roof; attached as she was to Louis, she would have been the last to condone it.

But Madame du Haussay, who went often to Quesnay's (some said they were lovers), related with her usual detachment an interesting conversation—a conversation which reveals the hatred and fear of the *philosophes* toward the religious party and the deep conflict of views which separated the liberals from the conservatives.

One evening [she said] I went to Doctor Quesnay's while Madame was at the theater. The Marquis de Mirabeau came in, and for a time the conversation was rather boring for me, being concerned only with economics. It soon became more interesting, however, when Mirabeau said, "I think the King looks very badly; he is aging rapidly."

"So much the worse," said Quesnay, "a thousand times so much the worse! It would be a catastrophe for France if he died." And he lifted his eyes to the ceiling and sighed deeply.

"I don't doubt that you love the King, and rightly so," said Mirabeau, "and I love him also; but I have never seen you so upset."

"Ah!" answered Quesnay, "I am thinking of what would follow."

"Well, what of it? The Dauphin is honorable."

"Yes, he is, and full of good intentions," said the Doctor, "and he has spirit; but the bigots will have an absolute empire with a King who looks upon them as oracles. The Jesuits will govern the State, as in the last days of Louis XIV, and you will see the fanatical Bishop of Verdun [the Dauphin's former tutor, Boyer] as Prime Minister. . . . Parlement will have no choice but to shut up, and it will not be treated any better than my friends the philosophes."

"But they go too far," interposed Mirabeau, "why attack religion so openly?"

"I agree," said the Doctor, "but how can one help being indignant at the fanaticism of the others, and how can one help remembering all the blood they have shed during the last two hundred years? Still, we must not irritate them too much, or France will be a repetition of England under Bloody Mary."

"You are right," agreed Mirabeau, "but after all the Dauphin is sensible and educated."

"It is the early part of his reign that I fear," insisted Quesnay, "when the imprudences of our friends will be shown to him in the most unfavorable way . . . and the Dauphine will egg him on . . . believe me, Monsieur, the times of John Huss and Jerome of Prague are coming back —but I hope that I will be dead before it happens!"

Although Quesnay was First Consulting Physician to the King and a devoted friend of the Marquise, his principal interest lay not in medicine but in rural economy. He is best remembered as the founder of the Physiocrats, who considered agriculture the most productive of all efforts and who urged the removal of governmental restraints on the distribution of agricultural products. In his *Tableau Économique* he argued these views, and although they were contrary to the Royal government's policy, a de-luxe edition of his book was printed at Versailles under the King's immediate supervision.

This was not so surprising as it appeared. Louis liked Quesnay because he kept aloof from Court intrigues and never sought to advance either himself or anyone else. Furthermore, the King was deeply interested in agriculture, and had a profound respect for the Doctor's superior mind. He nicknamed him *Le Penseur*—and when one saw Quesnay's face, looking like a kindly intelligent parrot, with his piercing small black eyes, large straight nose, and wide upper lip—the King's sobriquet seemed fitting. Doctor Quesnay was a level-headed man, a man hard to fool.

Generous as she was to all the *philosophes,* Madame de Pompadour went out of her way to placate Voltaire, her old acquaintance from Paris and Étioles. She was somewhat afraid of him, mistrusted his wicked pen and mercurial loyalty, and sought by a shower of favors to bind him to her.

The Marquise prevailed over Louis' aversion to Voltaire and had him appointed Historiographer of France— but that was not enough. Voltaire was insatiable in his demands. "I have treated him as well as Louis XIV treated Racine and Boileau," grumbled the King. "I made him a Gentleman of the Bedchamber, and gave him a pension. It is not my fault if he has made a fool of himself, aspires to be Chamberlain, to be given a Cross, and to dine with me. Such things are not done in France."

The truth is that Voltaire made a poor courtier. Ambitious as he was for recognition, avaricious as he was for money, he could not completely conceal his contempt for the fatuous emptiness of Court life, and he oscillated between extreme servility and excessive impertinence. He considered himself eligible for an Ambassadorship, and was outraged when the King refused to take his aspiration seriously. Despite his intelligence, he was petty and jealous and inevitably aroused the hostility of the other Gentlemen of the Bedchamber, who feared he would end up by ruling them all.

The Duc de Richelieu inflamed the King's suspicion that Voltaire was an ambitious flatterer and impious *philosophe*. Incongruous though it was for Richelieu to level the charge of impiety at anyone else, the shaft found its mark and the King came to despise Voltaire more than ever.

Voltaire wrote an opera, *Le Temple de la Gloire,* a brilliant story in which he compared Louis to the Emperor Trajan—worthy of the love of the world and to whom the temple of glory was a fitting abode—but his fulsome flattery fell on barren soil. After the performance the King pointedly ignored him, and Voltaire as usual overreached himself.

"Is Trajan satisfied?" he asked.

Louis froze with hauteur, and passed on without speaking.

Voltaire's enemies finally removed him by arousing his avid jealousy against Crébillon. The Marquise's former tutor had been a famous dramatist when Louis XIV was alive but was now half-starving in the Marais, one of the poorer districts of Paris. Voltaire's enemies told Madame de Pompadour that Crébillon was neglected because he was too honest for intrigues, and the Marquise, shocked, cried: "What! Crébillon forsaken!" She immediately obtained for him from the King a pension of 250 livres, and when Crébillon came to thank her she was enchanted by the octogenarian's fine tragic face and gallant charm. Being slightly ill, the Marquise was in bed, and just as the old man bent to kiss her hand, the King walked in.

"Ah, Madame," exclaimed Crébillon, "the King has surprised us, and I am ruined."

Louis was pleased by the adroit remark, and Crébillon's star rose again. He was granted quarters in the Louvre and appointed tutor to Madame de Pompadour's daughter. *Catilina,* his first work in nearly twenty years, was printed by the Louvre press at Royal expense, a signal honor which Voltaire had long sought and never attained. The courtiers, especially those who were enemies of Voltaire, were delighted at the venerable poet's success.

"He had dignity," they said, "but no pride, and still less conceit. His poverty was the proof of his honesty. He was an admirable character, and truly the man whose genius best honored the King's reign."

Voltaire fell into the trap prepared for him. He was so consumed with jealousy that he ceased to appear at Court and soon took himself off to Berlin to spend an uneasy two years with that masterly ruler and inferior poet, Frederick II. When Voltaire came to say good-by to Louis XV the King turned his back. Voltaire was so incensed at this contemptuous treatment that as soon as he was safely across the frontier he sent back his warrant as Historiographer.

The Marquise had requested Voltaire to pay her compliments to Frederick, and when he did so the misogynist King of Prussia replied coldly, "I do not know her." Voltaire reported the rude remark to Versailles in malicious haste, and Frederick acquired an undying enemy. During the Seven Years' War, when his back was to the wall and France was in the ranks of his foes, he must have regretted a thousand times the sarcastic remark that he had uttered about the Mistress of Louis XV.

Voltaire, still smarting at the favor which the Marquise had shown to Crébillon and forgetting or ignoring all that she had done for him, attacked her viciously in *La Pucelle*—far more viciously than Maurepas had dared in his infamous *Poissonade:*

> Telle plutôt cette heureuse grisette
> Que la nature ainsi que l'art forma
> Pour le bordel ou bien pour l'opéra,
> Qu'une maman avisée et discrète
> Au noble lit d'un Fermier éleva,
> Et que l'amour d'une main plus adroite
> Sous un Monarque entre deux draps plaça . . .

> Or rather like that lucky tart
> Whom nature as well as art has formed

For the bawdy house or else for the opera,
But whom her shrewd and discreet mama
Reared in a Farmer's noble bed,
And whom love with a more dexterous hand
Placed under a Monarch between two sheets . . .

It was not long before Voltaire and Frederick discovered
that the other's correspondence was more agreeable than
his presence, and they quarreled publicly and ludicrously
like two shrill women. Voltaire resented having to read
Frederick's clumsy poetry and complained that his job was
"to wash the King's dirty linen." When he was told that
his Royal host's comment had then been, "one may suck
the orange and throw away the peel," the Frenchman's
patience, all too short, gave way entirely.

He parted from Frederick, apparently calmly polite but
actually seething with inward fury, and found refuge in
Switzerland. There he was marooned, and Marmontel appealed to Madame de Pompadour, pointing out that Voltaire's return depended on her. "Ah, no," she sighed, "it
does not depend on me." She, usually so vindictive in
avenging an insult, had forgiven the incorrigible Voltaire,
but she knew quite well that she could never persuade
Louis, who said abruptly, "Let him remain where he is."
(Voltaire never returned to Paris during the lifetime of
Louis XV.)

Jean Jacques Rousseau, whose opera *Le Devin du Village* was a favorite in the repertoire of the Marquise's
theater, was present when his work was performed at Fontainebleau in the fall of 1752. The sage of Geneva arrived

looking like one of his "noble savages," unkempt and with a three days' growth of beard. The Marquise asked him to remain after the performance for presentation to the King, but Rousseau, so contemptuous from a distance of kings and nobility, was overawed by the magnificence which surrounded him and fled before the curtain came down. The next day he received a message saying that the King would like to receive him, but he ignored the Royal wish, probably fearing he would be ill at ease, and never came face to face with Louis. The next spring, when *Le Devin du Village* was presented at Bellevue, the last performance to be given there, the Marquise sent him 50 louis as a token of her admiration. Rousseau was lucky at that; royalties for composers were then unknown.

Buffon, the naturalist, although often attending Quesnay's dinners, never became one of the Marquise's slavish followers, but his independence was not, like Rousseau's, the result of unsociability. Buffon was faithfully attached to Marie Leczinska and thought that constant attendance upon the Marquise and the acceptance of favors from her would imply disloyalty and disrespect to the Queen. Although Madame de Pompadour was vexed that she could not win him over, she admired his principle, and when she died showed her trust by confiding to Buffon the care of her dog, her parrot, and her pet monkey.

Duclos, the historian, was another who had ample cause for gratitude to Madame de Pompadour, succeeding by her wish to the post of Historiographer so abruptly vacated by Voltaire; Montesquieu, author of *L'Esprit des Lois*, leaned gratefully on the assistance which the Marquise offered him; and Marmontel, only two years younger than the Favorite, owed practically his entire fortune to her unflagging support. Although he had written a number of pleasing verses about her and Louis, he first won her avowed favor when he wrote a laudatory poem on the completion of the École Militaire, which owed its inception to the Marquise.

Marmontel was exceptionally agreeable in manner, and the Marquise, always susceptible to personal charm, took an active interest in his writing and so added to *Les Funérailles de Sésostris* that it is almost her own work (it was a failure). When Marmontel, plagued by debts and despair, asked her for a position that would provide him a modest income, she found him a post under Marigny; but knowing her brother's touchiness and tendency to imagine slights when none were intended, she warned the young writer when he came to thank her: "Men of letters have an imaginary system of equality that often makes them forget decorum; I hope, Marmontel, that with respect to my brother you will not be guilty of this."

During this period Marmontel wrote his charming *Contes Moraux* to help Boissy, the editor of *Le Mercure de France*, increase its circulation. When Boissy died a few months later Madame de Pompadour, realizing Marmontel's talent, said to the King, "Sire, will you not give *Le Mercure* to him who has made it what it is?"

Louis consented willingly (he liked Marmontel's mixture of sunny cheerfulness and refined deference), and Marmontel received his discharge from Marigny. When he assumed the editorship of *Le Mercure de France*, he went to live at Madame Geoffrin's in Paris in order to be nearer his work.

Le Mercure de France was more than a mere literary paper. In addition to book reviews and news of fine arts and the theater, it printed articles on science and travel. It carried Buffon's pictures of natural history, articles by Leroi the architect and Cochin the engraver, and a discussion of the merits of inoculation. The eighteenth century was a period of intense interest in the natural sciences, and there were articles on chemistry, medicine (a new method for curing the bites of spiders), and astronomy (the return of Halley's comet). Furthermore, since the paper was subscribed to by provincials as well as Parisians, it was obliged, often to its editor's distaste, to print local news and samples of local poetical talent.

Because of an altercation with a nobleman, Marmontel fell into temporary disfavor, and *Le Mercure de France* was taken away from him; but the Marquise, although forced for a time to withdraw her active support, never deserted him. In 1763 a vacancy occurred in the Academy, to which Marmontel aspired, but the Immortals hesitated, fearing that the King would oppose his election. The Marquise then succeeded in extracting from Louis a promise not to oppose Marmontel, if he were chosen, and thus the writer owed the crowning recognition of his career to his patroness.

Undoubtedly the most famous literary work of the reign was the *Encyclopédie* edited by d'Alembert and Diderot. This epochal creation, eventually comprising seventeen volumes, was the work of many contributors, among them Voltaire, Quesnay, Turgot, Helvetius, Montesquieu, Rousseau, and Marmontel. The first volume appeared in July 1751, and its publication was greeted with cries of alarm from the Jesuits, who saw in its frank discussions of theology, philosophy, and government a threat to their power. It is undeniable that the *Encyclopédie* not only gave explanations but sought to guide opinion as well, and its views on religion were deistic, heretical, and even anti-Christian. It was not difficult for the Jesuits to persuade the King that the work was inimical to Church and State, and after three volumes were published the *Encyclopédie* was suppressed. The Jesuits then attempted to continue it themselves but soon gave up, finding, as Grimm said, that it was easier to destroy the *philosophes* than to complete the work.

Voltaire relates that one evening the King and some friends were dining at Trianon, and the conversation happened to turn to gunpowder; no one could agree on its composition.

"It is curious," remarked the Duc de Nivernois, "that we amuse ourselves every day killing partridges at Versailles, and sometimes killing men and getting killed ourselves on the frontier, and yet are ignorant of exactly what the killing is done with."

"Unfortunately," interposed Madame de Pompadour, "we are in the same predicament about everything. I don't know how they mix the rouge I put on my cheeks, and if anyone asked me how my silk stockings are made, I would not know how to answer."

"It is a pity," said the Duc de la Vallière, "that His

Majesty has confiscated our *Encyclopédies*. . . . We should soon find in them an answer to all our questions."

The King defended the confiscation, and said that he had been warned that the volumes that were to be found on every lady's dressing table were the most dangerous thing possible for France. He intended to find out for himself whether this was true or not before allowing people to read the book, [and] when supper was over he sent for the *Encyclopédie*. . . .

It was then seen from the article on "Powder" that the Duc de la Vallière's prescription for gunpowder had been right; while the Marquise found out the difference between the old rouge of Spain . . . and the rouge used by the ladies of Paris. She found that the Greek and Roman ladies were painted with the purple that comes from the murex, and that our scarlet is the purple of the ancients; that there was more saffron in the rouge of Spain and more cochineal in that of France. She also learned how her stockings were made by a loom, and the machine filled her with astonishment.

"What a wonderful book!" she exclaimed. "Sire, you have confiscated a veritable storehouse of useful information. If one possesses it, one has at one's command all the wisdom of your kingdom."

But Louis' distrust remained, and the Marquise, although fully sympathizing with the opinions of the *Encyclopédistes*, felt she was unable to do more to aid them. When Frederick II offered d'Alembert a pension of 1,200 livres, the Marquise begged Louis to double it, pointing out that Prussia's gain would be France's loss, but the King, horrified at d'Alembert's views on religion, refused.

Another of Madame de Pompadour's contributions to the welfare of France was the founding of the École Militaire. Drawing her inspiration from St. Cyr, which Madame de Maintenon had established for young ladies of noble birth, the Marquise conceived the idea of a military school where the sons of poor nobles could receive an education at the expense of the government.

Fearing the expense involved, the King was at first cool to the idea, and the Ministers and the public were openly hostile. But the Marquise, reinforced by Pâris-Duverney, persisted, and Louis finally signed the edict establishing the École Militaire on January 22, 1751. It was to be financed by a tax on playing cards and Pâris-Duverney was placed in charge of its construction.

Marigny, by now Superintendent of Buildings, resented this and quarreled fiercely with Pâris-Duverney, calling him a swindler and so offending him that the financier refused to have anything more to do with the project and demanded his money back. All the Marquise's tact was needed to persuade him to overlook the affront, but even so the enterprise almost collapsed from lack of funds. Madame de Pompadour had so set her heart on the school that she went heavily into debt and even pledged her income for a year in order to pay the workmen, but, as she wrote Pâris-Duverney, "it will make known to posterity my devotion to the State."

Her persistence and unselfishness were rewarded when the École Militaire opened its doors in July 1756. It had accommodations for 500 boys from the ages of ten to twenty, who, in order to be admitted, had to prove four generations of nobility on at least one side of their family. Exceptions were allowed, however, for the sons of officers who had fallen in battle or died of wounds; these orphans were given preference over the sons of nobles who had not served their country in war.

The cadets were formed into ten companies which were given distinctive insignia by His Majesty. When their education was completed they were commissioned as officers in the Army and given a pension of 200 livres to support their rank. Many able officers of France owed their educations and careers to the courage and foresight of a frail woman, among them one who did much to destroy everything for which her King had stood—a sallow undersized Corsican by the name of Bonaparte.

XV

LOVE TO FRIENDSHIP TURNED

IN JULY *1749* the Marquis d'Argenson wrote in his journal about the Marquise—for once accurately—that "she had a miscarriage during the past Lent, and that during that time the King never left her. His affection has redoubled, and since then she is more a Favorite than ever. . . ."

Since d'Argenson did not say, it is reasonable to assume he did not know that this was the third time the delicate Mistress had undergone such an ordeal since she came to Versailles four years before. The miscarriages, always dangerous in those unsanitary days of septic surgery, exacted an obvious toll, and d'Argenson went on to say, with more truth than malice, that "the Marquise de Pompadour is changed, and changes daily, so that she is now almost a skeleton."

It was true that the Marquise, although not yet thirty, was in a precarious state of health. The repeated miscarriages had thoroughly wrecked her already defective organs in ways that are impossible for us to ascertain, but undoubtedly the ministrations of eighteenth-century doctors, no matter how skilled, had damaged her physiologically as well as psychologically. Her nerves became more unstable than ever, and she found sleep unattainable without .the aid of drugs. At the slightest exertion she suffered violent palpitations of the heart, and she began to fear the loss of her sight. To a physician today her prominent eyes, labored breathing and irregular heart, combined with her chronic fatigue, fragile physique and large appetite, would indicate a toxic goiter; measured by even the limited medical knowledge of her time, it was obvious that her body was doing its best to burn itself up. No wonder the doctors warned her and Louis that their physical relations must come to an end.

The Marquise received this announcement with mixed emotions. The promise of surcease from physical contact, which had long been to her a necessary evil and almost an agony, offered to her aching body the rest it so desperately demanded. She knew too, as did no one else, how impatient Louis was growing at her cold caresses and absence of passion.

His eyes turned with increasing interest to other women, and Madame de Pompadour inevitably came to realize, as her friend the Maréchale de Mirepoix warned her, that "it is your staircase that the King is fond of. He is accustomed to going up and down it, but if he were to find another woman to whom he could talk about hunting and his other interests, it would all be the same to him at the end of three days."

The Marquise, determined that he should not find that woman, was now face to face with the most difficult problem of her life—how to exchange the ties of love for the

less exacting but more permanent ties of friendship. Louis'
nature being what it was, she knew that she must rely upon
his enslavement to habit and retain by her mind what she
could never hold by her body.

Gradually, almost imperceptibly, with infinite patience
and skill, she once again accomplished the seemingly impossible—but not without ineffable sadness. She knew
that her days of youth were gone and that her days of love,
at least love of the senses, were swallowed forever in
memory. No woman, no matter how frigid, can surrender
her lover without profound sorrow for the past and
measureless fear for the future.

Her devoted Marshal Saxe died in 1750, and the Marquise wept unrestrainedly when his last words were repeated to her: "This is the end of a noble dream." The
words of pathos seemed to apply to her own life, and when
she remembered the shining visions which had dazzled the
mind of Reinette and Madame d'Étioles—how long ago it
was!—she was filled with melancholy almost insupportable.

"Do not send me Marshal Saxe's funeral sermon," she
wrote to a friend. "When I think of his death I am overcome with sorrow." Certainly her grief for Maurice was
real, but there was also grief for herself and mourning in
her heart for a chapter in her life which was closed forever.

She had reached the summit, and although she was to
acquire more power than ever before, it was not to bring
her happiness. It never occurred to the Marquise to adopt
the simplest course and withdraw from Court—for her
ambitious nature such a retreat would have been worse
than death. Sincerely devoted to Louis and desperately

anxious to retain her possessions, privileges, and position, she clung to the King with all the determination of her tenacious mind, and before the Court realized what had happened, she had gracefully assumed her new role— that of the King's Friend.

As an unmistakable signal to the Court that her relationship with the King had fundamentally altered, the Marquise, in the spring of 1751, said farewell to her upstairs apartments—those small delicate rooms which had been the abode of love for nearly five years. A handsome new suite on the ground floor had been prepared for her. The new apartment, which was connected to the King's Little Cabinets by a private staircase, was handsomely decorated, its crowning glory being a room finished entirely in red lacquer.

This room, in which the Marquise was to spend much of the next thirteen years, gradually became an unofficial Prime Minister's office, the center of all power. Gone were the days when she held her public *toilette,* surrounded by a smiling group of envious courtiers—she had more serious work to do now, and the lacquer room came to know the highest State secrets. When she had been in every sense the King's Mistress, she could take or leave politics as she pleased, being careful only that no enemy was free to destroy her; but in her new role she was forced into greater political activity.

Now that she and Louis were no longer lovers, now that she did not have to rely upon a weak sexual impulse to maintain her position, the Marquise acquired over the

King a stronger hold than ever—a different hold but one far more durable. She became more than ever his confidante, his companion and, in a peculiarly European sense, almost his wife. Marie Leczinska was no more than a crowned symbol who had never understood Louis; it was the Marquise who gave him understanding and companionship. Realizing her keen knowledge of his nature and following long-ingrained habit, Louis talked to her as he could talk to no one else and knew that he could always rely upon her for disinterested advice and unfailing assistance.

Madame called me one day [wrote Madame du Haussay], and I went into her room, where the King was walking up and down with a preoccupied air.

"You must go," she ordered, "and spend several days at St. Cloud, to a place which I will show you. You will find there a young girl ready to give birth. You will run the house and preside like a goddess at the *accouchement;* you will assist at the baptism and indicate the names of the father and mother."

The King, who had remained silent, began to laugh, and said, "The father is a very honest man."

Madame added, "Loved by everyone and adored by those who know him." She then went to a little armoire and took from it a small box which she opened. It contained a diamond aigrette which she showed to the King, saying, "This is good enough for her; I think, for discretion's sake, that it should not be too handsome."

The King hugged Madame, saying, "How kind you are!"

She wept softly, and putting her hand on the King's heart, whispered, "This is all I ask for."

Tears came into the King's eyes, and I began to cry also without very well knowing why. . . .

"All of these little shop girls who have no education,"
the Marquise explained later, "do not frighten me. I would
not be so tranquil, though, if I saw some beautiful woman
of Versailles or Paris try to conquer him."

The little shop girls entered Louis' life in growing
numbers, sometimes augmented by girls of respectable
families from the lower-middle class. Next to the valet
Lebel's room in the Palace was a chamber which came
to be known as *Le Trébuchet*—the Bird Trap—and not
without reason. The King's valets, and sometimes the
subalterns of the guard, procured for the Master young
women whom they thought would appeal to his taste and
hustled them into *Le Trébuchet*. If the King was pleased
with a girl, he moved her to a house in the town of
Versailles, kept her there until he grew weary, and then
married her off with a generous dowry.

This continuous procession in and out of *Le Trébuchet*
was sordid, the first sign of the King's increasing debauchery, but it was managed with the utmost discretion. The
Marquise, understanding that Louis' affairs with these
ignorant girls were from habit rather than serious need,
could afford to be complaisant. That she acquiesced without jealousy is true, but that she lowered herself to become
the King's procuress is a lie invented by her enemies.
Louis did not require such a service from her—his valets
were only too diligent.

The Marquise had not chosen her new quarters hap-
hazardly; as with her every action, a soundly calculated
reason motivated it.

Madame de Pompadour is going to be installed in the apartments of M. and Madame de Penthièvres [wrote de Luynes] . . . no one says the reason, but it is not difficult to guess it.

Madame de Pompadour understands the King: she knows that he has religion, and that his reflections and the sermons he hears cause him remorse and uneasiness; she knows that he truly loves her but that serious thoughts prevail over everything with him . . . and that if he found within his family a congeniality which would keep him quietly and pleasantly occupied, it might be that, having no violent passion to get over, he would prefer to sacrifice his present relationship to his duty.

She had noticed his fondness for Mesdames. . . . As it is probable that Madame Sophie and Madame Louise will soon be returning from Fontevrault [the convent where Mesdames were educated] and that a rearrangement of accommodations will be necessary, it was easy to foresee . . . that the King might give these apartments to Mesdames Henriette and Adélaïde and get in the habit of going down there and even taking supper. It is precisely that which the Marquise wished to prevent.

Madame Henriette actually did want the apartments for herself. Usually good natured, she became extremely irritated when they were given to Madame de Pompadour and protested that "whether the Marquise is lodged on the top floor or the bottom, the King my father will go there none the less, and the only difference will be whether he goes up to come down or goes down to come up; but as for me, a Princess of France, I cannot live up there, in the attic."

The coveted rooms fell to the Marquise, but the year after she moved in, Madame Adélaïde was given the apartments next to her. (Madame Henriette, the King's most

intelligent daughter after Madame l'Infante, had meanwhile died of a putrid fever.) Nothing could more clearly
indicate the changed status of the Marquise than for the
King to make Madame Adélaïde her immediate neighbor,
for dissolute though Louis was, he was rigid when it came
to his daughters' purity. The Marquise remarked to Madame du Haussay that no punishment was too great for the
King to inflict on the man who seduced one of his daughters. It never entered His Majesty's head that hundreds of
his subjects must have felt the same sentiments toward him.

Shortly after Madame Adélaïde had returned from
school, she "saw a young guardsman, extraordinarily handsome and well built; she sent him a beautiful snuff-box
containing a note which read, 'Let this be precious to you
—you will soon learn from whom it comes.' The soldier,
astonished, carried the box to his captain, the Duc d'Ayen,
who told the story to the King. Louis asked to see the box,
and recognized it as one he had given his daughter. He
[gave] the guardsman a pension of 4,000 livres, and made
him promise to go for a long time to a distant part of the
Kingdom. One must expect such violent actions from a
young princess twenty years old, strong and healthy like
Madame Adélaïde."

Like father, like daughter; but Madame Adélaïde, unlike Louis, never found the freedom to indulge herself.
For the rest of her long life she was doomed to shrewish
virginity.

A rewarding result of the Marquise's transformation into
"The Friend" was her improved treatment by the Royal
children. They knew, as did everyone at Versailles, that

the secret staircase had been walled up and that when
the King now visited the Marquise he entered by the front
door—and only as a friend. Even the stubborn Dauphin
went out of his way, at Choisy, to be pleasant to the
Marquise in marked contrast to his customary rudeness.

"The next day," said Croÿ, "Mesdames and their ladies
came to dine at Choisy and spend the night. The Marquise,
having been drawn into the Royal Family during the last
two years and having won them over by her respectful
attentions, has so gained their confidence that she is on
good terms with all of them, especially the Queen."

Describing a visit to La Muette in the same year (1753),
Croÿ painted a picture of family affection that would have
been unthinkable if Madame de Pompadour had still been
the King's Mistress: "M. le Dauphin was there, Mesdames
came, and I saw almost all of the Royal Family that day.
Since the Marquise has arranged it, they come on all the
trips, and that evening, when she left the table with a headache, all of them, one after the other, went to ask her how
she was feeling."

The Marquise, spurned for so long by her lover's
children, must have felt a glow of satisfaction when they,
rather timidly and sheepishly, repaid in some small measure the respect and courtesy she had always displayed to
them.

The King, too, sensing the inevitable hurt which their
changed relationship caused to her woman's pride, and
grateful that she had effected the transformation so
smoothly, paid her unusual honors; in 1752 he granted
her the rank and privileges of a Duchess. She now had the

right to sit with the Royal Family at the public dinners; she was entitled to an armchair like a Princess of the Blood; and her coach, flaunting the ducal arms, could proceed into the innermost courtyards of the Royal Palaces.

For the garden of Bellevue the Marquise commissioned Pigalle to execute a statue to replace one which had represented Love. Marie Leczinska, happening one day to be strolling through the grounds, came upon the marble figure of a chaste nymph whose features bore a haunting resemblance to the Marquise. Noting with approval the statue's attitude of purity and dignity, the Queen asked the gardener by what name the spot was known.

"It is the Grove of Friendship, Madame," he replied. "It was once called the Grove of Love."

The Marquise had learned to fear the hidden sting, and she knew that the details of her private relations with the King would soon provide fuel for every arsonist of malice at Versailles. She had not long to wait.

"In the King's stables," wrote the relentless d'Argenson, "there is a hunting mare named La Marquise, which the King rode for a long time and now never mounts. Last week M. d'Ecquevilly, returning from a hunt and finding no place in the carriages, mounted a horse and rode home. The King asked him how he came back, and he replied, 'On that old Marquise Your Majesty no longer rides.' Everyone laughed uproariously at the allusion to the Favorite who is now only a friend."

The most serious danger that threatened the Marquise during the period when physical love was dying came not from any fair woman but from a rival infinitely more formidable—Mother Church. Although 1750 had been the Jubilee Year in Rome, its celebration in France was scheduled for 1751. A Jubilee Year was a period when the faithful were supposed to avail themselves of the merits of the Saints with special fervor and a time when flagrant sinners were supposed to be reconciled to the Church. Would Louis go to confession, and approach the altar rail to accept the Sacrament?

As Barbier observed: "The King can hardly remain at Versailles without making his Jubilee [communion]. Public opinion is carried to the point of respecting the Jubilee more than the Easter duties which are obligatory. If he makes his communion, he cannot return to the Marquise a fortnight later, and a month's absence would be dangerous."

Madame de Pompadour was indeed terrified that the King would receive the Sacrament, fearing it would mean her ruin. Had not Father Griffet based his Lenten sermon on the woman taken in adultery? She had afterward noticed that the King consulted frequently with the priest, and the Jesuits were boasting openly that they were saying fifteen masses every morning for the King's return to the Sacraments.

The Marquise knew only too well how much Louis dreaded the feasts of the Church and into what searchings of conscience and sadness of soul they plunged him. The Jubilee so affected him that he changed his hunting days in order to attend religious services, and one day, when sending alms to a poor man, he exclaimed, "Let this poor

man ask God to show mercy to me, for I greatly need it!"
As for Madame de Pompadour, she became almost ill from
the strain, and wags in Paris joked that she suffered from
"Jubilee fever."

In April of 1751, as if the atmosphere was not gloomy
enough, there occurred an event which held ominous implications for the Marquise's security—the death of Madame
de Mailly. The former Mistress had led an exemplary life
of charity and penance since leaving Versailles, and had
sought by her sincere humility to atone for her years with
Louis.

A workman, recognizing her one day in Church,
sneered, "There goes the King's discarded whore."

"Since you recognize her," replied Madame de Mailly
gently, "pray for her."

When she died it was discovered that she was wearing
a hair shirt, and when she was buried her body was laid,
according to her instructions, among the paupers of
Potter's Field. Her death, coming when it did, held a
dramatic quality which could not be ignored. Everyone
inevitably contrasted the Christian end of the Mistress
who had unselfishly loved Louis with the glittering,
gorgeously dressed Marquise whose every action seemed
to betray her extravagance and love of power. So it seemed
to the public; how, in this year of Jubilee, did it affect the
King, unduly morbid as he was even in normal times?
Would Madame de Mailly's untimely death provide the
necessary impetus to send him penitent into the waiting
arms of the Church?

When the news was broken to Louis, "he did not sup

with the courtiers in the cabinets, and he seemed much troubled and wept, but they say *that piety still does not enter into it.* The Marquise consoles him as best she can, and certainly we owe obligations to that lady for preventing the King from falling into one of those maladies that arise from *ennui;* it must be admitted that she benefits his health, forces him to move about, amuses him and encourages him."

The Marquise hovered over the King as a physician over a dying patient, snatching only a moment to write to her brother: "Poor Madame de Mailly is dead. I am really upset over it; she was unhappy, and the King is moved by it."

In order to lift Louis from his depression, Madame de Pompadour trotted forth from her stable of amusements every distraction she could think of—trips to Choisy and Trianon, plays at Bellevue, politics, plans for the beautification of Paris, and the launching of the École Militaire.

In her schemes to remove the shadow of remorse from the King's conscience, the Marquise was ably assisted by Machault. Together they concocted a diabolically clever subterfuge which would remove the necessity of Louis' taking communion.

"She will see to it," wrote the Prussian envoy to Frederick, "that the publication of the Jubilee is not effective at the same time for the entire Kingdom, but only by dioceses; so that, when the Jubilee is in effect in Versailles and Paris, the King will be at Compiègne, where it will not yet have been proclaimed, and then, when the time for it comes at Compiègne, the King of France will find

himself ready to return to Versailles, where the Jubilee
will already have been held."

How Frederick and his guest Voltaire, skeptics and
cynics to the core of their natures, must have shaken with
laughter at the spectacle of these devious devices designed
to restrain His Most Christian Majesty from approaching
the Table of his Saviour! But the Marquise won—1751
approached its end, the Archbishop of Paris declared the
Jubilee closed on December 29, and Louis XV had not
made his Jubilee Duty. Madame de Pompadour's danger
was over, but the memory of her fright led her to take steps
to conciliate her unyielding enemy, the Church.

There was another reason why the Marquise was anxious
to make her peace with the Church. No longer the Mistress,
she aspired to be the devoted friend, the dispenser of disinterested advice, and—if she could—the ruler behind the
scenes. She wished to invest her new position with respectability, and for this the good will of the Church was essential.

Bernis says that the Marquise did not hate the Jesuits
when she came to Versailles, although it stands to reason
that her views and theirs were antithetical. Although her
first approaches to them had been rebuffed, she decided
after the Jubilee Year to make another attempt. Consequently she summoned Father de Sacy, a Jesuit whom she
had known in Paris, and confided to him that she wished
to be reconciled to the Church. She explained that she and
the King were no longer lovers and that her desire to
remain at Court was motivated solely by the hope of being

a salutary influence upon him. Father de Sacy spent many hours discussing with her the attitude of the Church, and the Marquise listened with every sign of devotion and respect. She admitted that she did not feel that inclination and taste for devotion which she would like to have but that she hoped by prayer to obtain it.

The Prince de Croÿ saw her hurrying to Mass early one morning before the servants were up, "without affectation and manifesting a real piety." Croÿ, who really liked Madame de Pompadour and was willing to believe the best of her, said, "I have always foreseen and predicted for more than four years that little by little she would become pious with the King, and that then her favor would reach its peak."

Was the Marquise, then, really sincere in her new devotion to religion? In a sense, yes. She was willing to manifest the outward forms, and she was anxious to receive the Sacraments, but she had no intention whatever of changing her mode of life.

Father de Sacy was at first inclined to be lenient until sharply checked by his superiors. Madame de Pompadour never understood the Jesuits nor why they hated her, but the men of the Society of Jesus never labored under any illusions about her. Knowing that the Marquise was the devoted friend of the *philosophes,* they doubted the sincerity of her new-found religion; if they cloaked her with respectability by granting her Absolution they might prolong the power of one who could never be their friend.

Moreover, by appeasing the Marquise they ran the risk of alienating their devoted pupil the Dauphin, who was already bitterly protesting at de Sacy's leniency. The Jesuits sometimes despaired of converting Louis XV to a life of piety, and the King was now in his forties; but the Dauphin, of whose support they were sure, was young and the future lay with him.

The future they dared not risk, and so Father de Sacy was instructed to inform the Marquise that Absolution was impossible unless she withdrew from Versailles and returned to her husband.

Retirement from Court formed no part of the Marquise's plan, but at the suggestion of the astute Machault, she pretended to acquiesce and wrote to her estranged husband. She confessed the wrong she had done him (eleven years before) and begged his forgiveness.

"Already my sin has ceased, and all that is necessary is to end the appearance of it—something which I ardently desire. I am resolved by my future conduct to atone for my past wrongs. Take me back; you will find me anxious to edify the world by the harmony of our life as much as I scandalized it by leaving you"—a touching letter, ringing with sincerity—sincerity somewhat blunted, however, by a private message carried to M. Le Normant d'Étioles by the Prince de Soubise who informed the husband that, although his wife was truly penitent, the King would be highly displeased if M. d'Étioles accepted her offer to return.

Le Normant d'Étioles did not require the hint. Living happily with Mademoiselle Rem and their children, he considered his faithless wife dead and her threatened return to his bed anything but a favor. With a straight face, adopting the same tone as the Marquise, he replied on February 6, 1756:

"I have received, Madame, your letter in which you inform me of your determination to return to me and your desire to surrender yourself to God. I cannot but admire such a resolution. I can well understand that it would be very embarrassing for you to see me, and you must agree that my feelings would be the same. Your presence can only intensify painful memories.

"Therefore, the best course for us is to live apart. No matter how much dissatisfaction you have caused me, I believe that you are concerned for my honor, and I should regard it as compromised if I received you in my house and lived with you as my wife. You are aware that time cannot alter what honor demands."

Armed with her husband's refusal to take her back, the Marquise felt herself invulnerable. She had followed Father de Sacy's orders and it was not her fault if M. d'Étioles would have none of her. Nothing, she thought, now stood in the way of her receiving Absolution.

Unfortunately, Father de Sacy learned of the hint which had been conveyed to M. d'Étioles and, now adamant, insisted that the Marquise retire from Court if she wished Absolution. The Marquise flew into a rage and promptly dismissed him from her presence, warning "that he would do better to attend to religion rather than to intrigue." From that day she abominated the Society of Jesus, and within a few years its members would have good reason to regret their refusal to treat the Marquise de Pompadour as Christ treated the Magdalene.

The Marquise succeeded in finding a more understanding (secular) priest, discovered for her by, of all people, Barryer, her accommodating Lieutenant of Police! Her new confessor proved obligingly merciful, absolved her of her sins, and saw nothing wrong in her remaining at Court.

Bernis, no zealot but thoroughly shocked at this mockery, told her that the comedy had fooled no one, that she would only be thought false and hypocritical, and that as her heart was not touched, piety would soon end by tiring her. Moreover, she made herself ridiculous by taking up devotion and would make herself still more so by dropping it from boredom.

"My prediction did not please her," added the brave Abbé, "but it came true to the letter." And so it did, for having obtained what she wanted, the Marquise soon grew tired of simulating piety and going so often to Mass, and dropping her aspirations to become another Maintenon she reverted to what she was—Madame de Pompadour, darling of the *philosophes*.

The Marquise's apparent reconciliation with the Church, if not the Jesuits, brought about the realization of one of her most ardent desires—to be named Lady in Waiting to the Queen. When Louis had first requested the Queen to make the appointment, Marie Leczinska demurred, observing that a woman who was separated from her husband and denied the Sacraments of the Church could not decently fill so honorable a position. The King, having no answer, let the matter drop.

But after the Marquise found a confessor and made her Easter Duty, the Queen was again confronted with her husband's request. "It was pointed out to her that it would be an heroic act on her part to forget the past; that all scandal would be obliterated when it was seen that what retained Madame de Pompadour at Court was an honorable position, and that this would be the best of all proofs that nothing but friendship existed any longer between the King and his Favorite."

The submissive Queen yielded and sent the Duchesse de Luynes secretly to tell the Marquise of her promotion. "My dear," Madame de Pompadour said to Madame du Haussay one evening after she had gone to bed, "you are going to be very pleased; the Queen is making me a Lady in Waiting and tomorrow I am to be presented. You must make me look very handsome."

"This was the time," according to Madame du Haussay, "when Madame appeared to me to be the most contented."

She had reason to be; even the pious at Court for a time sang her praises and did not hesitate to visit her. Their attitude was summed up by a courtier who said: "It is conjectured that she will remain the King's Friend; she will be the conciliator between husband and wife, the arbiter and channel of favors to the Royal Family, regular in the practice of religion, if not devout, charitable and irreproachable in conduct, the friend of everyone—in other words, playing at Court a great role and one worthy of a noble mind."

That is the role the Marquise would have liked to play, and she succeeded—at least in part.

XVI

THE STORM-SWEPT GARDEN

*T*O *THE* casual observer, Madame de Pompadour's new life might have seemed preferable to the days when she had been forced to rely upon the unstable prop of simulated passion. Her relations with the Royal Family had immeasurably improved, and her political influence was approaching its summit; as the King's friend she reigned as unofficial Prime Minister of France, her power virtually unchecked except by an occasional rare mood of Royal stubbornness.

One by one she had destroyed or neutralized a long list of those who had stood in her path—Orry, the Marquis d'Argenson, Maurepas, and Richelieu. The courtiers concluded that her power would continue indefinitely, and while their hatred and envy were as strong as ever, they concealed their feelings beneath protestations of loyalty and smiles of friendship.

But the Marquise was too realistic to be deceived; she knew that she walked by day and by night on the brink of a precipice and that one false step would be her last. She searched the King's impassive countenance for telltale signs of ennui, and she listened with a little smile on her lips to the gossip of the Court, suspecting in every furtive whisper a plot against her. The price of her security was unceasing vigilance.

This perpetual struggle to maintain her foothold on the slippery steps which led to the Throne cost her untold emotional anguish. Her essential nature, once so soft, so gentle and agreeable, hardened in the relentless pursuit of ambition, and discordant notes of vengefulness and cynicism marred the harmony of her disposition. Her success clashed with her gentler self, and she must have felt guilty for her shortcomings as a mother.

Not that Alexandrine d'Étioles lacked for any luxury or, for that matter, affection from her mother—when she saw her. But the Marquise, her days crammed with distractions, intrigues, suppers, parties, and gambling, had all too little time to give to her child, and the uneasy knowledge of her neglect lay deep within her. She was too middle class not to feel a strong sense of responsibility for her daughter, and she knew that in a vital sense she was not living up to it.

Suddenly the cruelest loss a mother can experience struck the Marquise—a loss for which she was totally unprepared. Alexandrine, while at evening services in the convent chapel, became violently nauseated and was taken to her bed suffering from chills and fever. The child was bled, but such witless treatment was ineffectual against what was probably acute appendicitis, and the small patient lapsed into convulsions. The King sent two of his doctors, but they reached Paris too late; on June 14, 1754, less than a day after she became ill, Alexandrine was dead.

The grief of the Marquise was terrible to witness. Louis, ordinarily so shy in expressing sympathy, was the quintessence of kindness, and the considerate Queen sent a comforting message to the stricken mother, who was weeping incessantly and passing from one swoon to another. While the Marquise was grateful for the Royal Family's attentiveness, their compassion could not restore her child, and her heart lay desolate within her.

Alexandrine was buried in the Convent of the Assumption where she had disputed precedence over the other little girls, but within a few months her body was reinterred in the Church of the Capuchins, where the Marquise had purchased a handsome vault from the family of Créqui.

The Marquise had not recovered from her shock when she received another: M. Poisson, now seventy and griefstricken at the death of his adored grandchild, was carried off by an attack of dropsy less than two weeks after her death. For the Marquise her father's death was almost an anticlimax, but with his passing went the last remnants of her childhood. When Alexandrine and M. Poisson were lowered into their graves, another was buried with them—the tender, affectionate girl who had been called Reinette. There remained only the Marquise de Pompadour, clever, brilliant and still beautiful, bearing where her heart had been a storm-swept garden.

Alexandrine's death seriously affected her mother's health, increasing an already marked tendency to heart trouble. The right auricle of the organ became dilated, intensifying her palpitations, kidney complications developed, and her digestion, deranged by grief and constant worry, became unstable. Her respiratory system, always susceptible to infection, worsened, the tonsils became inflamed, and she endured agonizing paroxysms of coughing which left her gasping for breath.

The treatment which the doctors prescribed for these manifold ills of her body, while acceptable in the eighteenth century, were hardly therapeutic. For diseases of the heart digitalis was unknown, and bleeding was the accepted treatment—not a beneficial treatment for the Marquise, who was always inclined to anemia. To relieve her kidney ailment and costiveness, a diet of asses' milk and copious quantities of *eau de Miers,* a mineral water high in sulfur content, was prescribed; but the one treatment upon which all her doctors agreed, the one which would have most benefited her—complete physical and mental rest—was, from the strenuous nature of her life, impossible for her to follow.

There is a world of pathos in a letter which the stricken Marquise wrote to the King, accompanying the gift of a wallet which she had embroidered with silver thread and a piece of her own hair, woven into a garland:

"Sire, I am ill, dangerously perhaps. In the melancholy that overcomes me, I wish to leave you a souvenir which will always keep me in your memory. I have embroidered this wallet with my hair—accept it, and do not ever let it leave you. Put your most important papers in it, so that its contents might reflect the opinion you have of it. Will you not grant my prayer? Sign it, I beg of you, it is the whim of illness."

Underneath, in the King's handwriting, was his reply:

"This token of affection will never leave me. *Louis.*"

More than ten years later, after Madame de Pompadour was dead and Madame Du Barry shone radiantly at Versailles, the King carelessly gave her the wallet. Wonderingly, she took it to Madame de Mirepoix, who had been the Marquise's loyal friend. Together they extracted the letter and read, with tears in their eyes, the words which an unhappy woman had written in the hour of her deepest sorrow.

Slowly the Marquise recovered her physical strength and resumed the outward routine of her busy existence. She dried her tears and concealed the marks of sorrow, for the King grew restless and irritated in the presence of sustained grief. She knew that for her now there was no choice but to follow the ambitious road she had charted, sustained only by the King's trust and friendship. Even of that she could not be too sure, and her brother, the only one of her family remaining to her, was too moody and self-conscious to respond with warmth to her feeling for him. Meanwhile, she was troubled by the threatening presence of one powerful enemy she had not yet destroyed —the Comte d'Argenson, the most dangerous of all.

The mordant Minister of War had watched, incredulously and then with growing dismay, the successive ruin of his older brother and the other enemies of the Marquise. The Comte d'Argenson was a brilliant Minister who had, since taking office in 1743, thoroughly reorganized the Army and introduced into it much-needed reforms, although his older brother sneered that "he goes at great things by little means." He was the senior Minister of the Council and, because he flattered Louis and spared him the tiresome details of government, the Monarch's favorite. D'Argenson made the King believe that he alone was his friend at Court, assiduously furthered his influence, and in the fierce pursuit of his ambition to become Prime Minister met but one obstacle—Madame de Pompadour.

The Marquise had no reason to love d'Argenson, who had repeatedly ignored her suggestions in filling vacancies. And he knew that so long as her reign continued, his chances of advancement were hopeless; within his brain gnawed the incessant fear that she would eventually get rid of him as she had the others. He resolved to destroy her but he moved slowly, for he was a perfect courtier, as polished as his brother was crude, as earnest as Maurepas was flippant.

He dissembled his hatred, and although the Marquise was not deceived by his cordiality, she outwardly accepted his apparent friendliness at its face value. Knowing the King's attachment to d'Argenson, she felt that she too must move cautiously.

The courtiers were treated to the spectacle of the War Minister giving a dinner for the Favorite and were equally astonished when he was the only Minister invited to spend the night on the first visit of the King to Bellevue. But behind these amenities a fierce struggle was underway between the two antagonists for the allegiance of Machault.

The Comptroller-General owed his post as much to d'Argenson as to Madame de Pompadour, for at the time of Orry's fall it had been the Minister of War who had backed Machault for the post, blocking the scheduled appointment of a creature of the Pârises. Furthermore Machault's mistress, Madame de St. Florentin, detested the Marquise, and urged him to side with d'Argenson. In the end, however, the Marquise bought his loyalty by obtaining for him the coveted post of Keeper of the Seals. She could hardly have been disappointed later to discover that purchased loyalty is never more than transient!

The Comte d'Argenson, unknown to the Marquise, achieved a triumph of cunning when he simultaneously acquired a mistress and a spy—none other than her own cousin by marriage, the Comtesse d'Estrades. This fat and ugly woman owed everything to the Marquise—her position as Lady in Waiting to Mesdames and, still more valuable, her inclusion in the group of intimates who attended the Little Suppers. But Madame d'Estrades, far from being grateful, was devoured by jealousy and not only reported to d'Argenson everything she saw and heard in the Marquise's apartments (where she was a trusted visitor), but dared go further:

"This Madame d'Estrades, who would have been nothing had it not been for the kindness of Madame," wrote Madame du Haussay most indignantly, "ugly as she was, had the gall to try to seduce the King. One day at Choisy, when he was a little drunk—the only time, I think, that it ever happened to him—he went for a boat ride. Madame, being ill with indigestion, could not accompany him, and Madame d'Estrades seized her chance. . . . It was dark when they returned, and she followed the King into a secret room where she made advances to him. . . . That same night she told Madame that the King had followed *her* into the room and tried to violate her. She was safe in giving her version of the story, because the King knew neither what she had said nor what she had done."

Madame d'Estrades had a niece at Court, Madame de Choiseul-Romanet, a young bride of nineteen. Urged on by d'Argenson, the Comtesse filled the young girl's head with dreams of seducing the King and overthrowing the Marquise. In the beginning Louis was only amused at what he considered a meaningless flirtation, but his amusement changed to interest when Madame de Choiseul let it be known throughout the Palace that she would never be unfaithful to her husband *except with the King* (where had Louis heard that before?).

He made several appointments with the young woman, during one of which he fell on a dark stair and almost broke his leg, but to his bewilderment she steadily refused to surrender herself. Her reluctance was not attributable to virtue, but to the astute coaching of d'Argenson and Madame d'Estrades, who had instructed her to withstand the King's advances until she had secured his promise to dismiss Madame de Pompadour.

One night when Dr. Quesnay was sitting with d'Argenson and Madame d'Estrades, Madame de Choiseul burst into the room, with her dress in disorder and a look on her face which explained why.

Madame d'Estrades rushed to her and asked eagerly, "Has it happened?"

"Oh yes," answered the silly girl, "it has happened. He

loves me, he is happy, and she is to be dismissed; he gave me his word."

There was a shout of triumph from the conspirators. Only Quesnay remained silent.

"Doctor," said d'Argenson uneasily, "things will not change for you, and we hope sincerely that you will remain with us."

"M. le Comte," Quesnay replied coldly, "I have been attached to Madame de Pompadour in her prosperity, and I propose to remain so in her misfortune," and he left the room abruptly.

D'Argenson glanced uncomfortably at his mistress, who said airily, "Oh, I know him; he won't betray us."

Madame d'Estrades' faith in Quesnay was vindicated; he did not reveal the plot to the Marquise, but she discovered it in an unexpected way. Madame de Choiseul-Romanet imprudently showed a letter she had received from the King to her cousin, the Comte de Stainville, who was known to be an enemy of the Marquise. What she did not realize was that her ambitious relative had decided privately to come to terms with the Favorite at the first opportunity.

Stainville, inventing a pretext for keeping the letter, immediately went to Madame de Pompadour, who was naturally astonished to receive a visit from him. He explained that, although he was no follower of the Marquise, he was concerned for the welfare of the kingdom, and that Madame de Choiseul-Romanet was too young and foolish to assume the position which Madame de Pompadour was filling so commendably. Leaving the surprised Marquise to reflect upon the contents of the letter and his own forth-right honesty, the Comte de Stainville tactfully bowed himself out; it was not long before he was appointed Ambassador to the Vatican, and in less than four years he would become Duc de Choiseul and Foreign Minister of France.

Now that the Marquise knew of her danger, she met it boldly; her natural anger was doubled by this additional instance of treachery, for it was she who had arranged Madame de Choiseul-Romanet's marriage, secured her appointment as a Lady in Waiting to Mesdames, and in-cluded her in the suppers. Persuading the pliant Louis that he had been duped by a scheming woman, she secured the "little serpent's" dismissal from Court.

Although she perceived that the entire plot had been engineered by d'Argenson and Madame d'Estrades, they naturally refused to admit their complicity, and for the moment there were no measures she could take against them. But it was not long before the ugly Comtesse com-mitted one blunder too many.

The King wrote a long account describing his difficulties with *Parlement* to the Marquise, who being ill, read the letter and laid it on her bedside table. Soon after, Madame d'Estrades, still in the guise of a friend, paid her usual visit, chatted for a short time, and left. Evidently she took the letter with her, for a thorough search of the apartments failed to uncover it. The King was furious when he heard that a private letter of his had been filched, although he was still reluctant to dismiss Madame d'Estrades, believing that Madame Adélaïde was fond of her. But the Marquise, better informed than he on the gossip of the anterooms, knew that Madame Adélaïde was temporarily annoyed with her Lady in Waiting. Excusing herself from Louis, she went into the Princess's apartment and obtained from her the admission that she was "tired" of Madame d'Estrades; with that admission the doom of the Comtesse was sealed.

On August 8, 1755, Madame d'Estrades had been invited to dinner by the King, but not knowing the hour, she came to ask it of Madame de Pompadour. "At the usual time, Comtesse," replied the Favorite with a smile, knowing that the King had already ordered M. de St. Florentin to write her letter of dismissal. Madame d'Estrades was forbidden to appear at Court, but she was allowed to retain her salary. The Marquise had freed herself of a traitress, but the Comte d'Argenson, declaring that the dismissal of the Comtesse had been a direct affront to him, loathed her more than ever.

The worst of it was that his power was growing—he had won to his side the financiers of the capital, including the Pârises, who feared the financial policies of Machault, and had beguiled the Queen, the Dauphin, and the devout— in short he had become the focus of opposition for all those who opposed Madame de Pompadour.

Difficult though it was for friendship and loyalty to thrive in the poisoned atmosphere of the Court, the Marquise occasionally experienced the exquisite joy of staunch devotion. Madame du Haussay commented on her strong attachment for Madame d'Amblimont, and the Marquise replied that she was "a person unique in her honesty and in her loyalty to her friends."

Four days ago [the Marquise said] on her way to dinner the King came up and, pretending to tickle her, tried to give her a note. Madame d'Amblimont, pretending not to understand, put her hands behind her back, and the King was forced to pick up the note, which had fallen on the floor.

The Duc de Gontaut was the only one who witnessed this, and after supper he said to Madame d'Amblimont, "You are a good friend."

"I only did what I ought to have done," she replied, putting her finger to her lips in a gesture of secrecy.

It was he who told me of the little heroine's act of friendship; she has not said a word to me about it.

But the Marquise saw to it that the "heroine's" loyalty did not go unrewarded; at Choisy, a few mornings later, the King himself went up to Madame d'Amblimont and slipped around her neck a circlet of emeralds and diamonds.

Another firm friend of the Marquise was Madame de Brancas, whose lack of beauty was compensated for by her animated countenance. Her cultivated mind and facile choice of language made her a favorite with men of letters, and although kindhearted and unpretentious, she bore herself in a charming courtly manner.

The gay and witty Maréchale de Mirepoix won the Marquise with her air of sincerity and frank devotion. She was not pretty but had a fresh piquant look which charmed everyone with whom she spoke. In later years she was to be as loyal to Madame Du Barry as she had been to Madame de Pompadour.

For many years the establishment known as the *Parc aux Cerfs* was cited as the crowning example of Louis XV's debauchery. Although no one seemed to know exactly where it was or what it was, the King's enemies spoke knowingly of a mansion, almost a palace, where he indulged in boundless debaucheries. They wrote juicily of an interminable procession of young women, sometimes even of children of nine or ten, who were lured or kidnaped to the *Parc aux Cerfs* for the gratification of an aging licentious satyr.

What actually was the *Parc aux Cerfs?* It remained a mystery for nearly a century after the death of Louis XV, until M. Leroi, the Librarian of Versailles, discovered in the archives documents which effectively destroyed the tissue of lies.

The *Parc aux Cerfs*—so called because it stood on land which had once formed part of the Deer Park of Louis XIII —was in truth a small modest house, which far from being a mansion was so small that it could accommodate at most only two occupants in addition to the woman who supervised it (the widow of a clerk in the War Office). Its ground floor contained a coach house, a small stable, a large kitchen, and a bathroom, while upstairs there were only two rooms. The larger one was simply decorated, and except for the colored marble mantelpieces there was no sign of luxury.

This unpretentious house, then, of which Madame du

Haussay wrote that "there were almost never more than two women there, and more often only one," was the alleged "seraglio" where the King was said to grovel like an Oriental sultan in unrestrained lust. Certainly the *Parc aux Cerfs* was an amorous and by no means edifying retreat for the King, but it was less pretentious than that of many a private citizen, and the sums which it supposedly swallowed were grossly exaggerated.

The King's agents, looking for a more secluded place of assignation than *Le Trébuchet*, had come upon the house in 1755, and Louis had purchased it through a man named Vallet, who registered the property as his own and paid the taxes on it. The King owned the house for sixteen years, until his infatuation with Madame Du Barry made its retention unnecessary. When he sold it for 16,000 livres in 1771, he made the transaction openly as King of France.

The Marquise was well aware of the *Parc aux Cerfs*. Secretly her fastidious nature must have been revolted by the activities which proceeded behind its walls, but to have tried to change the King's habits would have been the wildest folly. No, so long as the *Parc aux Cerfs* was shelter for mere "nobodies," Madame de Pompadour ignored its sordid aspect and banished worry from her mind.

Its first occupant was the "little Murphy," not yet fifteen when Lebel discovered her apprenticed to a dress-maker. Surmising that her immaturity would appeal to the King's jaded tastes, the valet-procurer gave 1000 écus to her mother and 100 louis to her employer and took her to the *Parc aux Cerfs*.

Despite her youth the girl was not inexperienced and Louis was not the first man in her life; it was she who had posed as the Virgin in Boucher's picture "The Holy Family." Although not very bright, *la petite Morphise,* as she came to be known, was very beautiful, and her childlike ways delighted the bored Monarch. When she gave birth to a daughter, the affair became an open one; she visited Louis at the Palace and was given a suite of rooms at Fontainebleau. The Papal Nuncio went so far as to inform the Vatican that the influence of "the Irish star" was rising and that the reign of Madame de Pompadour was drawing to a close.

Madame d'Estrées, an avowed enemy of the Marquise, came to the same conclusion, and to hasten the fall of the Favorite she played upon the childish ambitions of Mlle. Murphy. One day when Louis was visiting her, she interrupted him and pertly asked how things were between him and his "old woman." The King was first astonished and then resentful and, suspecting that a hidden hand was pulling the strings, demanded to know who had put such an idea into her head. Mlle. Murphy, now in tears, confessed naïvely that Madame d'Estrées had told her to utter the piece of impudence.

When Madame de Pompadour was told, she realized that Mlle. Murphy, in the hands of mature enemies, could become dangerous, and so the girl was hastily married off to a M. d'Ayat, her banishment being softened by a present of 50,000 livres and a dowry of 200,000. Her infant daughter was granted a yearly pension of 8,000 livres and installed in a convent. Madame d'Estrées, upon whose head the real blame lay, was summarily dismissed from Versailles.

The Marquise once described another "nobody," Mlle. Dorothée, to the ever-attentive Madame du Haussay.

"She has been brought here," said Madame de Pompadour, "by a Gascon who is called Du Barry, who is the most contemptible subject in France. He builds his hopes on her charms, which he fancies the King cannot resist. She is undeniably pretty. . . the daughter of a Strasbourg porter. . . ."

"Is Madame worried about a creature like that?" asked Madame du Haussay incredulously.

"Anything is possible," replied the Marquise. "But I don't think the King wants a scandal. Fortunately Lebel (always watchful of the Marquise's interests) told the King that Dorothée's former lover was eaten up with a loathsome disease, and added, "Your Majesty will not get over it as easily as scrofula." Nothing further was needed to wreck the young woman.

But most of the transients of the *Parc aux Cerfs* were simple persons who caused no alarm to the powerful Mistress, ignorant girls such as the one at whose *accouchement* Madame du Haussay had officiated. That deluded young mother, whose identity has been lost, never knew that her lover was the King. Louis, after the Murphy liaison, began to go incognito to the *Parc aux Cerfs,* and if sometimes he forgot to remove the Blue Ribbon which he wore under his coat, he explained it away by saying that he was a Polish nobleman, a relative of the Queen.

But his secret was not inviolable and discovery once led

to infinite embarrassment. One of the girls, going through his coat pockets, found a letter from the King of Spain—and she was overwhelmed by the staggering realization that her "Polish nobleman" was in reality the King of France.

On his next visit she burst into the room where Louis was amusing himself with her successor, and throwing herself on her knees, screamed: "Yes, you are the Lord of the whole Kingdom, but that is nothing to me if you are not the King of my heart. Do not leave me, Sire, I think I will go mad."

The King was thoroughly disconcerted and attempted to calm the poor girl, placing her on his knee and absent-mindedly giving her a kiss. The chaperon, or "abbess" as she was called, rushed in and dragged the hysterical creature away; she was sent for some days to a madhouse, where she was told that her experience had been only a dream, and then married off in the country.

The women who paraded through the *Parc aux Cerfs* came there of their own volition, the daughters or apprentices of hairdressers and seamstresses. And, in most cases their stay was brief, for Louis, to the disguised delight of the Marquise, grew easily bored with them. When children were born, they were separated from the mother and usually placed in a convent or with some trustworthy family. Although the King showed no personal interest in his bastards, he provided them with a modest future, endowing them with an annuity of 10,000 or 12,000 livres; their mothers were given a respectable dowry and married off to some solid and not overparticular countryman. The *Parc aux Cerfs* saw them no more.

Generally speaking, the Marquise had little reason to fear the girls of the *Parc aux Cerfs*, but from ladies of the Court her danger was always intense and never more so than during the affair of the Marquise de Coislin. This beautiful and haughty woman had the powerful support of the Prince de Conti in her campaign to supplant Madame de Pompadour, and for some months the issue was in serious doubt. The Favorite's nerves were shattered, and she even wrote to Louis in a fit of depression, begging to be allowed to retire from Court. Of course, she did not mean it beyond the moment, but the low state of her morale was revealed by the fact that the letter was ever written at all.

What affected her most [Madame du Haussay commented] was the dread of being supplanted by a rival. I never saw her more irritated than one evening when she returned from Marly. She spitefully threw down her muff and coat and undressed with extreme haste; then sending aways her other maids, she said to me:

"I don't believe anyone can be more insolent than that Madame de Coislin. I had to play *brélan* with her tonight, and you cannot imagine what I suffered. Everyone seemed to take turns in coming to stare at us, and two or three times Madame de Coislin, looking at me, said in the most insulting manner, '*Va tout!*'

"I thought I would be ill when she said triumphantly, 'I have played Kings,' and you should have seen her curtsy when she left!"

When I inquired how the King had reacted, the Marquise replied, "You don't know him, my dear; if he were going to put her in my apartment tonight he would treat her coldly before people, and me with the greatest affection.

"It is the fault of his upbringing," Madame de Pompadour went on defensively, "for at heart he is frank and honest."

The struggle between the Favorite and Madame de Coislin had repercussions in the sensitive arena of foreign affairs and threatened to affect the impending alliance with Austria.

"The story of Madame de Coislin grieved me for the King's sake, for our friend's (Madame de Pompadour) sake, and for the sake of our Treaty," wrote Bernis, who had become Minister of Foreign Affairs, to the Comte de Stainville, now Ambassador in Vienna, "but I have been reassured. If that woman, counseled, and thank God, badly counseled by the enemies of Madame de Pompadour and of the State, had conducted herself better she would have ruined the Alliance before any of us were aware of it. Nothing is more important for the Court of Vienna than the preservation of our friend."

Bernis' concern led him to write directly to the King, pointing out that the replacement of Madame de Pompadour would offend the Austrian Court and cause it to question the stability of French foreign policy, and he added, with immense moral courage, that he "certainly would not work with another woman who had no rights of friendship and gratitude over me."

The King answered Bernis' letter kindly, promising to dismiss Madame de Coislin; it was not the Abbé's letter, however, but a private one, ostensibly written by a member of *Parlement* to a friend and extracted from the mails, which led to Louis' decision:

"It is all right that the Master has *une amie,*" the letter went on, "a confidante, as we all do when we wish; but it is desirable that he *keep the one he has.* She is gentle, harms no one, and her fortune is already made. The one that is proposed has all the arrogance of noble birth, and he will have to give her a million a year, because they say she is very extravagant. The King will have to make Dukes, Governors, and Marshals of her relatives, who will end by surrounding him."

The letter writer's allusion to Madame de Coislin's flagrantly mercenary nature was enough for the King; a few days later Madame de Pompadour was able to announce to the waiting Madame du Haussay that the "proud Marquise [de Coislin] has missed her chance. She frightened the King by her grand airs, and unceasing demands of money from him."

There were some among the cynical who whispered that the decisive letter had been inspired by Janelle, the Postmaster-General, a faithful adherent of Madame de Pompadour. But the Favorite, regardless of method, had crushed another rival and was free to enjoy her reign as *de facto* Prime Minister.

XVII

PRIME MINISTER IN PETTICOATS

N NOVEMBER 1755, only two months after the rout of Madame de Coislin, the Marquis d'Argenson conceded, almost with admiration, that Madame de Pompadour had reached in all but name the summit to which he and his brother had aspired for so many years.

"She has all the air of being the Prime Minister of France, and the King wishes it to be so, and to be outwardly apparent as well. Certainly it is better to see at the helm the erect figure of a beautiful nymph rather than that of a crouching old monkey like the late Cardinal Fleury; but these fine ladies have the tempers of white cats, which show signs of being pleasant enough at first, and then soon bite and scratch you from sudden caprice."

But three months later, after the Marquise had been named Lady in Waiting to the Queen, d'Argenson reverted to his accustomed criticism: "This woman is immensely rich, and we see her meddling in finances; we see also that foreign affairs are led by her flippancy. She wants to keep the King tranquil by hopes, never by the force and decision of his actions. . . . She is not an Agnes

Sorel, the inspirer of honorable and dignified resolutions... and the King is an enslaved and subjugated lover who fears to displease his Mistress. This one loves him after her fashion and dreads to offend him, but she has all the defects of her age, her low birth, and her trade of kept Mistress."

The Marquise should have been satisfied now that she was, next to the King, the most important person in the government of France. But power demanded its price, as Madame du Haussay bore witness: "Madame experienced many tribulations amidst all her grandeurs. Anonymous letters were often written to her containing threats of poison or assassination...."

For protection against these hidden dangers, the Marquise relied chiefly upon Berryer, the Lieutenant of Police. Bernis attests that "Madame de Pompadour was convinced that Berryer's vigilance had saved her a dozen times from poison or dagger; she had no liking for that coarse and middle-class man, but she believed he was necessary for her safety."

Janelle, the Postmaster-General, was another vital element in the Marquise's system of defense. The mails of the *Ancien Régime* were not inviolable, and Janelle maintained a watchful eye for letters which might prove of assistance to his patroness. Every Sunday he appeared at Versailles to "work with" Madame de Pompadour—that is, to show her copies of letters, threatening or informative, which he had opened and read. Armed with so effective an intelligence service, the Marquise was able to forestall with ease any adverse plots which her enemies were rash enough to commit to the postal system.

Janelle was not a savory character. Dr. Quesnay, usually a paragon of composure, almost foamed at the mouth when his name was mentioned and uncompromisingly stated that he "would not dine any more willingly with the Postmaster-General than with the public hangman."

Bernis, who in 1755 was being groomed for a role of utmost importance, watched the Marquise's activities with a loving and sometimes anxious eye. "With regard to the letter Madame de Pompadour had written to the King on the improvement of public affairs, I should never have supposed her capable of telling him the truth with such energy, and even eloquence. I loved her the better and esteemed her the more ... and I exhorted her not to weaken that style, but to continue to tell the truth with force and courage."

Aside from the feeble state of the kingdom's finances, the gravest internal problem that plagued the Marquise and the King was the vicious struggle between *Parlement* and the Jesuits over the religious question, a struggle which inevitably involved the Crown. When Machault in 1750 had instituted his salutary income tax, the *vingtième*, the clergy, invoking their feudal exemption, not only declined to pay it but refused to submit any accounting of their enormous revenues. Sensing the hostility which their negative attitude aroused, however, the hierarchy, led by the Jesuits, revived their old quarrel with the Jansenists, hoping to divert attention from their own obstructionist behavior.

Christophe de Beaumont, Archbishop of Paris, ordered the priests to deny the Sacraments to anyone who refused to accept the validity of the bull *Unigenitus* (which anathematized Jansenism), and among those so excluded was the Duc d'Orléans, son of the former Regent. Not satisfied with the sternness of this prohibition, the Archbishop went further and forbade his clergy to perform Catholic funeral services for anyone who had confessed to a Jansenist priest.

Parlement, overwhelmingly Jansenist in sympathy, was outraged at this revival of intolerance, and in its turn forbade the priests to obey the Archbishop, severely punishing those who did so. Madame de Pompadour, smarting from attacks by certain members of *Parlement,* at first sympathized with the clergy, and the King, naturally conservative in religious matters, strongly supported the Archbishop.

Louis annulled the edicts which *Parlement* had passed to protect the Jansenists and instructed the judges not to interfere in matters of religious doctrine. In reply the judges closed the courts, withdrew to the country and went on strike, refusing to perform their duties; consequently all litigation which was subject to the jurisdiction of the Paris *Parlement* came to a halt.

The following year, 1754, the recalcitrant judges returned, and the courts resumed their functions; a truce seemed to have been reached, and in September the King, declaring that there must be no more controversies, banned any innovations in religious practices. This seemed to strike a blow at the campaign against Jansenism, and now it was the turn of the Archbishop to be angry.

Christophe de Beaumont was a man of firm principles, great ambition, and violent disposition. He persisted in his intransigence against the Jansenists, and *Parlement* ordered his letters of reprimand burned by the public hangman. Finally, in a desperate attempt to unsnarl the impasse, Louis reluctantly exiled the Archbishop, "seriously disturbed that he had been forced to take such a step."

"What a pity," he often said, "that such a worthy man should be so stubborn."

"And so narrow-minded," someone added one day.

"Shut up," the King said brusquely. In his heart he still sided with Beaumont, although Madame de Pompadour had few regrets at the stubborn Archbishop's fall. Had he not expressed more than once the Christian desire to "see her burn"?

But the Archbishop's exile did not solve the dispute which continued to smolder, and in 1756 the King dissolved *Parlement,* exiling sixteen of its leaders. Many of the Jansenists blamed Madame de Pompadour, and one of the members of *Parlement,* Président Meinières, held two lengthy conversations with her in a futile attempt to reach a settlement.

At their first meeting the Marquise spoke long and eloquently of the misbehavior of *Parlement* in defying the King, and although she did not convince Meinières, he "went away filled with astonishment and admiration" at her grasp of the intricate issues involved.

The second interview took place a few days later, on February 8, 1757. Meinières argued persistently for the recall of the sixteen exiles, and although he failed to win her consent, the Marquise conceived the greatest admiration for his firmness.

Secretly, she was beginning to favor *Parlement*, perceiving in the Jansenists a potential ally against their mutual enemy the Jesuits; she exercised a moderating influence on Louis, and he ended by recalling the exiles and permitting *Parlement* to resume its functions in September 1757.

D'Argenson admitted that "it was through her that the King became reconciled to *Parlement* ... but her good counsels are expensive; mildness and equity are bought by luxury."

The successful conduct of foreign affairs is as vital to a nation's security as the solution of its internal problems, and it was in the realm of foreign affairs that Madame de Pompadour most conspicuously—and, according to some historians, disastrously—exerted her influence. To some extent her importance in the conclusion of the alliance with Austria has been exaggerated, but her name will forever be linked with that dramatic reversal of alliances known as the Diplomatic Revolution.

The Peace of Aix-la-Chapelle was not a lasting one. France gained nothing for her sacrifices, and the Empress Maria Theresa burned at the loss of one of her fairest provinces to Prussia. "Austria has never forgotten Silesia," said Frederick II, and he was right; he knew that the

Empress-Queen would never rest until she recovered it. Since the time of Francis I the traditional policy of France, elaborated by Cardinal Richelieu, had aimed at opposing the power of the Habsburgs, whether it be in Germany, the Low Countries, Italy, or Spain. Frenchmen came to look upon Prussia, Austria's chief rival in Germany, as their natural ally, and the slightest hint of a *rapprochement* with Vienna was abhorrent to most of Louis XV's Ministers.

The idea of an Austrian alliance did not originate with Madame de Pompadour. At the close of his long life, Louis XIV, having seated a Bourbon Prince on the throne of Spain, had advised his heirs to establish lasting peace with the Habsburgs. In Italy they were no longer a threat to French security; on the northeastern frontier their power was blunted by the French acquisition of Alsace and of Lorraine (which was ruled by Louis XV's father-in-law); in Belgium their hold was infirm and tenuous.

To any statesman not blinded by the anti-Habsburg tradition, it should have been clear that Austria, weakened and divided, had been succeeded as France's principal enemy by the maritime power of Great Britain, and that the rising power of Prussia at Austria's expense threatened to upset the balance of power in Germany and provide future misfortunes for France.

Louis XV was aware of this, but because of the head-strong opposition of traditionalists such as the Comte d'Argenson, Machault, and Marshal Belle-Isle, he characteristically hesitated to assert himself and dared not suggest an alliance with Maria Theresa. Personally he admired her as much as he disliked his nominal ally Frederick, to whom he was still bound by treaty.

The King of Prussia had proved himself unreliable during the War of the Austrian Succession, deserting France to conclude a separate peace with the Empress. A worse transgression, he scoffed at religion and Louis XV's private life with equal malice, and the King never forgave his Prussian colleague's cutting witticisms.

Nor could Madame de Pompadour ignore Frederick's heartless jokes at her expense, every word of which was repeated to her.

"I should deem myself culpable toward Your Majesty," the Prussian Ambassador in Paris warned his King, "if I did not inform you that everything Your Majesty does or says, even in your most private intercourse, is known at the Court of Versailles. . . . I venture therefore to entreat, Sire, that in this respect you will use the necessary circumspection; all the more so as Your Majesty is well aware that a single word, that has the power to sting, is sometimes the cause of more serious mischief than actions of even the greatest weight."

But Frederick treated his Ambassador's excellent advice with contempt and took a perverse pleasure in insulting the Marquise from the safety of Berlin. Even when servants were within hearing, he referred to her as "Petticoat II" or "Cotillion II," and upon the hound dog that shared his lonely bed he conferred a name of distinction: Pompadour. These churlish sarcasms of an asexual invert wounded the brittle vanity of the Marquise beyond appeasement and decisively influenced the future of Europe.

Regardless of the political and military factors involved, Madame de Pompadour, boiling with the outraged fury of a woman who has been gratuitously insulted, was emotionally receptive to an alliance with Austria against the hated Frederick.

The first significant step in the train of events which culminated in the reversal of alliances occurred when Maria Theresa chose Count von Kaunitz-Rietberg to represent her at the Court of Versailles. Kaunitz, who was to be surpassed only by Metternich in his untiring service to the House of Austria, was only thirty-nine when he arrived at Versailles in 1750, but in spite of his comparative youth he was already marked for a glorious career in diplomacy. Convinced that Austria's mortal enemy was Prussia, he had earlier persuaded the Empress, over the vigorous objections of her other Ministers, that Austria must abandon her traditional alliance with the maritime powers, England and Holland, and, with the fixed aim of destroying Prussia, ally herself with Russia and France. Maria Theresa had arrived at the same conclusion herself, and from 1749 Kaunitz served as her chief adviser.

"The Comte de Kaunitz, Ambassador of the Empress, presented his credentials today. He is said to be charming, and seems to be a very polished person." So wrote the Marquise to her brother in Italy, unaware that she was describing the beginnings of an epochal friendship.

And the courtly Austrian reported to his Empress: "I have not forgotten to pay my respects to Madame de Pompadour. I know that the King is much gratified, and that she herself is not insensible to my attentions."

From the beginning the Marquise was charmed—how the Austrian's behavior contrasted with that of the Prussian Ambassador, whom Frederick had forbidden to visit her! Kaunitz flattered her, and shrewdly divining her bitter resentment at the affronts of the Prussian King, encouraged her desire to play a great role in foreign affairs. In his long-range plans to draw France into an alliance he soon found a willing confederate in the Marquise; in fact, her enthusiasm was so immoderate Kaunitz felt impelled to remind her that Austria still had many enemies at Versailles and that, if their plans were to succeed, they must move slowly in the Council.

Kaunitz resided in splendor at the *Palais Bourbon,* where he gave delicious little dinners, ending the meals with an elaborate if somewhat terrifying ritual of picking his teeth before the startled guests; it was only one of his many foibles. He detested fresh air and the sight of an open window sent him rushing furiously to close it. Kaunitz was inordinately vain about his appearance, especially his hair and complexion. He wore three shades of wigs, and Marmontel surprised him one day after he had been riding, plastering his face with the yolk of an egg to remove the tan.

A friend of the Marquise once derisively alluded to the Count's practice of running about a room pursued by four valets armed with bellows, which were used to blow the surplus powder off his wig. Madame de Pompadour halted the laughter by remarking solemnly:

"It was Alcibiades who cut off his dog's tail to give the Athenians something to talk about, so that he could distract their attention from the things which he wished to hide."

Her comparison was pertinent. Kaunitz, in spite of his foppishness, was in deadly earnest, but he wished to conceal the real purpose of his mission to Paris under a cloud of powder. Marmontel once reproached him for visiting the wives of bankers and neglecting the nobility.

"My dear Marmontel," Kaunitz explained haughtily, "I am here for only two reasons—for the affairs of my Sovereign, which I transact properly, and for my pleasure —and on this last matter, I have only to consult myself. Showiness would weary me, and be a burden; it is for this reason that I avoid it. Of all the intriguing women at Versailles, there is not one worth the trouble of gaining. I have two persons at Court, the King and his Mistress. I am in favor with them both."

When Kaunitz returned to Vienna in 1753 to become Minister of Foreign Affairs, the Marquise bade him farewell with profound regret. She had come to be sincerely fond of him, while he, although loving no one, could remember Madame de Pompadour with a glow of satisfaction: his mission had been an unqualified success, and the new Austrian Ambassador, Stahremberg, would find in the King's Mistress a warm friend of Austria.

Events were moving rapidly in the interminable devils' race of European politics but the first overt act occurred far away—in the wilderness of North America. A small party of Virginians, led by a young surveyor named Washington, clashed in 1754 with a force of French and Indians

in the Ohio valley, which was claimed by both France
and England. In London and Paris, neither government
was ready for war, and while fighting raged furiously in
America, and the army of a British General named Brad-
dock was cut to pieces, the home governments indulged
in an elaborate pretense that peace still existed.

But a *dénouement* was clearly imminent; without a
declaration of war a British fleet attacked and destroyed
a French squadron, and the nations of Europe began to
choose sides. George II of England, also King of Hanover,
feared for his German possession and offered to renew
his alliance with Maria Theresa, but the Empress, hoping
instead for a French alliance, rejected the offer. Great
Britain then secretly concluded the Treaty of Westminster
with Frederick, who had affectionately remarked that his
uncle, George II, was "fit for the gallows."

Meanwhile, a fierce struggle was underway between the
partisans of Prussia and Austria at Versailles. The Comte
d'Argenson favored Frederick as always, while Machault,
now Minister of Marine, argued against any participation
in a continental war, pointing out that the critical struggle
with Great Britain lay on the seas and in the colonies.

Paralyzed by irresolution, Louis and the remainder of
the Council vacillated between the two factions; Madame
de Pompadour, passionately pro-Austrian, was engaged
in her struggle with Madame de Coislin, and until it was
resolved she dared not annoy the King with political
arguments. The Austrian Ambassador, armed with a treaty
of alliance, waited in an agony of indecision, not knowing
whether to place his bet on the Mistress or Madame de

Coislin. Kaunitz instructed him to use his own discretion, and Stahremberg continued to court Madame de Pompadour; his decision was vindicated with the destruction of Madame de Coislin.

The Marquise was now free to concentrate the weight of her influence on the King, whose inclinations toward Austria grew stronger. The more Maria Theresa flattered Louis, the more he contrasted her to Frederick, who referred to him as "Sardanapalus."

"He is a madman," complained Louis, "who risks his all to win or lose; he may win, though he has neither religion, morals, nor principles." It was easy for the King to convince himself that an alliance with Catholic Austria against Protestant Prussia would advance the cause of religion—and perhaps atone in a measure for his own sins. "He dreamed," wrote Henri Martin, "of a holy war from the recesses of the *Parc aux Cerfs.*"

Nevertheless, the King still hesitated to negotiate personally with the Austrian Ambassador and chose the Abbé de Bernis as his intermediary. The important point is that the choice of Bernis, who had proved a successful Ambassador to Venice, was Louis' own. For many years historians erroneously maintained that the Austrian alliance was the creation of the Favorite and that she alone dragged France into a disastrous war.

Certainly she was in favor of the tie with Maria Theresa, but to state that she was entirely responsible for it is to ignore, as many would like to do, the fact that Louis XV still retained final control of policy. His remark long afterward, "That was my doing," referring to the Austrian alliance, should have been enough to dispel the misconception that it was the exclusive handiwork of his Mistress.

In *The King's Secret,* Comte de Broglie, unfriendly to the Marquise but conscientious in his final verdict, agrees: "Heaven forbid that I should plead the cause of Madame de Pompadour, or even that I should invoke extenuating circumstances on her behalf . . . but the truth tends, and I am sorry for it, for the sake of morality, to the exculpation of her."

When the King asked Bernis his views on a possible alliance with Maria Theresa, the Abbé gave an equivocal reply. Secretly, he was not enthusiastic over a pact of friendship with the former enemy, and the King, sensing this, said angrily, "You are like all the rest, an enemy of the Empress."

Louis added, "I may as well make a fine compliment to M. de Stahremberg and tell him he will not be listened to."

Bernis denied that he was unalterably opposed to an Austrian treaty and expressed willingness to act as the King's secret negotiator with the Austrian Ambassador, "for the King did not conceal that what he had desired all his life was to have the Court of Vienna for his ally."

The amiable Abbé wanted to maintain peace as long as possible, for reasons of the utmost soundness which he listed in his memoirs:

The finances of the Kingdom . . . had only an appearance of good administration, for since the Peace of Aix-la-Chapelle the State had spent every year far more than its revenues; the burdens on the people were undiminished, and all the money of the kingdom was virtually in the hands of the financiers. Commerce was flourishing, but without support from the Navy.

We had many hulks, but few vessels. Our militia, though numerous, was neither well organized nor well disciplined; and our frontier forts, ill provided and out of repair, completed a very sad picture of the state of France.

In the Council, no union; open war between M. d'Argenson and M. de Machault . . . the Prince de Conti heading a virtually separate department, (*Le Secret*) yet not a Minister; Madame de Pompadour openly at war with him; the King holding the balance in the midst of these conflicts. Overflowing luxury of the most scandalous nature and the people poverty-stricken; no true intelligence in the Council, no citizen of courage at Court, and, on the eve of war, no generals by land or sea.

Notwithstanding his misgivings, the Abbé, the Marquise, and the Austrian Ambassador inaugurated in September 1755 a series of highly secret meetings in the summerhouse of Babiole, which was located on the grounds of Bellevue.

The chief criticism of these negotiations, which ultimately entangled France in a continental war, was that the overseas Empire in India and Canada would be starved of defenses; but it was clear to Bernis that in the impending struggle with Great Britain that nation, through Hanover, would launch a land attack against France. A continental ally was essential, and that ally could only be Austria; moreover it was reasonable to hope that the ensuing balance of power might still prevent a continental war. France hoped to preserve peace between the two German rivals, but what Bernis did not know was that Maria Theresa, determined to recover Silesia, had already agreed with Russia on the future partition of Prussia.

Louis, still striving to avert war in Germany, sent the Duc de Nivernois to Berlin early in 1756 with an offer to renew the Franco-Prussian alliance of 1741, which was due to expire. During his secret negotiations with Vienna, Louis had loyally insisted that Prussia be included in any guarantee of the status quo, and if hostilities had not broken out between Prussia and Austria, the bitter Anglo-French colonial struggle might never have spread to the continent.

Although Frederick received the French Ambasador with mocking courtesy, he declined his offer of a new treaty, saying with a smile of triumph that he had already concluded an alliance with England. This was the first public avowal of the Treaty of Westminster, and the Duc de Nivernois was struck dumb with astonishment. Before he could recover, the Prussian King contemptuously advised him to go to Vienna, since "an alliance between France and Austria is so natural."

The only rational explanation for Frederick's temerity in deliberately antagonizing so powerful a nation as France lies deep in his subconscious. Since childhood he had fawningly admired French culture and the French language, while despising that of his own boorish land; eager to be accepted as an equal by Louis XV, he resented being treated as a junior partner and resolved after Aix-la-Chapelle to break his ties with France. Frederick's conduct toward France revealed a love-hate complex which was repeated in William II's attitude toward England a hundred and fifty years later.

In spite of the remarkable military genius which earned him the title *The Great*, Frederick was extraordinarily neurotic. Madame de Pompadour was not the only woman to feel the sting of his adder's tongue. Frederick almost dug the grave of himself and his kingdom with that sharp instrument. His heart gutted of love by the flaming spectacle of Katt, the friend of his youth, shot down before his eyes, the frustrated Prussian monarch must have found a satisfying outlet for his bitterness in mocking the immorality—normal, nevertheless—of Versailles and St. Petersburg. For the Tsaritsa Elizabeth joined the mighty coalition against Prussia mainly because of Frederick's sardonic comments on her many love affairs, and the three most powerful women in Europe—Pompadour of France, Elizabeth of Russia, and Maria Theresa of Austria, "the three furies" as Frederick called them—almost destroyed the Hohenzollern and his upstart kingdom.

He must have been concerned at the mighty host assembling against him, but he concealed, not too effectively, his anxiety behind words which reveal a vicious hatred of women:

"Observe," he said to his perennial male companions, "how singular a fate is mine! My reverence for the fair sex is well known. On no occasion do I fail in the respect I owe them. Well, would you believe it, I, who give them no cause for offense, who occasion them no manner of restraint, who have no concern in common with them, and never meddle in their affairs, am condemned to carry on an open war with them. Here I am forced to enter the lists with three of them at once, and these the most illustrious Europe has to boast—the Empress Elizabeth of Russia, the Empress Maria Theresa of Austria, and the Marquise de Pompadour of France!

"And what, I pray you, is my offense? Can you conceive of anything more extraordinary? The three first whores in Europe unite together to provoke, beyond the bounds of endurance, the man who of all the world should be the most indifferent to them."

The government at Versailles was electrified by the news that Great Britain had secured Prussia as an ally; opposition to an Austrian alliance melted away, for now it was all too clear that if Frederick and Maria Theresa *should* be reconciled, France would be isolated. Admittedly Austria needed France, but France needed Austria equally as much.

The first Treaty of Versailles, of which Count Kaunitz and Madame de Pompadour had dreamed for five years, was signed on May 1, 1756. It stipulated that Austria would remain neutral in the quarrel between France and England and provided for a joint guarantee of each other's territories in Europe.

The French government hoped that the treaty would prove a deterrent to a European conflict, but the Empress, fortified by the new alliance, continued her preparations against Prussia. Frederick, having no intention of waiting to be attacked, suddenly invaded Saxony, without bothering to declare war, in August 1756. He demanded from

King Augustus III (the Dauphin's father-in-law) neutrality and permission to use Saxony as a base against Austria; Augustus indignantly refused, and threw in his lot with the Allies.

Thus began the Seven Years' War, in which Prussia, a small and poor kingdom supported only by British gold, held at bay the combined forces of Sweden, Poland, Saxony, Russia, Austria, and France. The war enshrined forever the reputation of Frederick the Great and ruined irreparably, in the eyes of the French people, that of the Marquise de Pompadour.

But before this war, in which she was to play so prominent a part, was thoroughly launched there occurred an isolated event, terrible in its suddenness, which carried the Marquise to within an inch of complete ruin.

XVIII

THE ATTEMPT OF DAMIENS

O N WEDNESDAY, January 5, 1757, at six o'clock in the evening, Louis XV descended the stairs from the Little Cabinets to enter his carriage, which was drawn up by the Marble Court. He was on his way, accompanied by the Dauphin, to rejoin Madame de Pompadour, who was at Trianon.

As the King, leaning on the arm of the Duc d'Ayen, emerged from the Palace into the flickering light of the torches, a middle-aged man suddenly thrust himself between two of the Guards of Honor who were lined up at attention and struck Louis a blow in his right side. The assailant, who wore a brown overcoat and had his hat on, darted back between the soldiers before they could stop him.

"Take off your hat," shouted the Dauphin at the retreating figure, "don't you see the King?"

"Duc d'Ayen," said Louis, "someone has just struck me with his fist." He then put his hand inside his coat, and withdrew it covered with blood. Upon seeing this, the valet who was holding the carriage door shouted, "The King is wounded!"

The rapidity of the attack had paralyzed everyone, but the valet's cry galvanized the stunned witnesses into confused activity. Several of the guards pursued the attacker, seized him by the collar, and dragged him before the King.

"That is the man who struck me," said Louis. "Arrest him but do not kill him."

The King's companions, including Marshal Richelieu, moved toward the wounded Monarch in order to carry him back into the Palace, but he waved them away, saying, "No, I still have strength enough to walk." He seemed perfectly calm and climbed the stairs unaided.

But when he reached his bedroom he suffered the unavoidable reaction of shock and loss of blood and grew very pale. "I will never come out of this," he murmured, his natural terror of death overcoming him. He gave orders to send at once for a surgeon and a priest.

As the Court was not then in residence at Versailles, almost every necessity was lacking—there were no sheets on the King's bed, and he was placed, wrapped only in a dressing gown, on the bare mattress.

At some time in his childhood, Louis had acquired the singular belief that, as a direct descendant of Saint Louis, it was impossible for him to be damned, provided that he received the Sacraments before he died. Convinced now that death was near, he asked once more for a priest. His confessor, Father Desmarets, could not be found, and a simple priest from the town, awed by the identity of the august sinner, was ushered into the room. The King confessed rapidly and demanded absolution, promising that he would confess at greater length when he had the opportunity.

The Dauphin's surgeon, Hévin, dressed the wound and bled the King; etiquette forbade that he do more. When Louis' own surgeon, La Martinière, arrived, he probed the wound as far as the rib and declared that it was only superficial. The assailant had used a crude knife having a four-inch blade on one end and a stiletto, somewhat shorter and narrower, on the other; it was the latter with which he had stabbed the King, inflicting an upward wound about three inches long, between the fourth and fifth ribs. The heavy winter clothing which Louis wore mitigated the force of the blow; otherwise the wound would have been more serious.

Notwithstanding La Martinière's reassuring diagnosis, the King's pessimism was undiminished and communicated itself to his family. Overcome by the sight of blood, the Dauphine fainted, while Madame Adélaïde rushed to and fro like one demented. Marie Leczinska was at first placid, thinking that the King had only suffered an attack of indigestion, but when she saw her husband's side covered with blood she too became ill.

The Dauphin, although weeping, managed to keep his head. He asked Bernis if he should summon the Council, and the Abbé answered, "Without a doubt, Monseigneur; never has it been more necessary to call it."

The Dauphin turned back into the King's room to receive his orders and asked his father if he suffered. "I would suffer more, my son," replied Louis, "if such an accident had happened to you." He appointed the Dauphin

Lieutenant of the Kingdom, giving him authority to preside at the Council, and handed the keys of his private
papers to the Comte d'Argenson.

Father Desmarets having by now arrived, the King
wished to confess for the third time. "He fears the devil,"
said a courtier, "and at the slightest ailment is frightened
at the thought of eternity and its horrors."

He made a full confession, and publicly "demanded pardon of his children for the scandal that he had caused
them and of the Queen for the wrongs he had done her.
He said to the Dauphin that he would reign now and
that the Kingdom would be in good hands."

Meanwhile, the assassin had been taken into the guard-
room and stripped. "All right," he shouted defiantly, "I
did it. There is no use looking for anyone else."

He denied that the knife was poisoned but muttered
ominously, "See that the Dauphin is well guarded!" When
asked if he had any accomplices he replied, "Yes, I have
them, but they are not here."

The man's ambiguous answers, coupled with the fact
that he had 35 gold louis in his pocket, caused Machault,
who was in charge of the interrogation, to suspect a widespread conspiracy. In an attempt to obtain more information he ordered torture applied, and the feet of the
miserable wretch were burned with torches. In vain; the
assailant refused to speak another word, and at last he
was taken off to the town jail of Versailles.

It was subsequently discovered that he was an unem-
ployed lackey named François Damiens, who had formerly
been in the service of a Counselor of *Parlement*. In his

employer's house he had listened to denunciations of the
King and the Jesuits, and being mentally unbalanced, he
decided to attack the Monarch. Damiens did not intend
to kill the King; he merely wished, by frightening him,
to persuade Louis to treat *Parlement* (then in exile) with
less severity.

In spite of his muddled statements, the mad attempt
was Damiens' own idea; he had no accomplices whatever.

Immediately after the attack a courier galloped to
Trianon to inform the Marquise, who returned at once
to Versailles, racked with fear for the King's life and
uncertainty for her own future. Would this prove to be
a repetition of the travesty at Metz? She knew quite well
that the Jesuits would play upon the King's fears and
push their advantage to the limit, and she envisioned
reliving the fate of Madame de Châteauroux.

Not daring to go to the King unless he sent for her, she
shut herself up in her apartments with Madame du
Haussay, and wept, and fainted, and wept again.

If ever she had a friend, she had one now in the Abbé
de Bernis. "I went down to see her," he recalled. "She
flung herself into my arms with cries and sobs that would
have touched the hearts of her enemies, if the hearts of
courtiers are ever touched."

The Abbé returned to comfort her every hour during
that first endless night of the King's illness and many
times during the days of suspense which followed.

Never once did Louis ask for the panic-stricken Marquise who waited in her apartments below; never once

did he mention to Bernis or anyone else the name of
the woman who had been his faithful friend. His thoughts
may have returned again and again to her, but the Marquise, not knowing what those thoughts were, waited in
terror. Would he yield to the prayers of the devout and
order her to leave Versailles?

The courtiers, quivering with curiosity, flocked into
the Marquise's apartment, pretending sympathy and
bringing disquieting gossip. "They came to see how she
took it," according to Madame du Haussay, "under pretense of interest, and Madame did nothing but weep and
faint away. Doctor Quesnay never left her, nor I either."

The people, who received the news of the attack on the
King with furious cries and the utmost despair, gathered
in crowds under the Marquise's windows, shouting insults
and threats at "the King's slut." By some mysterious proc-
ess of mass psychology, as in the days of his illness at
Metz, the people's love for the King returned with the
news of his danger, and their accumulated hatred fell once
more on his Mistress.

In the bedroom above, Louis was quickly recovering
from what after all had been a trivial wound, but his profound melancholy deepened. He had always believed that
his subjects loved him, and he was completely unnerved
by Damiens' attack. "It is here that I suffer," he said,
placing his hand on his heart.

The wound itself caused him no pain, and the only
inconvenience was having to sleep on his left side instead
of his right, as was his habit. In spite of his obvious im-

provement, Louis continued to regard himself as dangerously ill until he was unexpectedly jolted out of his hypochondria.

An old soldier named Landsmath, an officer of the King's Hunt who had known Louis since his childhood, lost patience with the gloomy atmosphere of the sickroom and the hysterics of the Royal Family, and bending over the bed said, "Order these women out of here, they only upset you. I have something to tell you."

Louis, who permitted Landsmath to say anything to him, waved the Dauphine and Mesdames out of the room, and the old man, speaking in a rough voice full of affection, turned to the King:

"These idiots have deceived you, Sire. In four days you will be out hunting, and as for the blade being poisoned, that is an old wives' tale. Even if there had been any poison, it would have rubbed off on your coat."

The veteran then took off his shirt and, pointing to his own terrible scars, said, "Look, Sire, these are the kind of wounds to be frightened at. I received them thirty years ago, and I am still alive."

He then insisted that the King sit up, and Louis was relieved to find that he could do so without any pain. Landsmath closed the curtains of the bed, and going into the anteroom, which was crowded with priests and weeping women, said rudely: "His Majesty desires to sleep. See that none of you disturbs him."

Five days after the assassination attempt, although Louis was still in bed, he was well enough to receive a deputation from Brittany, and the following day the ladies of the Court were admitted to find him in his dressing gown, freshly shaved and powdered, sitting in an armchair.

Although the King's danger was past, the anguish of Madame de Pompadour continued unabated. "It is a fact," wrote the Marquis d'Argenson, "that since the attempted assassination the Marquise has not seen His Majesty for a moment. She pretends not to feel her disgrace, but little by little people are forsaking her. She has neither seen nor received any message from the King, who does not appear to give her a thought. All this time he is having daily interviews with Father Desmarets, and has made many affectionate and virtuous remarks to the Queen. "All this," he added hopefully, "means a great change at Court."

Madame de Pompadour was sustained during her agonizing suspense by a few devoted friends—Madame de Mirepoix, Madame de Brancas, the Prince de Soubise, Marigny, Bernis, and Dr. Quesnay, who saw the King five or six times a day and reassured her that "there is nothing to fear." But where was Machault, the Keeper of the Seals, Machault, who owed everything to her and whom she intended to make Prime Minister? He was constantly with the King, but he, who could have dissipated her fears as no one else, did not come through the door of the red lacquer room.

In order to quiet the Marquise's nerves, Madame du Haussay sent her son every day to spy on what was happening in the King's apartments. One morning he returned to say that Machault was having a long conversation with the King, and Madame du Haussay sent him back to watch the Keeper of the Seals after he left the sickroom. Surely, if he was still loyal to the Marquise, he would come to give her information!

But the boy came running back half an hour later to report that Machault, after leaving the King, had gone straight to his own house, "followed by a crowd of people." Upon hearing this, the Marquise burst into tears, saying bitterly, "So that is a friend!"

Bernis said soothingly, "You mustn't be in too much of a hurry to condemn him at a time like this."

But the Marquise, certain that Machault had deserted her, remained inconsolable, and within an hour her fears were confirmed.

Machault appeared at her door, his face more cold and stern than usual, and asked, "How is Madame de Pompadour?"

"Alas, Monsieur," replied Madame du Haussay, "just about as you would imagine!" Machault went into the Marquise's room, where he remained alone with her for half an hour. Madame du Haussay recorded the results of the interview:

Madame rang, and I entered, followed by the Abbé. Madame was in tears, and sobbed, "I have to go away, my dear Abbé."

I made her take some orange-flower water, in a silver goblet, because her teeth were chattering.

Afterward she told me to call her equerry, and she calmly gave him orders to prepare her house in Paris, and to tell all her household to be ready to start.... She then told her friends that Machault "believes, or pretends to believe, that the priests will demand my dismissal and precipitate an open scandal, but Quesnay and all the doctors say that now there is not the slightest danger."

Madame de Mirepoix came in and exclaimed, "What are all these trunks for? Your people say that you are leaving."

"Yes, my dear friend, the Master wishes it; that is what M. de Machault said."

"And what is his advice to you?"

"That I should leave without delay," answered the Marquise.

"He wishes to be master, your Keeper of the Seals," exclaimed Madame de Mirepoix angrily, "and he is betraying you! He who abandons the game, loses it."

Madame de Pompadour was surprised and then gave her clever friend a thoughtful look. A short time later Marigny came into Madame du Haussay's tiny room and said cautiously:

"She is staying, but not a word to anyone! We will pretend that she has gone, in order not to arouse her enemies. It is the little Maréchale (de Mirepoix) who has done the trick; but the Keeper of the Seals will pay for this one day."

Bernis condemned Machault for his cold and neglectful treatment of the Marquise during the tense days of the King's illness but denied that the Keeper of the Seals had advised her to leave. If he did, then Machault was guilty of a blunder which was in sharp contrast to his customary shrewdness; for it should have been clear to him that if Louis had not dismissed the Marquise when he was afraid of dying, he would never do so now that he was convalescent.

The King was thoroughly weary of his dull family and priests for whom he had no further need, and his desire

to see the Marquise, which had evaporated only at the fear
of death, returned as soon as he was out of danger.

At last, one day [wrote Dufort de Cheverny] it was
nearly two o'clock, and the apartment was almost empty.
The King had on his dressing gown and night cap and
carried a cane, leaning on it lightly. Sometimes he glanced
out the window, sometimes he would stop, and stand lost
in thought. The Dauphin, to whom the King made no sign
of dismissal, was chatting with the Marquis de Muy; the
Dauphine could not summon courage to take her leave.

The King, being at last reassured that everyone else
was at dinner, gave the Dauphine the signal to depart.
She came forward, made the customary curtsy, and went
out. She was accompanied by several ladies, among them
Madame de Brancas, a friend of Madame de Pompadour.
The King said to Madame de Brancas, "Give me your
cloak."

She took it off and gave it to him. With a bow to her,
he put it around his shoulders, walked around the room
in silence, and then left the room. He turned in the direction of the Inner Apartments, and the Dauphin, who was
in the habit of going with him, took a few steps in the
same direction. He was not halfway across the room when
the King turned around. "Don't you come," he said. The
Dauphin obeyed, and returned to his own apartment for
dinner.

The King came back between three and four o'clock.
One would not have known that he was the same man.
His mind was alert and he had an agreeable look on his
face. A smile hovered around his lips, and he talked ani-
matedly, without a sign of ill temper. He had something
to say to all of us, made one or two joking remarks about
the cloak he was wearing, and then left, saying that he
was going to dine, and urging us to do the same.

He came back, and it was easy to guess that he had been
to see Madame de Pompadour. Just this one conversation

with a friend who was more interested in his welfare than anyone else in the Kingdom had soothed his troubled spirit which was more in need of comfort than his body.

Partially, but only partially, as the result of his equivocal attitude toward the Marquise, Machault was dismissed. Her resentment was justifiable, and his callous behavior had destroyed their friendship. But it is an exaggeration to say that she destroyed him; more accurately, she did nothing to save him. The Keeper of the Seals (and Minister of Marine as well) was feared and detested by the clergy as the originator of the *vingtième* and also by the courts as head of the magistracy. The King dismissed him only because he thought that the *Parlement* would never settle down in peace as long as the Keeper of the Seals was retained in office.

Louis' private feelings were unmistakable. "They have led me such a dance," he wrote to Madame L'Infante, "that they have forced me to dismiss Machault, a man after my own heart. I shall never get over it."

This sincere regret shines between the lines of the King's letter to Machault:

M. de Machault, although I am convinced of your integrity and the honesty of your intentions, present circumstances compel me to ask you to hand me back my Seals and to resign your position as Minister of Marine. Be assured always of my good will and friendship. If there is anything you would like me to do for your children, at any time, do not hesitate to ask me. It will be well for you to remain for a time at Arnouville. I shall continue to pay you your salary of 20,000 livres and am allowing you to retain your honorary rank as Keeper of the Seals.

While the Marquise was not sorry to see the government lose the competent services of Machault, she was far more preoccupied with the one enemy who remained, the enemy who was the most dangerous of all—d'Argenson. The proud Minister of War, who disliked equals and never unbent to inferiors, felt stronger than ever after the dismissal of his rival Machault.

The gentle Abbé, hoping to avoid an open clash between the Marquise and her powerful antagonist, called on d'Argenson and tried to persuade him to be more friendly, pointing out that the Favorite was willing to overlook the past. D'Argenson, taking the Marquise's overtures (which Bernis had spent hours persuading her to extend) as a sign of weakness, received the Abbé coldly and showed no interest in conciliation. Clever though he was, d'Argenson was falling into the error which had destroyed Maurepas—overconfidence.

"He is puffed up," said Bernis, "about Machault's dismissal, which leaves the field wide open to him. I am afraid it will only bring about a death struggle."

The incident which touched off the clash that Bernis had predicted was d'Argenson's obstinate refusal to conceal from the King letters which referred to Damiens' attack. The Marquise knew that Louis, who could not even bring himself to mention his assailant by name, merely referring to him as "Ce monsieur," wanted to forget his unnerving experience, and she ordered Janelle to omit, from the letters he showed the King, any which mentioned the attempted assassination.

D'Argenson was also Minister for Paris, thereby having

jurisdiction over the post office and the police, and when he learned of this, threatened the Postmaster-General with the Bastille if he obeyed the Favorite. Madame de Pompadour realized that the hour of decision had arrived. She went at once to the Minister of War and demanded an explanation of his threats to Janelle. The interview was stormy, and d'Argenson refused to rescind his orders, saying insolently, "I shall not change my opinion, Madame, and I am astounded that you, who have no authority to do so, presume to interfere in a matter which concerns myself alone."

"For a long time," answered the Marquise, "I have been aware of your feelings toward me. I see plainly that it is impossible to change them. I do not know how it will end, but one thing is certain: either you or I will have to go."

When Madame returned [reported Madame du Haussay] she was in a vile humor. She leaned on the mantelpiece, gazing into the fireplace. M. de Bernis entered, and said, "You look like a dreaming sheep."

She emerged from her thoughts, and throwing her muff on a chair, remarked, "The sheep is dreaming of a wolf."

The King came in a few minutes later, and I heard Madame crying. The Abbé asked me to bring some Hoffman's Drops, and the King sugared the dose himself, presenting it to Madame in a gracious manner. She ended by smiling, and kissed the King's hands.

The next day the Comte d'Argenson was exiled, his letter of dismissal being as brutal as Machault's was gentle:

M. d'Argenson, I have no further need for your services, and I command you to hand me your resignation as Minister of War and to retire to your estate at Les Ormes.

With the destruction of her principal foe, the triumph of Madame de Pompadour was complete, although her influence in his fall might not have been as decisive as she imagined. Louis, in the recesses of his devious mind, no longer held his high opinion of d'Argenson, blaming him for laxness in prosecuting the authors of seditious circulars, and was willing, indeed eager, to relinquish him.

But the departure of Machault and d'Argenson, though a brilliant triumph for the Marquise, was an unlucky day for France, which lost the services of a capable Minister of Marine and a superior Minister of War on the eve of a major war. D'Argenson was no friend of Austria, but he would have prosecuted the war vigorously, and Machault was highly popular with officers of the Navy; their successors, hopelessly incompetent, brought satisfaction to no one except Madame de Pompadour, whose creatures they were.

As for Damiens, the wretched lunatic whose harebrained action had unleashed such a train of fury, his punishment was more hideous than any man, even a sane one, should have had to bear. At four-thirty in the afternoon of March 28, 1757, he was taken to the Place de Grève, which was surrounded by a vast throng of people. First his right hand, the one which had struck the King, was plunged into boiling sulfur, causing him to utter a piercing shriek; his body was then torn with pincers, and molten lead was poured into the wounds, after which he was drawn and quartered.

His endurance was so extraordinary that after more than an hour he was still alive, and the strength of four horses was insufficient to tear his limbs from his body. Damiens, who usually swore profusely, made no sound except for intermittent screams of agony during his horrible punishment. Although he was not a religious man, he listened attentively to the two priests who comforted him and often turned his head to kiss the crucifix which they extended.

In spite of brutal lashings, the straining horses failed to pull Damiens apart, and finally, in desperation, the executioners hacked at his limbs with an axe. His left leg parted first, and the spectators, who until then had appeared indifferent, clapped their hands. Then the other leg separated from the still-breathing trunk, followed by the two arms; only then did Damiens' head fall back, and when the trunk and the severed limbs were piled up in a heap to be burned, the heart, said Croÿ, "still palpitated."

"Many persons, including women," said the disgusted Madame du Haussay, "had the barbarous curiosity to watch this execution, among them Madame de Préandeau, the beautiful wife of a Farmer-General. She rented a double window-space for 12 livres, and played cards while she was waiting. When someone told the King this, he covered his eyes with his hands, exclaiming, "Oh, the unspeakable creature!" But Louis was misjudging the Farmer-General's wife. Madame de Préandeau did have a heart, after all.

"Jesus!" she cried, when the executioners lashed the horses, "how I pity the poor animals!"

XIX

THE SEVEN YEARS' WAR

*T*HE Austrian Ambassador, Count von Stahremberg, who had said of Madame de Pompadour that "it is to her that we owe everything," in a letter to Kaunitz described the dismissal of d'Argenson as "a most fortunate circumstance for us." His elation was justified, for with d'Argenson disappeared the last of Austria's foes in the Council of Louis XV; henceforth the Austrian sympathies of the Marquise would reign unchecked.

Exactly a year after the first Treaty of Versailles a second and stronger one was concluded by the Allies, a treaty which envisaged the partition of Prussia. France agreed to increase her contribution of troops to the common cause and to pay a yearly subsidy to the Empress until her armies had recovered Silesia. In return France was to receive the ports of Ostend and Nieuport and later, contingent on Austria's recovery of Silesia, the fortresses of Ypres and Mons. Madame l'Infante's husband, Don Philip, was promised the Austrian Netherlands and Luxembourg in return for the cession of his Italian duchies to Maria Theresa.

This treaty was almost entirely to the advantage of the Empress, for if her arms were successful she would recover

Silesia and gain additional territory from Frederick, thus emerging from the war as the supreme power in Germany. As for the Netherlands (Belgium), Maria Theresa could well afford to relinquish them—they were nothing but a burden and their remoteness from Vienna rendered them almost indefensible. Stahremberg had not foreseen such a favorable treaty, and he owed his unexpected success to the friendliness of the Marquise.

Duclos, a poor historian, originated the story that the august Empress of Austria and Queen of Hungary, in whose veins flowed the proudest blood in Europe, had achieved her alliance with France by the simple but demeaning expedient of writing a flattering letter to Madame de Pompadour in which Maria Theresa is alleged to have addressed the Marquise as *Ma cousine*.

No such letter was ever written, nor was it necessary. Madame de Pompadour, devoted to Maria Theresa's interests, was already bound, heart and soul, to Austria. High as she had climbed, the Marquise knew that there were certain favors she could never expect, among them a personal letter from the brilliant and virtuous woman who ruled in Vienna.

But Maria Theresa, while thoroughly disapproving of everything which Madame de Pompadour represented in her personal life, was too consummate a diplomat to ignore her assistance, and in 1759 she presented to the Marquise a desk of fine lacquer, set with a portrait of the Empress surrounded by diamonds. The Austrian ruler would not stoop to write to her ally's Mistress, but Count Kaunitz performed the task with his habitual grace:

The Empress is touched, Madame, by the interest which you continue to take in Her alliance with the King ... and as she thinks that you will not be displeased, and that the King cannot fail to approve ... She is sending directions to the Count von Stahremberg to remit to you a small token of remembrance from Her, and begs that you will be pleased to accept it as a proof of Her esteem for you.

The Marquise's letter of thanks to the proud Habsburg is embarrassing in its servility and strikingly illuminates the unbridgeable gulf which separated an Apostolic Queen from a middle-class courtesan.

May I be permitted to hope that Your Imperial Majesty will deign to accept my very humble thanks and expressions of respectful gratitude for the inestimable portrait which has been sent to me? If to deserve this precious gift, nothing more is needed than to be penetrated to the depths of one's being with sincere admiration and enthusiasm for the entrancing graces and heroic virtues of Your Imperial Majesty, no one in the world can have a better claim than I. I venture to add that there is not one of Your Imperial Majesty's subjects who does not render homage to those rare and sublime qualities.

You are accustomed, Madame, to observe in all those who have the privilege of approaching you the sentiments which I have the honor to express, but I trust Your Majesty will condescend to remember mine, and to look upon them as inspired by the most profound respect with which I am, Madame, Your Imperial Majesty's most humble and obedient servant,

JEANNE DE POMPADOUR

The people of Paris did not share the Marquise's enthusiasm for Maria Theresa, and most of them heartily disliked the alliance with the former enemy. The war had hardly begun before another verse appeared in the streets:

> Versons pour la reine d'Hongrie
> Tout notre sang,
> Donnons-lui pour la Silésie
> Tout notre argent,
> Elle a su plaire à Pompadour.

> Let us shed for the Queen of Hungary
> All our blood,
> Let us give her for Silesia
> All our money,
> She has made herself attractive to Pompadour.

Having taken an important part in the reversal of alliances, the Favorite aspired to a more grandiose role— nothing less than to choose personally the generals who would lead France to victory. Ruled not by the merits of the Marshals but by her personal feelings toward them, her interference in military affairs is almost wholly indefensible, and here her critics stand on firm ground.

The Court of Vienna had requested the appointment of the Prince de Conti as French Commander in Chief, and the King had promised the post to him, but the Marquise, resenting Conti's support of Madame de Coislin the year before, influenced Louis to renege on his word. Not only did she deny the supreme command to the Prince, she refused to permit him to engage in any military activity at all. Her ability to thwart Conti, a Prince of the Blood and Director of *Le Secret,* is an indication of the enormous power which she had gathered into her hands; but her meddling was not to her credit, for Conti possessed more military talent than the rest of the Marshals combined.

The first commander of the French armies in Germany was Marshal d'Estrées, whose wife had been exiled from Court for inciting *la petite Morphise* against the Marquise. D'Estrées had no particular ability, but his opponent, the Duke of Cumberland, who commanded the army defending Hanover had even less. By luck rather than skill, Marshal d'Estrées gained the battle of Hastenbeck in July 1757 but was recalled the day after his victory. The enmity of the Marquise, added to the powerful hostility of Pâris-Duverney, to whom the Marshal had refused to confide his plan of campaign, accomplished what the Duke of Cumberland had failed to do.

The suspicious Parisians, guessing the real reasons for d'Estrées' recall, were furious, and their anger mounted when they learned that his successor was Marshal Richelieu. When the displaced commander returned to Versailles, Louis received him kindly but insisted that he call on Madame de Pompadour.

"It is by the King's command, Madame," said the demoted Marshal, "that I have come to pay my respects to you. I am perfectly aware of the sentiments you entertain toward me, but I have too much confidence in the justice of the King, my Master, to fear them." Without waiting to hear the Marquise's reply, Marshal d'Estrées turned his back and stalked from her apartment.

Marshal Richelieu had gained a certain reputation by his capture of Minorca and siege of Genoa during the previous war, and although he was less competent than d'Estrées, he inherited from his predecessor a ready-made opportunity to strike the enemy a crushing blow. The army of Cumberland had retreated into a *cul de sac* at the mouth of the Elbe, and its commander, seeing that his situation was nearly hopeless, concluded an armistice with Richelieu.

The Convention of Kloster-Seven, as the agreement was called, was signed on September 10, 1757, and by its terms the Duke of Cumberland agreed to disband his army, guaranteeing that his troops would take no further part in the war. The Convention was actually a military *capitulation,* but as Cumberland flatly refused to accept that word, Richelieu rashly acceded to his wishes. By doing so he exceeded his powers, for he was authorized to accept only a capitulation in the field and not a convention, which required subsequent ratification by the respective governments.

Worse still, Richelieu was incredibly foolhardy in neglecting to take any hostages or set any date for the execution of the convention. Louis XV reluctantly ratified it, but Bernis, who had become Foreign Minister in July, was filled with pessimism. "I shall not be astonished," he said, "if the whole of M. de Richelieu's fine convention goes up in smoke."

His surmise was all too correct. George II recalled his unsuccessful son, and as soon as Frederick II's military position improved, the English government disavowed the convention. The Hanoverian troops which Richelieu had carelessly permitted to escape were to inflict, a year later, a crushing defeat on the French at Créfeld.

Richelieu was more interested in plundering northern

Germany than in fighting battles, and his troops enthusiastically followed the example he set them. All standards of military honor seemed to have vanished from the armies of France, which were encumbered with the chefs, lackeys, hairdressers, and courtesans of incompetent officers; the baggage trains of the army, loaded with such military necessities as powder, pomade, and perfumes, stretched for miles across the German plain. An observer would have been justified in concluding that the entire Court of Versailles was on the move.

Henri Martin, in his *History of France,* wrote that "they resembled the cohorts of Darius and Xerxes rather than the armies of Turenne and Gustavus Adolphus. The officers permitted the soldiers to indulge in all kinds of depredations in order that their misery might not revolt against the spectacle of their leaders' magnificent luxury."

"Worst of all," wrote Bernis to Stainville, now French Ambassador at Vienna, "the lack of discipline in our troops, the sordid avarice of our generals, and their insatiable greed are turning the whole Empire against us. They respect no proprieties in the imperial towns, men are dying of famine because of their thefts, and they are dishonoring the name of France."

In spite of the gay progress of Richelieu's army, he was for the moment a powerful threat to Frederick, and had he been permitted to join the Prince de Soubise, together they might have freed Saxony and annihilated the King of Prussia.

But the Prince de Soubise was the darling of the Marquise, who it sometimes appeared, ran the war with the sole aim of elevating him to the supreme command. Soubise belonged to the great house of Rohan, and unlike Maurepas, he was the friend of all the King's Mistresses; lively and charming socially, he possessed no morals whatever.

As Soubise was younger than the Marshals and only a Lieutenant General, the Favorite dared not risk an open scandal by naming him Commander in Chief—not at the beginning of the war, anyway. But that was her ultimate intention, and Soubise persuaded her that his victories would reflect renown upon her name. Therefore Madame de Pompadour, wishing all the glory for her favorite and jealous of Richelieu, refused to permit the Marshal to join Soubise and ordered him to divide his army, sending only part of it to reinforce the Prince.

Richelieu had grave defects as a commander, but Soubise had more. He was incapable of enforcing discipline, and his army, a mutinous mob, pillaged and destroyed everything in sight including churches and convents. Soubise was personally courageous, but his excessive vanity and insatiable hunger for military glory was to be his ruin, as Bernis gloomily predicted.

"We are anxious about M. de Soubise," he wrote, again to the Comte de Stainville. "Though he is prudent and all his connections are excellent, we are afraid that the desire to win a battle, or the fear of retreating, may expose him to defeat."

At Erfurt Soubise joined his nominal superior, the Prince of Hildburghausen, who commanded the Imperial army, and together the Allies advanced on Leipzig. Before they had proceeded far, however, they encountered the

Prussian army under Frederick near the small Saxon village of Rosbach. Hildburghausen, who was as fatuous as the French general, wanted to engage in battle, but Soubise, although the Allies were more than twice as numerous as the Prussians, suddenly suffered a rare access of caution and advised a retreat. A last-minute letter from Stainville in Vienna, urging him to attack, changed his mind and ultimately destroyed what little military reputation Soubise had.

On November 5, 1757, the Battle of Rosbach opened with an attempt by the Allies to outflank the enemy, but the astute Frederick, pretending to withdraw, himself succeeded in turning the French flank; the troops, lacking confidence in their officers and deserted by their ineffectual Imperial allies, broke and fled in all directions. The defeat, which fell hardest upon the French, was catastrophic; all their baggage, artillery, flags, and drums fell into the hands of the Prussians, 5,000 were taken prisoner, and 3,000 were left dead on the field. Frederick, losing only 165 soldiers, had won a stupendous victory at a ridiculously cheap price.

A captured French officer, dining that night with his Royal captor, asked Frederick how he had won so easily. Smiling thinly, the King replied, "The Prince de Soubise has twenty cooks and not a single spy; while I, on my part, have twenty spies and but one cook."

Whatever the cause, there was no minimizing the extent of the disaster and Soubise, who at least was honest, did not try.

"I write to Your Majesty," he reported to Louis, "in a paroxysm of despair. Your army has been completely routed. I cannot say how many of your officers are killed, taken prisoners, or missing."

The Parisians were disgusted by the disaster, but reacting with their customary insouciance, hummed a little ditty:

> Soubise dit, la lanterne à la main,
> J'ai beau chercher, où diable est mon armée?

> Soubise says, lantern in his hand,
> I have looked in vain,
> Where in the devil is my army?

But popular fury rose against the Favorite, who was considered primarily responsible, and every day Madame de Pompadour received anonymous letters, mocking verses, insults, and threats of poison or assassination. She was overwhelmed at the defeat which had engulfed her protegé, and for a long time was plunged into the deepest melancholy, being unable to sleep without the aid of drugs.

Ten days after Rosbach she was still in such a state of depression that she made her will, believing that she had not long to live. But her hatred of Frederick grew stronger than ever, and she resolved to persist in the war until he was ruined and Prussia destroyed.

"Why does Providence leave him the power to make so many unhappy?" she wrote to Madame de Lutzelbourg, and to Kaunitz, "I hate the conqueror more than I have ever done. Let us put forth every effort; let us crush the Attila of the North."

But Bernis, who had lost whatever initial enthusiasm he might have had for the war, was convinced after Rosbach that France's position was hopeless and that to persist in the continental struggle would only mean the loss of the colonies. He tried to persuade the Marquise that Vienna should make peace with Berlin, but she, blind to the vast importance of Canada and India and obsessed with a desire to avenge Soubise, would not listen. The Abbé was in despair and confided to his journal that she "looked at all State questions like a child."

Marshal Richelieu was replaced in February 1758 by the Comte de Clermont, another choice of Madame de Pompadour. Clermont was gentle and affable, sincerely interested in the welfare of the ordinary wretched soldier but woefully inadequate for his gigantic task. He did make some attempt to restore discipline and court-martialed fifty officers who were absent without leave, but his attempts to reorganize the Army were foredoomed to failure.

"I have found Your Majesty's Army divided into three parts," he wrote in a despatch to Louis. "One above ground composed of bandits and robbers, another under the ground, and the third in the hospital. Shall I retreat with the first division or wait until one of the others has joined me?" The unruly mob which the unfortunate Clermont commanded was routed at Créfeld, a defeat as ruinous as Rosbach, and the Marquise, who now regarded herself as Minister of War, was plunged anew into despair. Clermont returned to Paris in disgrace and was succeeded by the equally incapable Marquis de Contades, who duly lost the Battle of Minden the following year.

By now Bernis was desperate, and he informed the Marquise that he would resign if the King did not urge the Empress to come to terms with Frederick. Madame de Pompadour was enraged at the temerity of her old friend, whom she had always considered a "plump white rabbit," and in the bitter atmosphere of defeat and despair their long friendship dissolved.

The Abbé's conduct as Foreign Minister came close to hysteria. The Marquise told Madame du Haussay that she realized after a week that his appointment had been a mistake and that the position was too big for him. Bernis' normally placid and somewhat smug nature was incapable of standing the strain, and his nerves went to pieces, as many of his letters to the Comte de Stainville plainly show:

November 22, 1757 [after Rosbach]: ... Sensitive, and, if I may dare to say so, sensible as I am, I am dying on the rack, and my martyrdom is useless to the State.

March 31, 1758: My reported quarrel or coldness with Madame de Pompadour has gone the rounds of Paris. The object is to set us at variance, but as I love her with all my heart, and abhor ingratitude, we shall always be intimate friends. . . .

May 1, 1758 [the second anniversary of the Treaty of Versailles, which the Abbé had negotiated]: I would buy peace with an arm and a leg if it could be had within three months.

June 6, 1758: ... The King will never abandon the Empress, but His Majesty cannot ruin himself with her. I am threatened in anonymous letters with being torn in pieces by the people. . . . Our friend [the Marquise] runs at least the same danger. . . .

August 1, 1758: Comprehend how much I suffer in finding myself perpetually represented as a man who is trying to destroy my benefactress and my friend. On the other hand, I should be the basest of men if I concealed from her certain truths.

September 3, 1758: Madame de Pompadour tells me sometimes to amuse myself and not make gloom. . . . I have converted the Infanta to peace; she feels the necessity for it. If her father is ruined, what will become of her?

Madame de Pompadour grew weary of the Foreign Minister's ceaseless sighings, and his insistence on telling her unpleasant truths, which in calmer days she could accept, increasingly irritated her. "I see plainly," he said, in pressing his urgings for peace, "that no one speaks to you in language as frank as mine; they all give you hopes. But I, who am not a courtier and who love you with all my heart, I who see what will surely happen—I have the courage to tell it to you."

The Abbé's defeatism, infuriating as it was to the Marquise, was fully justified, but her emotional involvement in the war, her pride, and her stubborn determination to offer another chance to Soubise blinded her to France's deteriorating strength. At all costs the war must continue, and Bernis, who opposed it, would have t go.

The Marquise had by now acquired another grievance against the Abbé. He had become a great favorite with the Dauphin and the Royal Family, and Madame de Pompadour pretended to believe that he was conspiring against her. Negotiations were underway with Rome to raise Bernis to the Sacred College, and she skillfully used that prospect to frighten the King. Louis said, "When a Cardinal sits in the council, he ends by becoming the head of it." The Marquise convinced him that Bernis aspired to be Prime Minister, and in October 1758 he accepted the Abbé's resignation.

To replace Bernis at the Foreign Ministry the Marquise chose the Comte de Stainville, who, upon his return from Vienna, was created Duc de Choiseul; only a few years earlier his decision to betray his cousin Madame de Choiseul-Romanet to the Favorite had proved itself one of prudent and profitable foresight.

Although Bernis was no longer Minister of Foreign Affairs, he remained a member of the Council for two more months, mainly because the Marquise needed his influence with the clergy to raise money for the war. But the Abbé's days at Court were numbered, and he knew it. On November 30th the King bestowed upon him the Red Hat of a Prince of the Church, saying with a smile, "I have never made so fine a Cardinal."

But Madame du Haussay, who knew what lay ahead for Bernis, wrote that the King "threw him the Red Hat as if it were a bone to a dog." Not two weeks later the new Cardinal received the letter which he had expected:

My Cousin, the repeated requests you have made me to resign the Ministry of Foreign Affairs have convinced me that in the future you would not properly discharge the duties you so desire to get rid of. It is from that reflection that I have determined to accept your resignation as Secretary of State.

But I have felt at the same time that you have not responded to the confidence I have shown you in such critical times, nor the singular favors which I have heaped upon you in so short a period. Therefore, I order you to go to one of your abbeys, whichever you choose, in twice twenty-four hours from now, without seeing anyone, and until I send you word to return. Send me back the letters of mine which you have, in a sealed package.

On which I pray God to have you, My Cousin, in His
Holy keeping.

At Versailles this 13th of December, 1758.

LOUIS

Most of the Foreign Ambassadors had expected Bernis
to become Prime Minister and were stupefied at his dismissal. He retired to the country, still bleating of his
loyalty to the Marquise and his sacrifices in her behalf; he
retired with the respect of almost everyone who did not
know him. Marmontel, whose knowledge of and dislike for
Bernis were equally intense, wrote a scathing description
of him "on the day when, in the habit of a Cardinal, in a
cap, red stockings, and with a rochet trimmed with the
richest point lace, he was going to present himself to the
King."

I traversed his Apartments between two long rows of
servants in new scarlet dresses laced with gold. On entering
his room, I found him as vain as a peacock, more chubby-
cheeked than ever, admiring himself in his glory, and
above all, unable to tire of looking at his rochet and scarlet
stockings.

"Don't you think me well dressed?" he said.

"Exceedingly well," I answered, "your new dignity sits
admirably on you, and I congratulate you."

These were the last words that ever passed between us,
and I easily consoled myself for not owing anything to him,
not only because I saw in him nothing but a coxcomb
invested with the purple, but because I soon beheld him
rude and ungrateful to her who had created him.

And so Cardinal Bernis, with his petulant mouth, enormous jowls, shrewd appraising eyes, and dainty fat hands,
went out of public life for twelve years. When the King

recalled him in 1770 to become Ambassador to the Vatican, the woman who had made his fortune—she to whom he had read his verses and given lessons in etiquette at Étioles so long ago—was no more.

A few months after his departure the Marquise, lying ill one night, said wistfully to Madame du Haussay, "I think of how I would have enjoyed his society and grown old with an amiable and faithful friend, if he had not become Minister."

The Duc de Choiseul was only a year older than the Marquise when he became Foreign Minister, and she soon discovered that he was a Minister after her own heart. He possessed enormous self-confidence, was loquacious, witty and good humored, and admired Voltaire whose views on religion he shared. Choiseul became at once the adored of the *philosophes,* the Jansenists, and *Parlement,* and it is almost astonishing that the King kept him in office and bestowed upon him such great power.

The answer lay partly in Choiseul's ability and partly in his charm. He was resolute and energetic, and so clear-headed that he towered over the rest of the Ministers. France had found her first Prime Minister since Fleury.

The Duc was in appearance plain, almost ugly, being short and red-haired, with a turned-up nose and small bright eyes which made him look something like an intelligent, malicious pig. But his charm was so great that he captivated men as well as women. "Never," said the Baron de Gleichen, "have I known a man so capable as he of spreading joy and contentment around his person."

The King, who differed from him as a borzoi from a terrier, fell under his spell, and the Marquise, who found his views in complete harmony with her own, gave him an affection that no previous Minister had ever received. The uninitiated whispered that they were lovers, but no rumor could have been more erroneous. The nature of her own disposition was refutation enough; moreover, Choiseul already had a mistress. But if Madame de Pompadour's affection for him was not physical, it was enduring, and before she died she relinquished into his hands most of the power she had striven so long to acquire.

Choiseul agreed that the war must be vigorously prosecuted, and his first act was to conclude a new treaty with Maria Theresa, each ally binding itself to conclude no separate peace with Frederick. The Prussian King, in spite of his brilliant victories, could fight at best only a defensive war. He ruled five million subjects, while his enemies held sway over a combined total of ninety million. They were numerous enough to survive defeat after defeat, while Frederick would have been ruined if he had suffered one Rosbach.

Writing to Voltaire on July 2, 1759, he cautiously opened the door to a separate peace with France: "It is to the King that you must address yourself, or to his Amboise in Petticoats." But the Marquise was as obdurate as ever and refused any thought of ending the war.

Provided it left him in possession of Silesia, Frederick would have welcomed peace at any time and never more than in 1759, which was the worst year of the war for him. A coalition of Austrians and Russians almost destroyed him at Kunersdorf, and a Russian army later in the year occupied Berlin and held it for ransom.

But if fortune smiled on her Allies, she turned a stony countenance to France. By 1759 Clive had won India for England, and in September General Wolfe defeated the Marquis de Montcalm and tore Canada from the feeble hands of the French.

At home the plight of the finances approached desperation. The King tried in vain to raise a loan from Spain, and money for the Royal Household became so scarce that the stables at Versailles lacked hay and oats. Silhouette, the Comptroller-General, resorted to heroic measures to lower the deficit by confiscating half the profits of the Farmers-General and reducing pensions. The King agreed to contribute his card-playing fund, but his action was nullified by Choiseul, who reimbursed him from the secret funds of the Foreign Ministry.

Silhouette taxed servants, horses, carriages, and bachelors and persuaded Louis, the Marquise, and the courtiers to send their silver to be melted at the mint. All in vain; M. Silhouette found it impossible to create substance where there was none, and when he suggested temporary bankruptcy, the accumulated resentment of those whose privileges he had curtailed burst upon his head. He was dismissed in November 1759.

In 1761 the Marquise threw a last opportunity in the path of the Prince de Soubise, giving him command of an army which was intended to cooperate with that of Marshal Broglie. Once again disaster struck French arms, and the two commanders blamed each other bitterly; Broglie (but not Soubise) was recalled in disgrace.

In that same spring occurred another abortive peace attempt. The new King of England, George III, was eager for peace, but William Pitt, the Prime Minister, was relentlessly determined to destroy France, and negotiations foundered. Choiseul then countered with the Family Pact between the two Bourbon monarchies, by which Spain agreed to enter the war against England in May 1762.

Spain was of no assistance to France—which was, indeed, almost beyond assistance—and Spain herself lost Manila and Havana to British fleets. But meanwhile two events had occurred which seemed to foreshadow peace: Pitt was overthrown and his successor, Lord Bute, wished to halt the war even though England was everywhere victorious; and the Tsaritsa Elizabeth died of a stroke in January 1762, leaving but two of Frederick's "furies" to plague him. Her successor, the insane Peter III, was openly pro-Prussian, halted Russian operations against Frederick, and even talked of joining him. Although Peter was soon murdered, his wife Catherine, who later appropriated the dubious title "The Great," refused to renew the war against Prussia.

By now even Madame de Pompadour realized that the war could not continue. Credit was exhausted, the Army was in tatters, and the people of France openly hostile. The Peace of Paris, signed on February 10, 1763, ended a seven years' war of unparalleled disaster which cost France 200,000 men, an empire in India and North America, and ultimately engulfed the monarchy. Frederick retained

Silesia and England emerged as the world's greatest Power.
It is small wonder that the people of Paris were not
amused when the Marquise ordered the sculptor Bouchardon to execute a triumphal statue of Louis XV for the
capital. The *Gazette de France* reported on June 20, 1763,
that the unveiling of the statue was received with "accla-
mations of joy" which amounted, in reality, to stony
silence.

Although the Marquise was mortified that the spectacle
was not more brilliant or more enthusiastically received,
the Peace of Paris did not arouse the resentment or even
the interest that might have been expected. One reason,
perhaps, for indifference to the treaty was the popular
absorption in another struggle which was still raging—the
fight against the Jesuits.

In 1757, while the great powers of Europe were struggling on the battlefields, remote and isolated Portugal,
tucked away in a corner of the Iberian peninsula, was the
scene of events which provoked a chain reaction throughout Catholic Europe and ultimately brought down the
Society of Jesus.

Pombal, the Portuguese Prime Minister, held the Jesuits
responsible for an insurrection which had occurred in
Paraguay in 1750 and also feared that they were conspiring
to thwart his reforms at home. In 1757 he issued an edict
forbidding members of the Order to approach the Court
without permission or to engage in commerce, preaching,
or the hearing of confessions.

In September 1758 an unsuccessful attempt was made on

the life of King Joseph I, and Pombal, declaring the Jesuits implicated in the plot, ordered their property seized in 1759, at the same time forcibly expelling them to Italy.

"There can be no doubt," wrote Bernis, about to become a Prince of the Church, "that certain Jesuits, friends of the conspirators, were either their confidants or their accomplices. This was the real origin of their expulsion from France in 1764, which might not have taken place if the Jesuits had behaved in a better manner."

When the astonishing news of Portugal's decisive action reached France, the enemies of the Order were electrified. During their long reign the Jesuits had mortally offended so many groups—Jansenists, *philosophes, Parlement,* and even other religious orders—that when their own hour of travail arrived they received support from no one. Bernis observed that "the whole nation had long been openly opposed to their Society."

The Jesuits themselves, with astonishing ineptness, handed their enemies a powerful weapon—an excuse to attack them for their far-flung commercial ventures. Father La Vallette, a member of the Order, ran a large and profitable trading company on the island of Martinique, and although the French government, prodded by the complaints of the inhabitants, remonstrated with his superiors, his activities continued unabated.

In 1755 Father La Vallette consigned a shipment of goods valued at 1,500,000 livres to the Marseilles merchandise firm of Leonci and Gouffre, to reimburse them for bills of exchange which he had drawn on them for that amount. The shipment was captured by the English, and

Leonci and Gouffre, facing ruin, appealed to the Jesuit authorities in Paris for repayment. As they obtained no relief, they were forced into bankruptcy, and their creditors thereupon successfully sued the entire Jesuit Order in France for the full amount of Father La Vallette's obligation.

Although the new General of the Society, Ricci, had at first been inclined to honor the obligation, the setback in the lower court convinced him that it would be a loss of face to admit responsibility for Father La Vallette's debts, and he swore that the good priest in faraway Martinique was operating a commercial establishment without the sanction of the Order, which, therefore, could in no way be responsible for his debts.

Ricci then decided to appeal the adverse decision not to the friendly Great Council but to the Grand Chamber of *Parlement,* a tribunal loaded with Jansenists. His audacity in placing the Society in the power of its fiercest enemies was a measure of his overweening confidence, but Bernis, who was observing developments with sharp attention, said "It really seemed as if a vertigo had seized them [the Jesuits] and made them no longer resemble their true selves."

Although Ricci swore that each establishment of the Order was self-governing in financial affairs, the Grand Chamber in May 1761 affirmed the verdict of the lower court and ordered the Jesuit Order in France to pay not only the full amount of Leonci and Gouffre's claim but 50,000 livres additional for damages. Then, realizing that its antagonists had put their heads in a trap, *Parlement* ordered an investigation of the constitutions of the Society of Jesus.

At this point Madame de Pompadour and Choiseul, both bitter opponents of the Jesuits, urged the Jansenists on in their attack. Choiseul needed the good will of *Parlement* in his attempts to raise new taxes and saw that he could best obtain it by supporting their action against the Jesuits. As for the Marquise, she only realized that here, finally, was the opportunity to avenge herself on the men who had repeatedly rebuffed and humiliated her. The motives which inspired her to encourage Choiseul and *Parlement* were far from honorable, but at least they are understandable.

A commission of *Parlement* reported that the constitutions of the Society contained provisions which were dangerous to the state and quoted, out of context, passages purporting to justify regicide. In reply the Jesuits published a defense, pointing out 758 misstatements and outright lies, but the Courts seized the publication and prevented its sale to the public.

In an attempt to afford the Order a respite, the King appointed a commission to judge the Jesuit constitutions. His commission recommended not outright suppression of the Society in France but the imposition of certain restrictions, such as consent to regular inspections of the Jesuit colleges and a guarantee not to import foreign Jesuits into France without the consent of the King.

Ricci might have saved his Order by acceptance of a compromise, but, referring to the constitutions, he grimly commanded, "Let them be as they are, or not at all!"

In 1762 *Parlement* forbade members of the Order to wear their distinctive habit or to correspond with their superiors, nor could they teach or hold public office unless they took an oath to the King. Louis was reluctant to suppress the Society, and his reluctance was strengthened by the sighs and moans of the Queen, the Dauphin, and the Dauphine, but he could not withstand indefinitely the combined pressure of Choiseul and *Parlement,* much less the malicious arguments of the Marquise.

At heart Louis would have agreed with Cardinal Bernis, who wrote to Voltaire: "I do not believe that the destruction of the Jesuits will be useful to France. I think it would have been better to govern them properly, without destroying them."

"If they [the Jesuits] should become wiser," Bernis added prophetically, "more modest, more politic, more chastened in their moral writings, less contemptuous of the other orders, more submissive to the Bishops, less presuming with the Clergy, and—above all—if there should rise among them great writers, learned men, good preachers, it is not impossible that they might recover from their fall."

For fall they did; in November 1764 the Society of Jesus was suppressed in the Kingdom of France, and in 1767 its members were banished. But even before the first event the woman whom they had hated so long had escaped from their impotent fury into a mercy they had never accorded her.

XX

THE MARQUISE GOES AWAY

*H*ER DREAMS of glory shattered by the Seven Years' War, Madame de Pompadour rapidly lost interest in the intrigues around her, of which she had been the mainspring for nearly two decades. That unflagging ambition which had spurred her onward through the years at Versailles seemed to wilt, and even the successful campaign which she and Choiseul were waging against the Jesuits held only her spasmodic interest.

Her portrait by Drouais, begun in 1763 and finished after her death, shows a middle-aged woman who appears much older than forty-two. Dressed in a simple flowered gown, she is seated at her embroidery stand, on which her small black dog has placed his forepaws. Her head is almost covered by a white shawl, evocative of those worn by the Queen, and here the Marquise looks Marie Leczinska's age. Her face is full and reveals an unmistakable double chin, and the swelling on the left side of her throat suggests a goiter.

There is nothing in her placid and resigned expression to recall the brilliant Mistress, and no trace of Reinette at all except in her eyes, which retain their alert and quizzical charm.

One day she reminded Madame du Haussay of the visit which they had paid some years before to the seeress, Madame Bontemps. The Marquise wryly recalled the disguise under which she sought to hide herself, "a false nose delicately made of a bladder, which rendered it impossible to recognize the face, and yet did not present a shocking appearance, a wart under her left eye, and her eyebrows painted." She asked the fortune teller how she would die, and the woman replied, "You will have time to prepare yourself."

Remembering the prediction, the Marquise turned to her faithful companion and said wearily, "The fortune teller said I should have time to prepare myself. I believe it, for I am dying of melancholy."

The people of France loathed her as much as ever but that was of little moment. Her enemies were scattered, and she had put her rivals to flight, from the boudoir and the Council Chamber. Her influence and her power were unchallenged, and even the Royal Family regarded her with respect.

And yet she was not happy and grew indifferent to her usual interests. From the dizzy height of her achieved ambition she gazed about her and beheld only emptiness. Her feelings might have been summed up in the words of an ancient Japanese poem which lay among her many rare books.

> I have so long been sick, I cannot tell
> What path the Spring has taken, yet I fear
> That long ago the Cherry Blossom fell
> For which mine eyes had waited all the years.

The skillfully concealed avarice, the fierce desire for possessions with which to reassure herself—all these had dissolved, and the exhausted Favorite was left with only her memories and her wasted body. Her feebleness increased and after climbing a short flight of steps she complained that her heart felt as though it would leap from her body.

The Court spent the latter part of February 1764 at Choisy. One evening Madame de Pompadour suddenly started from her chair, complaining of a pain in her chest; she fainted, and one of the lackeys carried her to bed. She had suffered a hemorrhage of one lung, and the fit of coughing which followed brought on a heart attack. The next day she developed chills and fever and the inflammation of her lungs grew worse. She had contracted bronchial pneumonia, especially dangerous to her dilated heart.

When the Court returned to Versailles, she was far too ill to be moved, and the doctors were pessimistic. The King was intensely frightened and returned nearly every day to visit her; when he could not come, he sent special couriers to keep her informed of affairs.

The Marquise slowly improved; her breathing became easier and the doctors assured her that she was recovering. She felt well enough to take a carriage ride in the park, and in a few weeks she was strong enough to return to Versailles. Her friends were overjoyed, and the poet Favart penned a pretty little verse on an eclipse then current:

Le soleil est malade,
Et Pompadour aussi,
Ce n'est qu'une passade,
L'un et l'autre est guéri.

Le bon Dieu qui seconde
Nos voeux et notre amour
Pour le bonheur du monde
Nous a rendu le jour
      et Pompadour.

The sun is sick,
And Pompadour also,
It was nothing but an interlude,
Both of them are healed.

The good God who favors
Our wishes and our love,
For the happiness of the world
Has given us back the day
And Pompadour.

But Favart's optimism was premature, and Madame du Deffand did not share it. "Madame de Pompadour is much better," she wrote to Voltaire, "but her illness is not nearly over, and I dare not entertain much hope."

Her fears were prophetic. The Marquise was hardly installed at Versailles before she suffered, on the 7th of April, a terrible relapse. The wet spring weather chilled the cavernous Royal residence which was dark and damp, the worst possible place for the sick woman. The inflammation of her lungs recurred in an aggravated form, and the doctors reluctantly informed her that the end was near.

Her will to resist had left her, and she received the news

with undisturbed calm. Her friends flocked to visit her, and she received them fully dressed, sitting upright in a gilt *bergère*. Reclining, it was impossible for her to breathe; even supported by the chair, her agony was evident to her distressed visitors.

Although the Marquise was no longer concerned with the labyrinthine life of Versailles, she made a supreme effort to be cheerful to her friends. Her *toilette* was as fresh as ever, and her sunken cheeks were carefully rouged in an attempt to conceal the ravages of the disease which was destroying her. Of her former beauty only the eyes, with their quick alert expression, remained undimmed.

Of all her gifts, she still retained the one which was her greatest charm—the desire, and the ability, to please. Dying, she remained the trained courtesan. Louis came to see her every day, as he had done through all their years together, and she, knowing how he disliked illness, forgot her pain and played once more the role which had become through inveterate practice instinctive to her: the role of Disinterested Friend, listening attentively to the bored King, interposing at the right moment the precise amusing or smoothing remark that would distract the thoughts of the gloomy egotist from himself.

The Marquise was still supreme in the King's heart, as friend, companion, and confidante. That was what she wanted. Habit had bound him to her, habit and what for Louis passed as love. He and Madame de Pompadour had arrived years ago at one of the rarest and most satisfying relationships which can unite two human beings: they were bound together by the indissoluble ties which link those who have bridged the gap between passionate love and platonic friendship.

During the affliction of this final illness, the King presented to the curious eyes of the courtiers his usual impassive countenance. Neither by word nor expression did he betray his hidden thoughts, and there were some who accused him of indifference to his imminent loss. They were sorely mistaken; Louis had been schooled since childhood to conceal his real feelings, and he fell back upon this training now.

But to his son-in-law he unburdened himself: "My anxieties," he wrote to Don Philip, "have not decreased at all, and I confess to you that I have little hope of a complete recovery, and great fear of an end too near. Almost twenty years of companionship and sure friendship! In the end, God is Master, and it is necessary to bow to his will. M. de Rochechouart has learned of his wife's death after long suffering; I pity him, *if he loved her.*" This letter of a lonely man poignantly discloses the feelings which his cold exterior hid from those around him.

On the 13th of April the doctors abandoned hope, and Louis himself broke the news to the Marquise. No one knows what words were spoken between them, but the former lovers must have felt a depth of emotion beyond words. Madame de Pompadour, anxious even in her extremity to follow the King's wishes, asked him if she should see a priest, and Louis insisted that she do so.

The Curé of the Madeleine, in whose parish the Hôtel d'Evreux was situated, visited her on the night of April

14th. At last Madame de Pompadour was coming to terms with the Church, and this time there was no question who had the upper hand. She complied with every condition the priest exacted and even sent for M. d'Étioles. But her husband had ceased to think of her, and he declined to visit the dying woman, pleading illness.

The Curé made his preparations to administer Extreme Unction, and to the suffering Marquise the ceremony seemed inordinately prolonged. She begged him to hurry, and then asked his pardon for her impatience.

After she had received the Sacrament, the King paid his usual visit, entering her chamber through the lacquer room from which she had ruled France for thirteen years. The Marquise spoke gently, almost cheerfully, to Louis who was almost speechless with sorrow. His sense of conformity to the ritual of the Church was satisfied by his Mistress' reconciliation to God, although his own repentance lay ten years ahead when, rotting with smallpox, he would make his peace with a patient God. After a short time, Louis bade her good night and departed. It was the last time he would see the woman who had illuminated one third of his life with grace and charm.

April 15th, Palm Sunday, broke gray and chill. Madame de Pompadour had not slept for want of air in her starved lungs and sat propped up in her chair, suffocating. The full-length windows facing northward on the wet green park were closed, covered by the brocade draperies. The sickroom's atmosphere was stifling with the smell of burning tapers. All was quiet. She was alone except for the comforting presence of Madame du Haussay—alone with her thoughts in the early-morning hours before the Royal beehive began to hum.

Her forty-two years seemed to her more like a hundred. So far had she traveled, along that devious road that led from her birthplace in the rue de Cléry to the Royal château of Versailles! For her, however, that road had been straight as an arrow, pursued unswervingly since her visit to the fortuneteller when she was nine. "Almost a Queen!" Madame Lebon's prophecy had been fulfilled beyond her unbounded imagination.

The winning charm of Reinette had smoothed the upward path, snared the King of France, ruled his kingdom, and transformed a gentle, kind bourgeoise into the rich and powerful Marquise de Pompadour. Her memory rolled back to that distant springtime of Fontenoy, when Louis had loved her as a woman, her ambitions had all seemed realized, and she was still good in heart.

Never such pure happiness again! That was before the whirlpool of Versailles swept her into its frenzied vortex where survival was possible only by stepping on the necks of others; where poisonous calumny, cancerous hatred, and dissolute living left their indelible scars—shattered health, suspicious mind, stained soul, and saddened heart. Was it for this that she had spurned a loving husband and abandoned her former simple life?

As her memories surged through her brain and she fought for breath, she could only answer honestly, as she always answered herself, *yes*. Crushed though she was, tired now and ready to die, she faced within herself the knowledge that she would climb the path again, step by agonized step.

She had fulfilled the destiny charted by her mother and M. de Tournehem, marked out for her when she was still a child. Luck, of course, and her own cool brain had helped her. She had been given every advantage, taught everything a charming young woman should know, everything, except the basic concept of right and wrong.

Wrong? There was no wrong except blunders and stupidity. Reason, reason alone, was the sole compass of conduct and faith, and morals were passé. The *philosophes* had discarded them; and Madame de Pompadour had always been disciple as well as patroness of the *philosophes*. As she sat in the *bergère* awaiting death, she accepted its coming philosophically.

She had made her peace with the Church, yes. That was good form, good manners. Versailles still lived by protocol, and the code demanded that one die in the Ancient Faith —and the King insisted upon it. But she confessed to herself that she had never attained Louis' religious faith, nor, thank God, his religious terror.

No, looking back she felt no regrets save one: that her small daughter, replica of her own cool charm, had not outlived her. If only Alexandrine were alive, married into one of the great families of France, perhaps even joined on the side sinister to the Blood Royal, the Marquise could consider her life complete. The blood of Poisson elevated to the peerage, insured of perpetuation!

But Alexandrine lay in the Capuchin vault, and Madame de Pompadour would never know the boundless pride

Madame Poisson had known when *her* daughter slipped into the arms of Louis XV.

As her mind played with the past, with what was and what might have been, she asked for her will. Its date, November 15, 1757, carried her back to those fearful days following Rosbach, when she had been sure she would die of humiliation.

Slowly the Marquise read its provisions:

"In the name of the Father and of the Son and of the Holy Ghost.

"I, Jeanne-Antoinette Poisson, Marquise de Pompadour, separated wife of Charles-Guillaume Lenormant, *écuyer*, have made and written this present testament and ordinance of my last will, which I desire shall be executed in its entirety...."

The Marquise made no change in the terms of her testament, but desiring to leave special remembrances to certain of her friends, she dictated a codicil to Collin which read:

"I desire to make bequests as tokens of friendship and as souvenirs of myself to the following persons: To Madame du Roure, the portrait of my daughter. Although my daughter had not the honor of being related to her, she will serve to remind her of the friendship which I have entertained for Madame du Roure. To Madame la Maréchale de Mirepoix my new diamond watch. To Madame la Duchesse de Choiseul...."

As the Marquise listed the intimate gifts, Collin burst into tears. He wrote with difficulty and made many mistakes, which she patiently corrected; then, summoning her remaining strength, she signed the codicil.

The King, his presence required at the prolonged religious ceremonies of Palm Sunday, did not come again. But the Marquise's friends continued to circulate through her rooms, marveling at her composure. Even her perennial opponent, the Dauphin, was moved to reluctant admiration.

Writing that afternoon to Boyer, now Bishop of Verdun, he conceded, "She is dying with a courage rare in either sex. . . . Every time she draws breath, she thinks it is her last. It is one of the saddest and most cruel endings that one can imagine. . . . The King has not seen her since yesterday."

Toward evening, the Duc de Choiseul came into her room again. He came not only as a devoted friend; as Prime Minister of France it was his duty to guard against the loss of any state papers which might be in her possession. Without attracting her attention, he tactfully slipped the papers on her desk into his portfolio.

He was soon joined by the Prince de Soubise and the Duc de Gontaut. They waited, profoundly moved, as death came nearer. On the dying woman's sunken cheeks the two spots of rouge flamed, accentuated by the spreading pallor underneath. Sensing the end, she gently dismissed them, saying, "It is near, my friends; leave me to my confessor and my women."

Her maids wished to change her linen, but she refused. "I know you are very skillful," she whispered, "but I am so feeble that you could not help hurting me, and it is not worth it for the little time I have left."

Not a word of complaint, not a gesture of impatience escaped her. Expression still showed in her brilliant eyes, and she continued to talk with the Curé, who had remained.

As the priest rose to go, she halted him with a slight gesture of her hand. "One moment, M. le Curé," she smiled, "and we will go away together."

When the King was told of the Marquise's death he cancelled the public dinner and at once shut himself up in the Little Apartments with her closest friends.

A few minutes later, two men bearing a plain stretcher left the Palace by the side door of the Chapel and hurriedly went off in the direction of the Marquise's private house in the town. The Duchesse de Praslin, watching them pass beneath her window, saw the body of a woman, "covered only with a sheet wrapped so tightly that the shape of the head, the breasts, the stomach and legs were distinctly outlined." She sent a servant to find out who it was, and upon hearing that it was Madame de Pompadour, she burst into tears.

The haste with which the body of the Marquise was removed from the Palace was not motivated by callousness; the regulations of the Royal household were inflexible, and they forbade keeping a corpse overnight in a Royal Palace. For two days Madame de Pompadour's body lay in state in the bedroom of her house in Versailles, the walls of which were covered with black hangings.

On Tuesday evening at six o'clock the funeral procession of the Marquise, followed by hired mourners, formed outside the church of Notre Dame de Versailles, where the preliminary services had been held. In accordance with the instructions of her will, her body was to be placed beside that of Alexandrine, in the Capuchin Church. (When this church was demolished, in 1806, to clear space for the rue de la Paix, the bones of Madame de Pompadour were removed to the Catacombs and placed in a private ossuary.) In order to reach the highway to Paris, the procession had to pass directly in front of the Palace, in full view of the Royal Apartments.

At that same hour the King's chief valet Laborde hastened to light the candles in the *Cabinet de Travail* and to draw the blinds in order to spare his Master the sight of the mournful convoy. But he was too late. Louis was already in the room, fully aware of what was occurring outside. He ordered the door locked and, taking his other valet Champlost by the arm, stepped out on the balcony into the stormy night.

Silently he stood heedless of the rain beating on his uncovered head. His velvet coat was soaked, and yet he made no move, watching the solemn procession pass slowly in front of Versailles. It reached the Paris road and turned east, gradually fading from his view among the distant trees. Only when it had entirely disappeared did he turn and re-enter the room. Champlost, who tells this story, was touched to see tears streaming down the King's face. In a low voice he murmured, "They are the only tribute I can offer her."

Louis XV has suffered so cruelly at the hands of malicious historians that it is not surprising how little known is this account of his reaction to the Marquise's funeral. Scribbling a vicious little pamphlet in 1790, Jean François de La Harpe gives a different version. The King, he wrote, stood on the balcony watching the procession disappear; turning to go inside, he shrugged his shoulders and indifferently remarked, "The Marquise has a wet day for her journey."

But Champlost's version is indisputable, and he refuted La Harpe's slur, an act of high moral courage at a time when the Revolution had deluged the Monarchy. With loyal precision, Champlost wrote his account for posterity: "I went into the King's room in order to light it and close the shutters myself, and I found the King looking at the sad spectacle in front of his eyes with a distress which was *proved by his tears,* bidding a last farewell to her whom he would never see again. If you call that *insulting indifference,* I shall be tempted to believe, sir [La Harpe], that you have been mistakenly named one of the masters of the French language."

The Marquise was hardly in her tomb before the irrepressible Parisians were busy composing another Poissonade. Death did not quench the consuming hatred they felt for their city's most successful daughter:

> Ci-gît qui fut vingt ans pucelle,
> Sept ans catin, et huit ans maquerelle.

> Here lies one who was twenty years a maiden,
> Seven years a whore, and eight years a panderer.

But if the capital was pitiless, those who knew her better felt differently. "In general," said the honorable Prince de Croÿ, "she was regretted, being kind and having done good for almost all of those who asked favors of her. She never had dismissed more than the three or four Ministers who had wished to supplant her or to stand haughtily on their own legs, and she had never done any evil other than necessarily, but there came to France many misfortunes of all kinds in her time, and much useless expense!"

Voltaire, that imp of genius who had remained faithful except in a moment of transient pique, wrote: "Be assured, dear colleague, that true men of letters, true philosophers, ought to mourn for Madame de Pompadour. Her opinions were *in harmony with ours;* no one knew it better than myself. She is in truth a great loss." And later, in another letter: "I am greatly afflicted by the death of Madame de Pompadour; I weep when I think of it. It is very absurd that an old scribbler like myself should be still alive, and that a beautiful woman should have been cut off at forty in the midst of the most brilliant career in the world. Perhaps if she had tasted the repose which I enjoy, she would be living now."

And Diderot the atheist, whose *Encyclopédie* the dead Marquise had tried to protect, wrote: "What will survive of her? The Treaty of Versailles, which will last as long as such things may; the *Amour* of Bouchardon, which will be admired to the end of time; some graven gems which will perplex the antiquaries; a good little picture by Van Loo which will be occasionally looked at; and a pinch of ashes." But Diderot was wrong. Much more than these remain to us of her fragile life; most of all the memory, illuminated by some of the world's loveliest portraits, of the woman who was a charming century's most exquisite ornament, the woman who was the last of the great *reines à gauche.*

A few days after the funeral, the Queen unburdened herself to Président Hénault: "Finally," she wrote, "there is no more talk here of her who is no longer than if she had never existed. Such is the way of the world: it is very hard to love it."

But was Madame de Pompadour so soon forgotten? The King's mask betrayed nothing of what he felt. Had he thrust from his mind all thought of the woman who had soothed, with sympathy and understanding, his tedious existence? The answer lies in his confidential letter to Don Philip: "My preceding letter will have given you an idea of why I have not answered yours until today. All my anxiety is over, in the saddest way of all. You will easily divine the truth."

No, Louis the Well-Beloved had not forgotten. His selfish heart could still know sorrow, although not for long. Instead of turning to God, as the pious Dauphine so ardently prayed, he reverted to the transitory inmates of the *Parc aux Cerfs* in a desperate attempt to dissipate his lonely boredom.

And four short years after the Marquise de Pompadour left Versailles forever, the blonde radiance of Madame Du Barry rose like the spring sun to illumine the aging King's final years.

APPENDIX

Excerpt from the Account Book of the Marquise de Pompadour

State of My General Effects

I have silver plate worth	537,600 *l.*
Furthermore in gold plate	150,000 *l.*
She has spent for her pocket money	1,338,867 *l.*
For food during the 19 years of her reign	3,504,800 *l.*
For the King's trips, extraordinary expenses, comedies and operas given in different houses	4,005,900 *l.*
Wages for my servants for 19 years	1,168,886 *l.*
Pensions that I have always paid until my death	229,236 *l.*
My cash box containing 98 gold cases each worth 3,000 livres	294,000 *l.*
Another cash box containing all my diamonds	1,783,000 *l.*
A superb collection of engraved stones at my house by Guay, given to the King and estimated at	400,000 *l.*
Different pieces of old lacquer	111,945 *l.*
Old porcelain	150,000 *l.*
Purchase of fine stones to complete the collection	60,000 *l.*
Linen for draperies and table for Crécy	600,452 *l.*
More for my other houses	400,325 *l.*
My wardrobe, everything included	350,235 *l.*
My kitchen utensils for all my houses	66,172 *l.*
My library including a number of manuscripts	12,500 *l.*
Presents given to the ladies who have always accompanied me	460,000 *l.*
Given to the poor during my reign	150,000 *l.*
Gifts of dresses, coats and material to the concierges	100,000 *l.*
For my Father's affairs, settled by M. de Machault	400,000 *l.*
For pictures and other whims	60,000 *l.*

Expenses for candles during 19 years	660,000 *l.*
Expenses for lanterns and candlelight . . .	150,000 *l.*
For beautiful mares, saddle-horses, carriages, and sedan-chairs, in all	1,800,000 *l.*
Fodder and care of my horses during 19 years .	1,300,000 *l.*
For all of my livery in all my houses	250,000 *l.*
For the purchase of Crécy	650,000 *l.*
For the purchase of La Celle	260,000 *l.*
Purchase of Aunay	140,000 *l.*
Purchase of the Barony of Tréon (near Crécy) .	80,000 *l.*
Purchase of Magenville	25,000 *l.*
Purchase of St. Rémy	24,000 *l.*
Purchase of Oville	11,000 *l.*
Purchase of Hôtel d'Evreux, Paris	650,000 *l.*
Purchase of land beside the above	80,000 *l.*
Spent at Champs during 3 years	200,000 *l.*
Spent at St. Ouen during 5 years	500,000 *l.*
Medals of gold or silver	400,000 *l.*
Collin, in charge of the servants and secretary .	6,000 *l.*
Dr. Quesnay	3,000 *l.*
du Haussay, chambermaid	150 *l.*
Couraget, chambermaid	150 *l.*
Neveu, chambermaid	150 *l.*

The Will of the Marquise de Pompadour

In the name of the Father and of the Son and of the Holy Ghost.

I, Jeanne-Antoinette Poisson, Marquise de Pompadour, separated wife of Charles-Guillaume Le Normant, *écuyer,* have made and written this present testament and ordinance of my last will, which I desire shall be executed in its entirety.

I recommend my soul to God, beseeching Him to have mercy upon it, and to accord me grace to repent and to die in a state worthy of His clemency, hoping to satisfy His justice through the merits of the precious blood of Christ, my Saviour, and through the powerful intercession of the Holy Virgin and of all the saints in Paradise.

I desire that my body be carried to the Capuchins of the Place Vendôme in Paris, without any ceremony, and that it be buried there in the vault of the chapel which they have allotted me in their church.

I leave to M. Collin, in recognition of his attachment to my person, a pension of . . . . 6,000 livres.

To M. Quesnay . . . . 4,000 livres

To M. Nesmes . . . . 3,000 livres

To M. Lefevre, overseer . . . . . . 1,200 livres

To my three maids, to Mademoiselle Jeanneton, to my three *valets-de-chambre,* to my men-cooks, officers, steward, butler, and concierge, each the income at ten per cent on 500 livres; and to make myself clearer, I am going to cite an example. Madame Labbaty has been with me twelve years; she would be paid 600 livres a year for life, in other words twelve times fifty at ten per cent on a capital sum of 500 livres, provided that for each year of service it will be increased by an additional 50 livres.

I leave to my footmen, coachmen, porters, ushers, gardeners, and wardrobe-women the sum of 300 livres, from which they will be paid the interest in accordance with the plan which I have explained in the preceding clause.

I bequeath to the rest of my servants who are not included in the two above-mentioned clauses, 500 livres of capital, from which they will receive pensions in the manner I have already explained.

Further, I direct that all the pensions and endowments created during my lifetime be paid without any deduction. And, further, I give to my maids everything in my wardrobe—gowns, underclothes, dresses, and laces.

Further, I bequeath to my third maid a legacy of 3,000 livres in addition to her annuity; and also to the wardrobe-woman in daily attendance upon me a legacy of 1,200 livres, in addition to her annuity.

Further, to my three *valets-de-chambre,* a legacy of 3,000 livres.

I beg the King to accept the gift which I am making him of my hôtel in Paris, it being suitable for converting into a palace for one of his grandchildren. My desire is that it should be for Monseigneur le Comte de Provence (later Louis XVIII).

I also beg His Majesty's acceptance of the gift which I am making him of all my engraved stones by Guay, whether bracelets, rings, or seals, to augment his cabinet of engraved precious stones.

As for the residue of my movables and immovables, of whatever kind and wherever situate, I give and bequeath them to Abel-François Poisson, Marquis de Marigny, my brother, whom I name and appoint my sole legatee; and in the event of his decease, I appoint in his stead M. Poisson de Malvoisin, quartermaster in the Army, and at present brigadier in the Carabineers, and his children. [Marigny died without issue in 1781, and the estate of Madame de Pompadour devolved to his cousin, Poisson de Malvoisin. With the death of his daughter in the early Nineteenth Century, the Poisson family became extinct.]

I appoint as executor of this testament M. le Prince de Soubise, whom I empower to act and to make all arrangements which he may consider necessary for the due execution of the said will, and especially to set aside such moneys, rents, and effects belonging to my estate as he may deem suitable for the payment in full of all the annuities bequeathed by me; and in case he should find them insufficient for the purpose, I empower him to provide from the sale of my movables a sufficient sum to acquire securities or annuities, the funds from which will serve to discharge the said pensions, and also to select and nominate such person as he shall deem suitable, and to pay him such salary as he may deem sufficient, to collect the revenues set apart by the executor of my will and to pay the aforesaid annuities to each of the aforesaid legatees, who, in virtue of this assignment and appropriation, will have no power to lay claim to anything, nor have any rights or charges upon the rest of the property belonging to my estate.

However troublesome M. de Soubise may find the commission I am giving him, he ought to regard it as a sure proof of the confidence with which his probity and his virtues have inspired me. I beg him to accept two of my rings, one my large aquamarine colored diamond, the other an engraving by Guay representing Friendship. I flatter myself that he will never part with them and that they will recall to his memory the person who has entertained for him the most tender of friendships.

Executed at Versailles, November 15, 1757.

JEANNE-ANTOINETTE POISSON
Marquise de Pompadour

Codicil I

I bequeath to Abel-François Poisson, Marquis de Marigny, my brother, the land belonging to my marquisate and peerage of Ménars and whatever he will find there at my death, and after him to his children and grandchildren male, to the eldest in all cases. If he has only daughters, the entail will lapse, and the land must be divided among them.

In the event of my brother dying without issue, I appoint in

his stead, subject to the same conditions, M. Poisson de
Malvoisin, at present brigadier in the Carabineers.

March 30, 1761

Codicil II

I desire to make bequests as tokens of friendship and as
remembrances to the following persons:

To Madame du Roure the portrait of my daughter. Although
my daughter had not the honor of being related to her, she
will serve to remind her of the friendship which I have entertained for Madame du Roure.

To Madame la Maréchale de Mirepoix my new diamond
watch.

To Madame de Château de Renaud a box containing a
portrait of the King set with diamonds.

To Madame la Duchesse de Choiseul a silver box set with
diamonds.

To Madame la Duchesse de Grammont (sister of Choiseul)
a box on which is a diamond butterfly.

To M. le Duc de Gontaut a wedding-ring of rose and white
diamonds, tied with a green knot; and a carnelian box which
he has always much admired.

To M. le Duc de Choiseul an aquamarine-tinted diamond
and a black box piqué and a cup.

To M. le Maréchal de Soubise a ring by Guay representing
Friendship; it is his portrait and mine for the twenty years
I have known him.

To Madame d'Amblimont my set of emeralds.

If I have forgotten any of my people, I pray my brother to
attend to them, and I confirm my will. I hope that he will
approve of the codicil which friendship dictates to me, and
which I have directed M. Collin to write, as I have only sufficient strength to sign.

At Versailles, April 15, 1764

LA MARQUISE DE POMPADOUR

Acknowledgments and Bibliography

The author wishes to express his sincere appreciation to Mr. John Hall Jacobs and Mr. George Logan, Librarian and Assistant Librarian of the New Orleans Public Library, and their staff; to Dr. Garland Taylor, Librarian of the Howard-Tilton Memorial Library of Tulane University, and his staff, especially Miss Marguerite Renshaw; to Mr. James Dyson, Librarian of Loyola University of the South, and his staff; and to the Library of Congress, for immeasurable assistance in the research which this book entailed.

A special debt of gratitude is due to Mrs. Frances Gardiner, of the Medical Library of the University of California, for her opinions and advice on the health of Madame de Pompadour, and to Dr. Julian G. Michel, of the Department of Modern Languages of Loyola University of the South, for suggestions on certain translations from the French.

Following is a partial list of the sources consulted:

Abbot, Willis J., *Notable Women in History*. John C. Winston, Philadelphia, 1913.

Argenson, Marquis de, *Memoirs and Letters*. P. F. Collier, New York, 1901.

Barbier, E., *Chronique de la Régence et du Règne de Louis XV*. Charpentier, Paris, 1857.

Bernis, Cardinal de, *Memoirs and Letters*. P. F. Collier, New York, 1901.

Boutaric, M. F., *Corréspondance secrète inédilée de Louis XV*. Henri Plon, Paris, 1866.

Broglie, Albert, *The King's Secret*. Cassell, Petter, and Galpin, New York, 1879.

Campardon, Émile, *Madame de Pompadour*. Henri Plon, Paris, 1867.

Capefigue, Jean Baptiste, *Madame la Marquise de Pompadour*. Amyot, Paris, 1867.

Caraman, Duc de, *La Famille de Madame Pompadour*. Leclerc, Paris, 1901.

Carre, Henri, *La Marquise de Pompadour*. Hachette, Paris, 1937.

Cheverny, Comte de, *Mémoires*. E. Plon, Nourrit et Cie., Paris, 1886.

Collé, Charles, *Journal et Mémoires*. Firmin Didot Frères et fils, Paris, 1868.

Cordey, Jean, *Inventaire des Biens de Madame de Pompadour*. Les Bibliophiles François, Paris, 1939.

Croÿ, Duc de, *Journal*. Flammarion, Paris, 1906.

Dietrich, Auguste, *Les Maîtresses de Louis XV*. A. Keiss, Vienna, 1881.

Ferté-Imbault, Madame de, *Le Royaume de la rue Saint-Honoré*. Ségur, Paris, 1897.

Gaxotte, Pierre, *Louis XV and His Times*. Lippincott, Philadelphia, 1934.

Goncourt, Edmond de, *The Woman of the Eighteenth Century*. Firmin Didot Frères et fils, Paris, 1862.

Haggard, A. C. P., *The Real Louis XV*. D. Appleton, New York, 1907.

Hausset, Madame du, *Mémoires*. Flammarion, Paris, 1891.

Hill, Cecilia, *Versailles, Its Life and History*. Little, Brown, Boston, 1925.

Imbert de Saint-Amand, Arthur Léon, *Les Femmes de Versailles*. E. Dentu, Paris, 1886.

Jullien, Adolphe, *Histoire du Théâtre de Madame de Pompadour*. J. Baur, Paris, 1874.

Leroi, J. A., *Curiosités Historiques*. Henri Plon, Paris, 1864.

Leroy, Alfred, *Madame de Pompadour et son Temps*. A. Michel, Paris, 1936.

Malassis, Paul Emmanuel A. P., *Corréspondance de Madame de Pompadour avec son Père et son Frère*. J. Baur, Paris, 1878.

Marmontel, Jean François, *Memoirs*. Nicholls, London, 1895.

Mowat, R. B., *A History of European Diplomacy*. Longmans, Green, New York, 1928.

Nolhac, Pierre de, *Louis XV et Madame de Pompadour*. Manzi, Joyant, Paris, 1903.

Nolhac, Pierre de, *Versailles au dix-huitième siecle*. Conard, Paris, 1926.

Perkins, James Breck, *France under Louis XV*. Houghton Mifflin, Boston and New York, 1897.

Potiquet, Dr. Henri Albert, *Un Document inédit sur la santé de Madame de Pompadour*. Chronique Médicale, Paris, 1903.

Reboux, Paul, *Madame de Pompadour, reine et martyre*. Flammarion, Paris, 1933.

Richelieu, Duc de, *Mémoires*. Société de l'histoire de France, Paris, 1918.

Soulavie, Jean Louis, *Madame de Pompadour*. Sturgis and Walton, New York, 1910.

Tinayre, Marcelle, *Madame de Pompadour, A Study in Temperament*. G. P. Putnam's Sons, New York, 1926.

Trouncer, Margaret, *The Pompadour*. Faber and Faber, London, 1937.

INDEX